PERSPECTIVES

ON THE WORLD CHRISTIAN MOVEMENT

Study Guide

1999 Edition

By

Steven C. Hawthorne
Curriculum Development
Institute of International Studies

William Carey Library

P.O. Box 40129
Pasadena, California 91114

paternoster
publishing

European Distributor
Paternoster Press
Carlisle, United Kingdom

Rights and Permissions
William Carey Library
P.O. Box 40129
Pasadena, California 91114

Published by
William Carey Library
1705 N. Sierra Bonita Ave.
Pasadena, California 91104
Phone (626) 798-0819
ISBN 087808-290-5

European distribution by
Paternoster Press
P.O. Box 300
Kingstown Broadway
Carlisle, Cumbria, UK CA3 0QS
E-mail: postmaster@paternoster-publishing.com

Cover Design: Chad M. Upham
Cover photos courtesy of Caleb Project

1999 Edition

Seventh Printing - June 2006

Printed in the United States of America

Contents

Introduction

Perspectives: A Course of Vision, Hope and Passion

As the name implies, the Perspectives course is about vision. It's the same vision which empowered Jesus to live His life with joy, hope, and single-hearted passion. This course explores that vision and will help you respond to Christ's invitation to live for the same purpose and significance that He did.

There's joy in this vision. Jesus told His first followers that the value of living fruitfully for His Father's glory was "that My joy may be in you, and that your joy may be made full" (John 15:11).

What was the vision? Jesus summed up the vision in one of His final prayers to His Father, "I glorified You on earth, having accomplished the work that You gave me to do" (John 17:4). Jesus' life purpose was to bring about God's glory on earth. Throughout His life, Jesus kept the vision of God's greater glory before Him. He believed His Bible as it told the story and described the prophetic certainty that God would be delighted by worship from every people. The vision of God's glory focused His life choices and filled His daily affairs with immense significance. Passion for God's glory energized and integrated His life. Life with purpose was so satisfying that He said, "My food is to do the will of Him who sent Me, and to accomplish His work" (John 4:34). As He set His life toward the hope of finishing God's work, His life became a daily feast of purpose. This course aims to help you live strategically toward that same hope.

"Missions" is a loaded word for most Christians. Many people are exposed to missions in the context of appeals for volunteers or funds. Missions has often been reduced to a limited question of whether you will be a missionary or not. Most Christians would admit that they don't really know enough about what missions is to know what they would do or be if they were to aspire to be a missionary. Even less clear is how someone can live for God's global purpose without being a missionary.

The point of this course is not to persuade you to become a missionary. Neither is it to train you in skills you need to serve as a missionary. We simply want to show you practical examples of how missions can be done wisely and well.

The primary idea is that God will fulfill His purposes. The certainty that He will see it fulfilled makes His invitation to join Him in His mission a matter of heart-blazing hope. We are not called to perform dull religious duties. He is enlisting His followers to lead lives of huge significance.

We are convinced that God has a "world-sized" role for every Christian in His global purpose. Whether people go to distant countries or stay at home is a secondary issue. The primary issue is what most people are hungry to discover: vision to live a life of purpose. Discovering that vision makes this course valuable, and perhaps crucial, for any Christian.

What's In This Course?

The course is designed around four vantage points or "perspectives"—Biblical, Historical, Cultural and Strategic. Each one highlights different aspects of God's global purpose.

The Biblical and Historical sections reveal why our confidence is based on the historic fact of God's relentless work from the dawn of history until this day. That's why the essence of this course is the record of what God has been unfolding for thousands of years toward a certain, and perhaps soon-coming, culmination.

As we wind our way through history, we will meet the largest and longest-running movement ever in history—the World Christian Movement. You will find that virtually every innovative approach you can think of has been attempted by those who have gone before us. We are in league with the most substantial movement of creative and self-sacrificing people the world has ever seen.

The Cultural and Strategic sections underscore that we are in the midst of a costly, but very "do-able" task, confirming the Biblical and Historical hope.

The Biblical Perspective

1. **The Living God is a Missionary God**
   God's purpose is three-fold: against evil—kingdom victory; for the nations—redemption and blessing; and for God—global glory in worship. God's purpose revealed in promise to Abraham. Exploring God's purpose for the nations: Blessing to the nations described.

2. **The Story of His Glory**
   Exploring God's purpose for Himself: How God has been steadily unfolding a plan throughout all nations and generations to bring about His greater glory, ultimately drawing to Himself the worship of all the peoples. Passion and prayer for God's glory.

3. **Your Kingdom Come**
   Exploring God's purpose regarding evil: How God has accomplished a defeat of evil powers in order to open a season of history in which the nations can freely follow Christ. The kingdom of God as the destiny of all history. Christ's mission seeks a hindering of evil to bring about a sign of the coming peace of the kingdom of God. Our prayers contend with evil in order to bring about the transformation of society with Christ's kingdom in view.

4. **Mandate for the Nations**
   Jesus shows great strategic interest in Gentiles; wise strategic focus by initiating a global mission on a few disciples among the Hebrew people. The Great Commission and the ways of God's sending in relational power. Dealing with the ideas of pluralism (all religions the same) and universalism (all persons saved).

5. **Unleashing the Gospel**
   The first followers of Jesus: obedient in costly, foundational ways. The climactic act of book of Acts is the freeing of the gospel to be followed by Gentiles without Jewish traditions as a requirement. A foundational act of God which speaks to the situations where the gospel is hindered today. Strategic suffering and apostolic passion.

The Historical Perspective

6. **The Expansion of the Christian Movement**
   The story of God's purpose continues relentlessly from Abraham's day until the present moment. An overview of the largest and the longest-running movement ever in history—the world Christian movement. How the gospel surged through the peoples and places of the world. Important insights for our own day.

7. **Eras of Mission History**
   The greatest explosion of growth ever has taken place in last 200 years in three "bursts" of activity. Why we could be in the final era of missions. The global harvest force comprised increasingly of non-Western missionaries.

8. **Pioneers of the World Christian Movement**
   Today we anchor the race by continuing what others have begun. It's a day of finishing. All the more reason to learn the wisdom and the heart of ordinary people who did extraordinary things in earlier generations. Reading the writings of William Carey and other leaders to discern what these people have left to us. Exploring the contribution of women in missions throughout the centuries.

9. **The Task Remaining**
   God's pressed His purpose forward until the present hour of amazing opportunity. Understanding the concept of "unreached peoples" to assess the remaining task. Recognizing the imbalance of mission resources shapes strategic priorities. The basic minimal missiological achievement in every people group opens the way for working with God against every kind of evil so that the gospel of the kingdom is declared and displayed with clarity and power. The need and opportunity of urban mission.

The Cultural Perspective

10. **How Shall They Hear?**
    Culture and intercultural communication of the gospel. Communicating the gospel with relevance at the worldview level helps avoid syncretism (blending of cultural error with God's truth) and also enables powerful movements of the gospel. Sensitive missionaries will look for ways that God has preserved or prepared people to hear the gospel, often finding redemptive analogies for God's truth.

11. *Building Bridges of Love*

The incarnation as a model of missionary humility. How missionaries can enter appropriate roles in order to form relationships of trust and respect to develop a sense of belonging, and thus to communicate with credibility for understanding. Recognizing the dynamics of social structure in order to initiate growing movements of ongoing communication throughout the society.

The Strategic Perspective

12. *Christian Community Development*

A survey of world need. Dynamic balance of evangelism and social action. Hope for significant transformation as a sign of Christ's Lordship by Christian community development. Exploring the charge that missionaries destroy instead of serve cultures. Healing the wounds of the world between the peoples.

13. *Spontaneous Multiplication of Churches*

Church planting which saturates and moves throughout a people group as a people movement is anything but happenstance. Missionaries can plant multiplying churches that reach entire families and communities. The vision for saturation church planting.

14. *Pioneer Church Planting*

The hope of planting churches among unreached peoples. How the breakthrough of the gospel in an unreached people requires that the gospel be "de-Westernized." The difference of contextualizing the message, the messenger and the movement.

15. *World Christian Partnership*

What it means to integrate life for Christ's global purpose. Developing a war-time lifestyle. Exploring the roles of going, and sending. Mobilization as a strategic aspect of the most effective sending. Wisdom in pursuing partnerships with local churches, mission agencies, non-Western missions and more. Seeking and knowing God's will with matters of cause vs. career. Doing our utmost and seeking His highest. Practical hope and wisdom to live for God's global purpose.

Improvements Over Earlier Versions

This is the third major edition of the curriculum called *Perspectives on the World Christian Movement*. The first edition of the curriculum appeared in 1982. A second edition was released 10 years later, in 1992. The 1999 version is the most thorough revision ever and is significantly different from earlier versions. Nearly half of the readings are new and most of the original readings have been updated and edited.

The Changes in This Version

The Perspectives movement has already helped thousands of people live in world-changing hope. For those who have used the Perspectives material before, watch for surprises! Many articles which have been part of the curriculum for years have been greatly revised. We have also sought to add more biblical substance to the course so that the paradigm shift of hope is a more forceful, life-integrating vision. You will also find more about suffering, more clarity in response to pluralism, more about freeing the gospel from Western traditions, more about partnership with a global mission force, and overall, more about a life of passion.

Different Published Formats of the Same Material

The *Notebook* version of the curriculum is an abbreviation of the standard curriculum. The standard curriculum contains every word found in the *Notebook* plus the additional readings required for graduate and undergraduate credit. The standard curriculum appears in the format of two volumes: a textbook of readings and this *Study Guide*. The *Reader* and *Study Guide* format is also by far the most flexible tool for guided study with a mentor. The *Reader* contains about 40% more reading material than the *Notebook*. The *Study Guide* is identical to the "guide notes" part of the *Notebook*, except that guide notes are extended to cover the extra readings in each section.

How to Use This Study Guide

Follow the Guide Notes

The Guide Notes summarize the main points of each lesson. In a very real sense, the Guide Notes constitute the course. Liken them to the interpretive guide in a museum who helps you to understand and thereby appreciate and remember what you see. The Guide Notes integrate the readings. In some cases they add to the material found in the readings.

Enrichment Readings for Non-Credit Students

Some will want to work through these materials for personal enrichment rather than for academic credit. For these students, we've grouped the essential portions at the first part of every lesson. We call this essential part, containing many of the highlights, the "Key Reading" section. In most lessons, the "key readings" comprise about 15 pages. The end of the key readings is marked by this bar.

Conclusion of Key Readings for this lesson.

Don't let the above marker stop you from going on to study every part. Many of the most fascinating highlights are in the material beyond the key readings. We encourage you to ransack (skim for highlights) every article as you are able. Don't be surprised to find that the readings are engaging and meaningful. We've not only gathered material from some of the best authors and leaders, we've sifted and edited their writing. Every page contains valuable vision and practical insight.

Study the Readings

The Guide Notes will cue you to read selections from the Perspectives Reader. You will often be asked to read portions of articles. You will find the range of pages with beginning and ending points described not only by the page number, but by a letter. The letter indicates which quadrant on the page you will find the starting or the ending point. Most of the starting and ending points are at break points above sub-headings. The diagram to the right shows which letter corresponds to which quadrant. If there is no letter, assume you need to read the entire page.

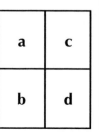

a	c
b	d

Three Sections Per Lesson

Each lesson has three parts of roughly equal length. This feature may help you gauge your study time. The three sections offer more flexibility in working through the entire lesson with a mentor or classmate.

The sections are marked with a bar at the end of the Key Readings and the Certificate Level Readings. e.g.

Conclusion of Certificate Level Readings for this lesson.

Focus on the Objectives

Each lesson opens with important introductory paragraphs and a list of objectives. This list should help focus your attention on the basic ideas.

Take In the Key Word

The "key word" at the beginning of each lesson is designed to stimulate interest and signal what may be of primary value to you. It is not intended to be a one-word summary of the content of the lesson.

Reflect on the Review Blocks

Sometimes we invite you to stop and reflect on an idea, look elsewhere in the notebook for an illustrating story from another article, or examine some scripture that will deepen your grasp of the topic.

You'll find these "Review Blocks" shaded with a gray screened box like this.

Learn from the Quizzes

The quizzes are designed to be completed with an open book and open Bible, if you prefer. There is no time limit to completing the quiz.

The left column is designed to help you prepare for class discussion with your written answers. The right "review" column is designed for you to write down information gleaned from class or mentor discussion which corrects or extends your answers.

1 The Living God is a Missionary God

God is a God of global purpose. God has already put in our hearts the longing to be a friend to a great God, to somehow become a co-worker with Him, living in the dignity of a purpose larger than ourselves. We really want to serve God in the biggest way we know how. What prevents us? Although we know better than to treat God as if He were a personal problem-solver, it's still common to regard Him from our point of view, as if He were on call to help us whenever we face difficult circumstances.

Our problem may be a matter of shriveled vision. We cannot devote ourselves to that which we cannot envision. Our vision is limited by the horizon of our own concerns and culture. But, there is a better destiny—a larger purpose. We can lay hold of it by knowing and following God toward a vision which extends far beyond ourselves.

In this lesson we'll begin a journey to discover what God has revealed about His purpose through the story of the Bible. His purposes make best sense when they are stretched out end-to-end on the timeline of the Bible's story. Walking with God through the story of the Scriptures will catapult us into the center of the significance of the rest of history.

The later it gets in history, the better God looks, because it's all coming about as He promised. Because He is a God of grand purpose, and because there is a mission He has set Himself to fulfill, our God is a missionary God.

PURPOSE
We were made to live for purpose. God Himself lives for purpose. The way to live with significance is to devote your life to a purpose that is larger than your life.

I. God's Promise Reveals His Purpose

God could have revealed His purpose in the form of direct commands about what He wanted to see done. Instead, God chose to reveal His purpose in the form of a promise, a promise that was both personal and immensely global: to bless all the families of the earth.

> **Open your Bible to Genesis 12. This is the hinge point of the Bible. Flip through the pages of Genesis 1-11. What kind of things are taking place in those passages? For what nations or peoples? Now page through Genesis 12 and onward. Do these portions concern peoples other than the Hebrews? What is the central difference between what happens in Genesis 1-11 and what takes place from Genesis 12 throughout the rest of the Bible?**

The Lord had said to Abraham, "Leave your country, your people and your father's household and go to the land I will show you.

"I will make you into a great nation and I will bless you;

I will make your name great, and you will be a blessing.

I will bless those who bless you, and whoever curses you I will curse;

and all peoples on earth will be blessed through you."

—Genesis 12:1-3

A. **God's Promise:** A mandate is better than a mere command. Because God extended His mandate initially in the form of a promise instead of as a direct imperative command, the emphasis is on what God would do far more than it was on what Abraham was expected to attempt. God emphasized the outcome that He wanted to see happen among all of earth's peoples rather than ordering Abraham to do a job with step-by-step directives. When you think about it, what better way could God use to convey His purpose to an entire faith family that would be co-working with God for thousands of years?

The promise reveals God's intentions more clearly at each stage of the fulfillment of the promise. God brings about successively greater fulfillments of His promise. John R. W. Stott describes a triple fulfillment. First, the promise was partially fulfilled in Abraham's day, and throughout the period of the Old Testament. Secondly, the promise was fully portrayed in the life of Jesus. Finally, the promise will be perfectly fulfilled at the end of the age. It is even now being fulfilled as He builds His Church. Through this promise of God we see Him as the God of history, the God of covenant, and the God of mission.

> **Read Stott, "The Living God is a Missionary God," pp. 3-8 (all)**

In the open spaces below, describe some of the details of the triple fulfillment of God's promise to bless the nations.

Progressive Fulfillment of God's Promise

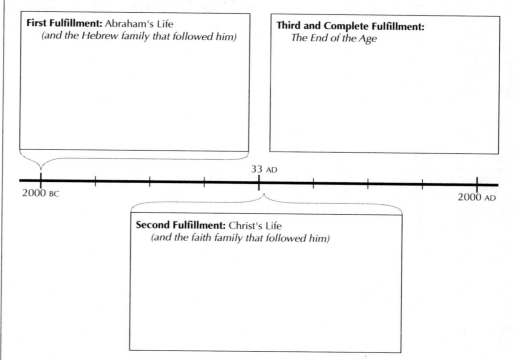

First Fulfillment: Abraham's Life
(and the Hebrew family that followed him)

Third and Complete Fulfillment:
The End of the Age

33 AD

2000 BC   2000 AD

Second Fulfillment: Christ's Life
(and the faith family that followed him)

B. God's Promise Repeated. God's desire to bring blessing among all nations is not a small, add-on idea that pops up in the New Testament. God's purpose is embedded in the very formation of the people of God. God repeats His promise five times to Abraham and his family.

Read in your own Bible Genesis 12:1-3, 18:18, 26:4, 28:14. What is the significance of God repeating the promise directly to Isaac and to Jacob?

C. God's Promise Confirmed. God could have revealed His purpose by assigning to Abraham a list of tasks that needed to be done. Or God might have indebted Abraham with blessing in a way that would have obligated Abraham to repay His kindness by doing expressly "missionary" tasks. But God apparently does not use obligating contracts to enforce the servitude of His people in His mission purpose. Instead, God "gambles" that He will gain their loving obedience. In Genesis 22, Abraham demonstrates that he would freely obey in faith, letting the God who gave the promise determine how and when He would keep His promise. At that moment God declares that because of Abraham's obedience, God's promise for Abraham's part in the global destiny was sure to come forth.

Read the story of Genesis 22:1-18. Why do you think God declared that the promise for the nations would come forth because of this particular act of obedience? What did Abraham prove?

II. God's People Formed to Participate in His Purpose

Even though the promise emphasized that God Himself would do a marvelous thing among the nations, Abraham and his descendants were not to be passive spectators.

A. Not Passive, but Active Communicators of Blessing. The statements of promised blessing came with a clearly connected purpose: "*so that* you will be a blessing" (verse 2) and "*so that* in you all the families of the earth will be blessed" (verse 3). The express purpose for God's choice of Abraham was for him and his family to play the key role in His global purpose.

B. True Significance. In contrast with the people of Babel, who wanted to "make a name" for themselves (Gen 11:4), God assured Abraham that He would make Abraham's name great. The way of highest significance in life lies not in acquiring security and self-made prestige. As with Abraham, significance lies in being a blessing to the nations. We are blessed to be a blessing. It is far more than a duty, it is our destiny.

> **Read Kaiser, "Israel's Missionary Call," pp. 10-13a**

C. Participating with God as His Priesthood. God's covenant at Sinai reveals God's purpose for His people. This is not an isolated verse of Scripture. The Exodus and the covenant made at Sinai were together the most definitive occasion of Israel's history. God's people were constituted for a purpose. Peter makes it clear that God's intentions remain the same in New Testament times and beyond. First, God's people are to be distinctive, a holy people of unique value among the peoples of the world. Second, God's people are to be God's priesthood declaring God's glories to the world.

D. Proving His Purpose. The songs of the Hebrew people reflect their understanding of God's mandate upon them to bring blessing to the nations. Psalm 67 shows that Israel knew that the nations were watching them as a spectacle of what God wanted to bring forth among all nations. The destiny of the nations— not some, but all the nations—is to sing praise to God.

God's purpose is the resolute focus of the Psalm: "God blesses us" with a purpose: "so that all of the ends of the earth may fear Him." God's ultimate purpose is that the nations would glorify Him in open recognition of two things: His redemptive, life-giving blessing (verse 1-2 and 6-7) and the supremacy of His kingship (verse 4).

> **Read Kaiser, "Israel's Missionary Call," pp. 13b-16**

III. What is God's Purpose?

God pursues one singular purpose which is reflected in Psalm 67: that He be glorified in global worship. To accomplish that end, God acts with a determined purpose that will not only affect all peoples, but defeat evil spiritual powers. Grasp the three directions of God's mission:

A. Toward God. God desires that worship will come *to Him* from every nation. Therefore, world evangelization is ultimately for God.

B. For People. God intends to bring redemptive blessing *to every people.* He will redeem a people from every people.

C. Concerning Evil. God will overcome evil powers in order to liberate people and ultimately, to bring all things under His everlasting and complete governance. This kingdom reign is the substance of the blessing He brings to the nations.

> **God's Purpose Summarized: For His glory in global worship, God purposes to redeem a people from every people, and to rule a kingdom over all kingdoms.**

Conclusion of Key Readings for this lesson.

IV. God's First Promise Displays His Final Victory

Long before Abraham, God had already promised to vanquish evil and to redeem people. Stanley Ellisen helps us understand the background for the promise found in Genesis 3:14-15, which is often called the "proto-evangel" (first gospel).

A. Two-fold Problem. Ellisen summarizes the double challenge of evil as being a two-fold problem:

1. **A satanic counter-kingdom** arose, bent on usurping God's reign by stealing the allegiance of people, and then deceiving and destroying people.

2. **Humans in rebellion** abdicated their regal position as appointed caretakers of the earth, and ironically, in a bid for greater power, succumbed to the lie of Satan's counter-kingdom, which resulted in the slavery of sin and death.

B. God's Two-fold Strategy for a Single Purpose. His strategy and His purpose are prefigured in the "proto-evangel" in what Ellisen calls "two crushings." God pledges that a human figure would entirely destroy the devil, "crushing" him. In the same breath, God states that Satan would wound that human figure, prefiguring the redemptive suffering of Christ. It's important to see that God overcomes both problems together in one mission: He redeems in order to rule. And He rules (gains victory) in order to redeem. Those two strategic emphases have one single, overriding purpose: God's greater glory in worship.

God's Ultimate Purpose: To draw loyal worship from every people, displaying His greater glory and manifesting His fullest love.

God's Two-Fold Strategy: While God's purpose ultimately concerns His glory, He has worked decisively and relentlessly with an integrated strategy *against* Satanic evil and *for* people.

1. **Concerning Satan:** God wages a war of liberation upon the satanic counter-kingdom, thwarting the darkness in order to rescue humankind, and ultimately destroying every work of Satan (the "Kingdom Program" according to Ellisen).

2. **Concerning people:** God redeems a people from every people, bringing them under the rule of Christ through the cross and resurrection of Christ (the "Redemptive Program" according to Ellisen).

> **Read Ellisen, "Everyone's Question: What is God Trying to Do?," pp. 17-20 (all)**

God's Purpose Summarized: For His glory in global worship, God purposes to redeem a people from every people, and to rule a kingdom over all kingdoms.

An Introduction to the Rest of Perspectives

This course is organized around four basic dimensions or "perspectives" on the world Christian movement: Biblical, Historical, Cultural, and Strategic. Stott's words can serve as an introduction to the rest of the course. Stott's summary of the story of the Bible helps us get launched through both the *Biblical* section (Lessons 1 through 5) and the *Historical* section (Lessons 6 through 8). Of course, we'll be exploring the biblical story in much more depth in the upcoming biblical lessons, but our pathway through history follows many of the same themes and approaches to observing a continuity throughout the ages toward a fulfillment of God's purpose. Stott also effectively introduces the *Cultural* section (Lessons 10 and 11) and the *Strategic* section (Lessons 9, 12 through 15) with his comments about the Bible modeling and empowering mission. Scripture reveals much-needed wisdom about effectively communicating the gospel cross-culturally. The Bible also sets out basic parameters of wise strategic thinking about completing the entire task in the power and ways of God.

V.   The Whole Bible as the Greater Mandate

A. Mandate for Mission. The biblical mandate for missions is not limited to a few Bible verses. We should never rely on a few apparent proof texts of a cause. We must look beyond isolated verses to see the mandate through and through the entire story of the Bible. Along the way we'll note many of the references of God's concern for the whole world. And of course, we'll examine the relatively few passages in which God gives an explicit command for missionary activity. But we will see the huge mandate for world mission best as we walk through the entire story of the Bible.

Read Stott, "The Bible in World Evangelization," pp. 21-22c

B. Message, Model and Power for Mission. The Bible reveals what God has been doing and what He wants done. God has shown us in the Bible how we can accomplish God's purpose in God's ways.

Read Stott, "The Bible in World Evangelization," pp. 22c-26

Conclusion of Certificate Level Readings for this lesson.

Credit Level Guide Notes continue...

**After studying this
section you should
be able to:**

- *Describe how Isaiah's
"Servant Songs" show
God's purpose.*

- *Explain what "blessing"
meant in Abraham's day
and what this means for
understanding the mission
mandate of Genesis 12.*

VI. The Biblical Foundation in Themes

Johannes Verkuyl presents five themes that run throughout the Old Testament that substantiate the idea that Jewish people "from their earliest days had heard and understood their call to witness directly as well as by their presence."

A. The Universal Motif. To enjoy this section you need to open your Bible to scan some of the passages.

1. **Table of the Nations.** Look over Genesis 10, which lists the peoples who were scattered at Babel in Genesis 11. The nations are a key part of the biblical drama. God is always concerned with the whole of humanity.

2. **Election of Israel.** The election of Abraham and Israel reveal that God's eye is on the nations.

3. **Breakthrough during exile.** Roughly 400 years before Christ, God scattered the Jewish people among the nations. Seventy years later, some were gathered back to the land again in what some biblical authors consider a second Exodus. Verkuyl points out the Jews' maturing of vision for the world that took place during the time of exile.

B. The Motif of Rescue and Liberation. That God redeemed Israel was foundational. That God would redeem the nations was a louder theme of the prophets and psalmists as the generations unfolded. Isaiah's "Servant Songs" presented God's purpose to bring salvation to the nations (42:1-12; 43:1-13; 49:1-13; 52:13-53:12).

Read the four "Servant Songs" listed above. Look for recurrent themes. Consider the missionary mandate embedded in the promise of these passages. Was the Servant a single person? Or did the Servant refer to the entire people? Or both?

C. The Missionary Motif. Verkuyl offers his view about the charge that Israel was only to be passively present among the nations and God would do the rest. Note that parts of the Bible itself were written in language and in forms that would have been meaningful to the surrounding nations.

D. The Motif of Antagonism. God is at war with His enemies in order to rescue His servants. This corroborates what Ellisen has stated about God's program to defeat evil. Notice particularly how the blazing zeal of God against His enemies is linked to the grand vision of the coming kingdom. God's warfare is linked to God's ambition for His glory to be revealed, which is actually a fifth motif.

E. The Doxological Motif. This theme is barely mentioned by Verkuyl, but he does mention the doxological theme. "Doxological" refers to God's greater glory. The word "doxological" comes from the Greek word for "glory."

Read Verkuyl, "The Biblical Foundation for the Worldwide Mission Mandate," pp. 27-30c

VII. The Biblical Foundation in the Story

Tracing themes throughout the Bible is valuable. However, the most crucial foundation for mission is the biblical story itself. All the verses, passages and biblical truths have even greater force when they are seen in the context in which they were written, and even more thrilling, when they are seen in connection with each other. When the stories are allowed to find their natural connection to each other, using the very themes that are mentioned above, a fascinating single story emerges of God triumphing over His enemies to rescue people from every nation for His glory. Ralph Winter describes the force of this story.

A. The Single Drama. The entrance of the kingdom of God is the central story of the Bible, and of all subsequent history. Every part of the Bible has some connection to the saga of God reconquering and redeeming the earth. It follows then, that this is still the dominant story unfolding in human history.

B. The Plan of Blessing. Winter's description of blessing is important. The concept strikes many Americans as simply things that are given free. That might be the case, says Winter, if God only referred to blessings (plural). But God speaks of the power of His blessing (singular), which includes blessings and gifts, but has more to do with the conferral of a family identity, responsibility and destiny. Such blessing was regarded as very desirable, but it carried obligation and responsibility to fulfill a family purpose. Inheritance was to increase and multiply through the generations. It was not at all thought of as a pile of remaining wealth to be squandered. This is why Jesus' parable in Luke 15 about a son spending his father's inheritance is so scandalous. The older brother was doing what was expected with inheritance and blessing. What this means for the nations is that God was forming a huge global family to be encompassed by His blessing. It also meant that persons who were blessed carried responsibility to fulfill the family purpose.

Read Winter, "The Kingdom Strikes Back," pp. 195-196d

2 The Story of His Glory

Studying this lesson will help you:

- *Explain how the entire story of the Bible unfolds toward a purpose of God's glory in global worship.*

- *Value worship as a relational act that reveals and delights God and fulfills His love for people.*

- *Explain the story of the Bible as God revealing glory to the nations in order to receive glory from the nations.*

- *Show how several of the main events of the Bible's story cohere around the theme of God's unfolding plan to bring about global glory by worship from the nations.*

- *Recognize the mission purpose found in the "Lord's Prayer."*

- *Explain the sentence: "Missions exists because worship doesn't."*

- *Explain how both an expansive and an attractive force have always been used by God to advance His mission purpose.*

- *Describe how the mission objective of planting churches in unreached peoples brings about God's greater glory.*

- *Explain how compassion for people's needs can be integrated with passion for God's glory.*

- *Grow with biblical passion for God's glory and kingdom.*

Most of us learned the Bible using a story-by-story approach. Lessons from these stories are usually applied to our personal concerns. Because of this we may have wrongly assumed that the Bible is a loose collection of stories with no overriding, integrating purpose. Furthermore, we may be quite selfishly mistaken to conclude that the Bible is all about our personal lives. The reality is that the Bible is far more about God than it is about people. With God at the center and the end of it all, the Bible can be seen, not as a disjointed collection of ancient stories and statements, but rather as a single driving saga. It's a story that runs right through every part of Scripture—and it's still unfolding today.

This all-encompassing story of the Bible is about what God began and what God will finish. As we behold God at work throughout the Bible, we will encounter God's own zealous passion. Christ wants us to share in His passion in order to enter His mission.

A well-known mission leader once declared, "Let my heart be broken by the things which break the heart of God." We'll explore some of the matters which strike the heart of God with grief, but we'll do it later in the course. However, at this point, we'll start with what thrills God. Let our hearts first be rejoiced by the things which rejoice the heart of God! Then, as we have aligned our hearts' desires with His, we can find our hearts broken by that which breaks the heart of God.

PASSION Passion is the heart set free to pursue that which is truly worthy. Those who set their hearts on that which is most worthy – the glory of God – live with joy-filled abandon. Their hearts are both seized and satisfied with the ambition for Jesus to be ardently worshiped. That love comes to dominate and integrate all other desires so as to live in the freedom of single-minded purpose.

I.   The Story of His Glory

The story of the Bible is a story about God more than it is about people. In order to see how the biblical stories coalesce into a single prolonged story, we'll need a fresh grasp of three biblical terms:

- **Glory:** intrinsic worth, substance, brilliance and beauty.

- **God's Name:** Beyond the function of reference and revelation, the public reputation and open renown of God.

Read Hawthorne, "The Story of His Glory," pp. 34-35d

Complete the exercise on the next page.

- **Worship:** that which glorifies God by recognizing His glory and by honoring Him with the offerings of the lesser, but worthy glories of the nations. Worship not only delights and reveals God, it fulfills God's love for people by bringing them to a place of their highest honor before Him.

Double Direction of God's Glory. God's mission purpose throughout the story of the Bible can be seen in the double direction of God's glory: God reveals His glory *to* all nations in order to receive glory *from* all nations. World evangelization is the fullest expression of God revealing His glory *to* the nations. The purpose of world evangelization is for God to receive glory *from* the nations.

Read Hawthorne, "The Story of His Glory," pp. 35d-37c

A. **Abraham: A People for His name.** Abraham opens the story by openly honoring God's name. His life provides a preview to the later history of the faith family: He made God's name known in worship. God made His name great by dramatic redemptive power. The result was an occasion of multi-national worship with the messianic figure of Melchizedek presiding. Abraham was blessed to be a blessing—with further purpose—in order that the nations would bless God Himself with their grateful worship.

B. **The Great Display:** God makes Himself known by name to the nations at the Exodus. The subsequent establishing of Israel in the land and the opening of the temple made His purpose even more clear.

1. **The Exodus:** the pivotal moment when God revealed Himself globally by name, distinguishing and honoring His name above any other god.

2. **The Conquest:** God's way of establishing the purity of worship to Himself.

3. **The Temple:** God's way of signaling that people from every nation could encounter and worship Him personally.

Read Hawthorne, "The Story of His Glory," pp. 37c-42a

Look up the verses and describe the reputation God seeks for himself by filling in the *last column*. *The first three are filled in for you as examples.*

God's Fame Among the Nations

	Name-Tag Name *Function: Reference* words used to refer to God	**Fame Name** *Function: Reputation* the public report for God's global renown
Melchizedek—Genesis 14:1-20 In the presence of Abram, the king of Sodom and other kings	**God Most High**	**Genesis 14:20** "... who has delivered your enemies into your hand."
Jethro—Exodus 18:7-12 After the delivery from Egypt	**the LORD (Yahweh)**	**Exodus 18:11** "... now I know that the LORD is greater than all the gods..."
Gibeonites—Joshua 9:3-10 Canaanites pretending to be a people from a distant land who heard of God's name.	**The LORD your God**	**Joshua 9:9-10** "... because of the fame (literally name) of the LORD your God, for we have heard the report of Him and all that He did in Egypt."
Moses—Exodus 33:15-34:8 At Sinai after God said that he would pass by Moses and proclaim His name	**The LORD God**	**Exodus 34:6-7** *Write what God proclaimed to be His name:*
Moses—Numbers 14:1-21 After God said He would destroy the people, Moses prayed, arguing on the basis of God's name	**The LORD**	**Numbers 14:14** *What the nations had heard:* **Numbers 14:15-16** *What the nations would conclude if God destroyed the people:* **Numbers 14:17-18** *What Moses knew God wanted as His reputation among the nations:*
Jonah—Jonah 3:4-4:2 The truth about God that Jonah did not want to disclose to a Gentile nation	**God (Elohim)**	**Jonah 4:2** *Compare to Moses above:*
Malachi—Malachi 1:11-14 God describing how pure whole-hearted worship reveals His kingly glory	**Lord of Hosts**	**Malachi 1:14** "I am a great _____ and my _____ is to be _____ among the _____."

Also the foreigners who join
themselves to the LORD,

To minister to Him, and to love
the name of the LORD,

To be His servants, every one
who keeps from profaning the
sabbath,

And holds fast My covenant;

Even those I will bring to My
holy mountain,

And make them joyful in My
house of prayer.

Their burnt offerings and their
sacrifices will be acceptable on
My altar;

For My house will be called a
house of prayer for all the
peoples."

—Isaiah 56:6-7

C. The Great Delay: Just when it looked as if Israel was going to make God's name widely known among the nations, Solomon led the way in idolatry. Idolatry profaned, or made common, the name of international renown that God had sanctified, or exalted, in the view of the nations. Then began centuries of up and down struggles with idolatry. God finally removed the people from the land, sending them among the nations into a time of captivity known as the Exile.

D. God's Persistence and Renewed Promise. God never ceased to pursue His original promise and purpose. The people were brought again into the land, the temple was rebuilt, and a Messiah was expected. God's word about this restoration is clear; it was all for the fulfillment of His global purpose. Many other expressions of the psalmists and prophets clarify God's purpose to be worshiped.

E. The Glory of God in Christ. Jesus fulfilled God's purpose to reveal His glory to the world in order to receive glory from the nations.

 1. **Prayers for the Name.** By the prayer He taught and the prayers He prayed, we can see how Jesus aimed His entire life at fulfilling the ancient purpose of making God's name known. For God's name to be "hallowed" or "sanctified" is for His namesake to be distinguished, exalted and honored. No prayer could be more basic to the mission purpose of God.

 2. **A house of worship from all peoples.** The text in Isaiah that Jesus quoted in the temple makes it clear that God rejoiced to receive worship arising *from* nations other than Israel. The temple was destined to become a place of worship that all peoples could easily access in order to meet God, bringing Him their prayerful worship.

Read Isaiah 56:6-7 carefully to see the context of the statement "For my house shall be called a house of prayer…." Note the references to prayer in verse 7. What kind of prayers are described? Who is offering these prayers? Jesus did not just quote this verse. He taught about it at what was likely the most public hour of His ministry (Mark 11:17). What kinds of prayer was Jesus wanting to see? This passage is often used to encourage prayer on behalf of the nations. This is fine, but it may miss the point of Christ's passionate teaching and temple-cleansing: the hope that the nations will themselves pray in full-hearted worship.

Read Hawthorne, "The Story of His Glory," pp. 42c-44

What did God do for His glory at each of the successive points of the story? Either finish writing out the verse in the space provided, or add another note describing God's actions and intentions.

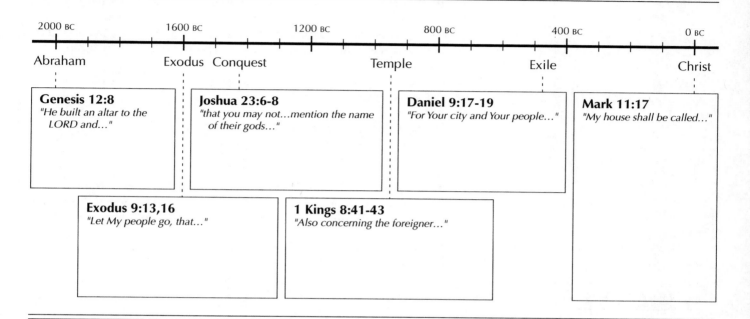

II. God-Centered Mission

We've explored how God's purpose for glory unfolds on the timeline of history. John Piper restates the case for focusing our motive in mission on God's glory in the worship of the nations. Piper says that world evangelization is a secondary, means-to-an-end activity. God's glory is the primary purpose for mission. Missions exists because worship doesn't.

A. God's Passion. God's supremacy over other gods provides clear rationale for mission. But an even stronger motive is ours in God's inexhaustible enthusiasm that there be praise arising from the nations. Worship is the fuel as well as the goal of missions.

B. God-centered Compassion. Calling the nations to worship is to seek their best interest. Understanding the redemptive value of worship can energize our acts of mercy even when, at times, feelings of love for others fade. As the nations see the dignity of worshiping the living God, His call to come near to Him by worship becomes the highlight of all the blessings He bestows. It becomes the most sharable message in the world.

Read Piper, "Let the Nations be Glad!" pp. 49-54 (all)

III. Fulfilling The Missionary Task

How was Israel supposed to fulfill the mission mandate inherent in God's promise to bless the nations through her? It might appear that Israel was to play only a passive role, attracting the nations to God's worship. Some have concluded that there was not an active mandate to go to the nations until the days of the New Testament. Look again at the biblical record to see the steady, relentless plan of God, both sending His people to the nations to declare the truth of His name, and as well, attracting the nations to join His people in worship.

A. **Two Forces.** Jonathan Lewis describes two mechanisms, or forces of mission, which were constantly at work.

1. **Expansive or centrifugal.** There is found throughout the story of scripture the outward-bound dynamic, which Lewis calls the expansive force. Others have called this the centrifugal force of missions, or a "go" structure of mission.

2. **Attractive or centripetal.** There is also found throughout the Bible the inward-bound dynamic, which Lewis calls the attractive force. Others have called this the centripetal force of missions, or a "come" structure of mission.

Read Lewis, "Two Forces," pp. 60-61

Conclusion of Key Readings for this lesson.

B. **Jonah.** Jonah is one of several people in the Old Testament that were sent by God beyond the borders of Israel. Johannes Verkuyl does not consider the sending of Jonah to be an exception, but an example of the self-centered attitude of God's people. He believes that, by the Holy Spirit, the book speaks to the Church today. Follow his exposition through the eight scenes of Jonah. Take note of how he describes Jonah's anger that God extended mercy beyond the borders of Israel even though He knew God's namesake was to be globally known as a "gracious and compassionate" God. Notice Verkuyl's description of Jonah's refusal to acknowledge the purpose of God's covenant with Israel for the salvation of the nations.

Read Verkuyl, "The Biblical Foundation for the Worldwide Mission Mandate," pp. 30c-33 (the Jonah section)

IV. Co-Working with God's Passion

Motives matter. The biblical vision for God's glory and kingdom energizes us with steady zeal.

A. **Beyond Duty.** Tim Dearborn explores some commonplace attitudes toward mission motivation.

1. **No longer a duty.** He exposes the inadequacy of being compelled by human needs. Instead, he describes how the passions of God's heart can propel our hearts. He suggests that there is one singular passion. What is that passion?

2. **God on mission.** He says that it is far better to affirm that "the God of mission has a Church in the world" than it is to say that "the Church has a mission for God in the world." How does this idea compare with what Piper and Hawthorne have stated?

3. **The Kingdom.** Dearborn begins to describe the theme of our next lesson: The Kingdom of God. How is the Kingdom another expression of God-centered mission?

Read Dearborn, "Beyond Duty," pp. 90-93 (all)

B. **Passion for God's Glory.** Paul was motivated by the hope that God would be glorified among the nations. How was Paul's mission as described in Romans 15, a mission that he aimed to finish? Can or should that be our vision today? Steve Hawthorne describes three changes in practice worth considering for us as we recognize our part in the ongoing story of God's glory.

1. **Deepen our motive base.** When mission is merely a compassionate response to human need, motivation can be limited to feelings of concern toward people. Some mobilization can be limited to stirring up guilt. But when mission is defined primarily as an enterprise that brings about something for God, and secondarily as something which brings about something which benefits people, then both our motivation and our mobilization can be more balanced. Compassion may actually run deeper. We can be deeply moved by needs while acting boldly for God's highest purpose.

2. **Define the task.** Focusing on God's glory helps us see the value of planting churches among people groups which become an expression of the sanctified best of that particular culture. This may be one of the best grounds for planting church movements among every people group. The people group *approach* is not as important as setting our vision on the people group *result*.

3. **Integrate efforts.** Which is more important? Evangelism or social action? This is a false dichotomy, in large part answered by lifting vision beyond what happens *for people* (which is usually emphasized in both evangelism and social action) and aim instead at bringing about glory, thanks, praise and honor *for God*. A single vision for God's glory can integrate and motivate efforts to serve people in their present-hour need as well as save people from eternal loss.

Read Hawthorne, "The Story of His Glory," pp. 45-47

Conclusion of Certificate Level Readings for this lesson.

Credit Level Guide Notes continue...

V. God's Mission

David Bosch introduces an important phrase. Don't let its significance be hidden by the Latin. The phrase is *missio Dei*, and it means God's mission, or the mission of God. It's surprisingly important to focus on God as the author of mission. Can you imagine how different it would be if people were merely responding to each other's needs as they saw fit? What if it was up to human ingenuity and mercy to engineer the changes that are needed in the world? That generally describes the attitude of the world outside the Judeo-Christian tradition. Think about it. Without mission, the world is a pretty bleak place. The only glimmer of hope would be some grandiose ideas about human progress or vague ideas about evolution. When these ideas and other ideas are seen to fail, the world becomes ripe with yearning for someone to be sent, for someone to redeem.

It's no wonder that the prayer Jesus prayed was for the Church to be one with God in mission so that the world would come to know that God had sent Jesus. John 17:11-23 is commonly misunderstood as if the world was to be attracted to God because the Church enjoys relational closeness. The context is all about Jesus leaving and sending His followers, even as He was sent. It's very likely that the idea of being "one even as we are one" refers to a collaborative intimacy in mission rather than an essential unity or a task-free relational closeness. Think about it!). In any case, it is good news that God is on mission Himself. It is also marvelous that He would ever condescend to send others on His behalf. In this section we'll seek to grasp some of the wonder of this awesome way of knowing God.

David Bosch occasionally uses technical words, but the meanings are usually nearby. For example, the word "prolepsis" is followed immediately by its meaning, "an anticipation."

A. God the Author of Mission. Bosch explains more about the light of the Servant of the Lord in Isaiah. He points out that the mechanism of mission works in two directions with the Servant. Light flows from the Servant to the nations. And yet, in response, the nations come to the light and are gathered into a larger people by the attractive power of the light. The main point is that God is the author. Israel never appointed itself as a missionary nation. The Jews did not have a habit of sending themselves on errands of salvation. They were called by God to do so.

B. The "Tender Mystery" of God and People on Mission. Bosch explains why both mechanisms were at work throughout both the Old and New Testaments. It would seem that centripetal or attractive force is God's work. A careless reading of the story at this point would lead one to conclude that centrifugal or expansive mission is man's work. This is a crucial mistake. To highlight the error, he uses the almost ridiculous phrase "God and Man as Competitors?".

To sum up the issue: If God is the author of only centripetal, or attractive mission, then that seems to imply that people need to undertake the initiative for centrifugal mission. The mistake is compounded when everyday zeal is added to the mix, or American pragmatism that assumes we can do anything if we just put our mind to it. Mission is not to be treated in this spirit. Mission is a "tender mystery" of God and people co-working, though God is always the author. Take special note of the series of paradoxes which illustrate this "tender mystery."

This is not an inconsequential issue. There are two extremes to avoid. If God is the sole initiator, not enlisting any collaboration from people, then there is resignation: Let be what will be. On the other hand, if God's mission is a command waiting for someone to finally be obedient, then there are waves of fanaticism: It all depends on us.

C. More Than A Command. This marvelous co-working of God and His people is exactly why the Great Commission is not stamped on every page, but almost presumed throughout the New Testament. Bosch says, "Mission in the New Testament is more than a matter of obeying a command. It is, rather, the result of an encounter with Christ. To meet Christ means to become caught up in a mission to the world." Bosch is not saying that the Great Commission does not have tremendous force. He is saying that the entire Bible supports the Great Commission in greater ways than finding parallel statements from God issuing direct imperative commands.

Read Bosch, "Witness to the World," pp. 59-63 (all)

VI. God Initiates Mission

Henry Blackaby and Avery Willis explore God's ways in accomplishing His mission. Examine the examples they mention of God initiating an act of advancing His mission by revealing what He was going to do. In every case, God gave His people something to accomplish, and yet, God was the one who accomplished everything. Why does God choose to do things in this way? Blackaby and Willis assert that God desires a a loving but purposeful relationship with His people in mission.

Read Blackaby/Willis, "On Mission with God." pp. 55-56d

3 Your Kingdom Come

Studying this lesson will help you:

- *Define and use the concepts comprising the theme of the kingdom of God in the Bible.*

- *Explain the surprise of "the mystery of the Kingdom" in terms of the Messiah coming not just once, but twice.*

- *Explain how Christ intended the missionary enterprise to extend His "D-Day" victory at the cross.*

- *Explain the mission significance of a "two-tier" timeline of history, in which a present evil age persists even though it is invaded by a coming kingdom age.*

- *Explain what it means to advance the gospel of the Kingdom.*

- *Explain how Matthew 24:14 gives hope and focus for completing world evangelization.*

- *Understand how Jesus pursued his life-work guided by a vision of the kingdom of God as a fight against evil.*

- *Pray with bold hope and with strategic purpose for God to restrain evil powers in order for people to hear the gospel and to hope for lasting change.*

To accomplish God's mission, or to enter it at all, we must be convinced that God is not merely managing evil, He is destroying it. Without such hope, we will not likely enlist ourselves in the spiritual war that we see raging. We are likely to explain away the present hurricane of darkness, acquiescing to it as if it were a passing outbreak of bad weather. But we know better. The Bible is clear about the extravagant price God has already paid to reconcile people who were enemies. The Bible is clear about God's determination to dismantle every evil power, with present-hour manifestations of the forthcoming triumph.

Jesus had one prevailing theme in His teaching: the kingdom of God. He used that theme to call people to follow Him. He used that language to enlist His friends to follow Him further – into the final stages of the global war against evil.

His kingdom focus challenges us with matters of huge significance in this war. It is no small thing to establish communities of kingdom life as outposts of light in the midst of spiritual darkness. Because of the surpassing certainty of the inbreak of the Kingdom, it is not rare to find Christ's servants loving their own lives so little that death does not threaten them. These people pray and labor for nothing less than His kingdom coming on earth as it is in heaven. Such a pursuit of Christ's kingdom is the heart of all true hoping. It is the soul of all praying. The kingdom of God is the core of all mission.

HOPE   God has called us to live our lives as a bold act of hope. To hope is not merely to wish for small improvements of personal circumstances. Hope expects all things, large or little, to be overwhelmed and filled with the immense glory of Christ. Thus, true hope pursues global glory and total triumph over evil. Lives of hope can face great evil with relentless courage, since there is no telling how soon God will break through with ultimate victory.

We've already seen God's ultimate purpose to be a crescendo of glory from all peoples. We've traced the outlines of His purpose for worship through the major turning points of the entire story of the Bible. Now we'll focus more closely on the way God liberates people from a kingdom of satanic darkness to serve Him as worshiping priests from all nations.

I. Basic Kingdom Concepts

A. The Meaning of "Kingdom." We commonly use "kingdom" to designate a king's geographical domain or people belonging to such a realm. The Bible uses the term in a different and dynamic way: "Kingdom" is the right to rule, rather than royally-owned real estate.

B. The "Kingdom of God" is the exercise of God's kingship, His authority, His right to rule based on His might, power, and glory.

Read Ladd, "The Gospel of the Kingdom," pp. 64-66b

II. Basic Kingdom Conflicts

A. The Mystery of the Kingdom. Jesus used the idea of "the mystery of the Kingdom" to describe a time of mercy for the nations before final judgment. The surprise that defines the mystery is that the expected kingly Messiah figure was to come not once, but twice. He will come in a blaze of glory as the Son of Man (Daniel 7). But this coming is preceded by His first coming in humility and hidden form as the Suffering Servant of God (Isaiah 42, 49, 53).

1. The Old Testament perspective saw the Kingdom coming as a single cataclysmic event of judgment on God's enemies, opening a time of God's peace and power.

The Vision of the Kingdom

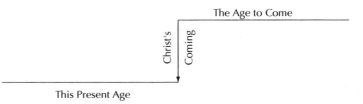

The Messiah brings God's Day of Peace and Power

2. God's kingdom comes in two stages:

• **With Jesus' first coming:** The Kingdom has already arrived! But it operates in a more hidden way, breaking satanic power, delivering people of all nations from the grip of evil's power and offering spiritual blessings of God's rule.

• **At the end:** It will come openly, in all the world's view, crushing all earthly powers, destroying every human attempt to usurp God's rightful rule, purging all sin and evil from the earth. This vision fulfills the Old Testament perspective.

The Mystery of the Kingdom

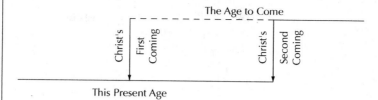

The Messiah Comes Twice

B. The Victory of the Kingdom. God's kingdom is a progressive victory over satanic dominion to rescue people of all nations from the power of darkness. This "present evil age" has already been invaded by "the age to come" of God's kingdom. Satan has already been defeated but he is destined to be destroyed in "the age to come." We are now living in the overlap of the ages. We work between the "already" of Jesus' first coming and the "not yet" of His second coming. The time between the two comings is fundamentally a time of conflict resulting from the overlap of the ages. The missionary task of the Church (evangelizing the nations) is the primary reason for this interim period. The Kingdom victory is accomplished in three great acts:

• **Christ's first coming:** breaking Satan's power—Jesus' mission on earth by His life, death and resurrection

• **Between His comings:** undoing Satan's works—Jesus continues His mission with the Church to the nations

• **Christ's second coming:** destroying Satan's kingdom—Christ comes in full glory

Read Ladd, "The Gospel of the Kingdom," pp. 66b-69c

Read Blue, "D-Day before V-E Day, p. 72

III. The Mandate of the Kingdom

George Ladd finds enormous mandate force in Matthew 24:14. We emphasize this verse not because we are predicting a specific time of Christ's return, but to emphasize that God apparently intends to wait until all peoples have had opportunity to respond to an adequate testimony of the gospel of the Kingdom.

A. Message of the Kingdom. The gospel of the Kingdom declares and displays God's triumph over the three enemies that have been the ruin of people throughout history: death, Satan and sin. They have each been defeated by His first coming and they will each be destroyed at His final coming.

The gospel of the Kingdom announces what God has already done, and is now continuing to do to conquer the enemies of sin, death and the devil. God intends to bring substantial healing and lasting transformation in the present day, and eternal life in the eternal kingdom. The gospel of the Kingdom is not only an announcement, it is a promise of what God will do to reconcile all things under the kingly headship of Christ.

B. The Mission of the Kingdom. Matthew 24:14 is the only verse in scripture in which Jesus gives his disciples a specific description of what *must* be accomplished *before* his second coming and the end of the age. World evangelization is an explicit condition for His return. The gospel of the Kingdom must be proclaimed in all the world. Only then will the end come. What constitutes an adequate " witness" or who constitutes "all the peoples" by Christ's understanding cannot be discerned with precision. Should we not take seriously any significant barrier between peoples which may block the flow of the gospel so that none of "the peoples" mentioned in Matthew 24:14 are bypassed? Should we not labor to establish the fullest "witness" possible — an ongoing community of obedience under Christ's Lordship?

1. **Meaning to history.** This truth, that God is holding history open in order for the Church to complete her task, gives meaning to history and gives enormous significance to the obedience of the Church.

2. **Motive of the Kingdom.** If it is true that the coming of the Messiah is in some way contingent upon the Church proclaiming the gospel of the Kingdom to all peoples, then we have great motivation: Final victory awaits the completion of the task. No greater hope can be conceived. Ladd asks and answers the question, "Do you love his appearing? Then you will bend every effort to take the gospel into all the world."

Read Ladd, "The Gospel of the Kingdom," pp. 69d-77

IV. The Prayer of the Kingdom

The essence of intercessory prayer as taught by Jesus is to argue a case in God's court. It is not a matter of explaining or acquiescing to evil, but rather fighting against it. Leading theologian David Wells exposes some assumptions that are deeply held on a worldview level. He declares that the Hebrew/Christian worldview denies that the evil we find on earth is God's will and plan. Instead, Jesus charged His followers to "rebel" against the status quo by intercessory prayer. We are to pray that His name be honored, sanctified, and blessed, even where it is denied. We are to ask that His kingdom rule become effective, even where it is defied and that His will be accomplished even where it is opposed by His enemies.

Read Wells, "Prayer: Rebelling Against the Status Quo," pp. 142-144

Conclusion of Key Readings for this lesson.

Now when John in prison heard of the works of Christ, he sent word by his disciples, and said to Him,

"Are You the Expected One, or shall we look for someone else?"

And Jesus answered and said to them, "Go and report to John what you hear and see:

the blind receive sight and the lame walk, the lepers are cleansed and the deaf hear, and the dead are raised up, and the poor have the gospel preached to them.

And blessed is he who keeps from stumbling over Me."

—Matthew 11:2-6

...in order that what was spoken through Isaiah the prophet, might be fulfilled, saying,

"Behold, my Servant whom I have chosen;

My Beloved in whom My soul is well-pleased;

I will put My Spirit upon Him,

And He shall proclaim justice (literally, judgment) to the Gentiles.

He will not quarrel, nor cry out;

Nor will anyone hear His voice in the streets.

A battered reed He will not break off,

And a smoldering wick He will not put out,

Until He leads justice (literally, judgment) to victory.

And in His name the Gentiles (literally, nations) will hope."

—Matthew 12:17-21

V. The Messiah on Kingdom Mission

Imagine Jesus reading His Bible. What would He have come to understand about God's purpose and His own part in it? There's no question that when Jesus began His ministry, the kingdom of God was more than a mere topic of His teaching. The reality of the kingdom of God set the stage for all that He did, said or prayed. He knew that He was the key figure in the global struggle between good and evil. He knew that He had been sent into the kingdom war. When He sent His followers He gave them a clear picture of the drama of God at war to redeem the nations.

A. The Day of the Lord. H. Cornell Goerner shows how the Book of Malachi probably shaped the vision and the ministry of John the Baptist as well as Jesus.

1. God's Day of Judgment. Malachi had warned Israel that God's judgment would fall on Israel first, rather than the nations, who were perceived to be God's enemies. Why judgment on Israel? Because of God's desire to be worshiped by all nations (Malachi 1:10-11). Israel had failed to fulfill the most rudimentary regimens of worship and the fear of God's name (Malachi 2:1-3; 4:1-6).

2. John's warning of the Kingdom. Malachi described a classic expression of the Old Testament vision of God's judgment arriving in a single stroke of destructive power against God's enemies. John the Baptist warned people of a vast coming judgment.

3. Jesus' Word of the Kingdom. Jesus continued this same message, calling for repentance because the turning point in history was at hand ("The time is fulfilled, and the kingdom of God is at hand; repent and believe in the gospel." Mark 1:15). As John and others looked on, they expected, after the model of Malachi (Malachi 3:1-5), that the Messiah would boldly confront the leading priests and governing powers, even to the point of throwing off the Roman empire's control.

4. The surprise Messiah. But Jesus disappointed John the Baptist. Instead of a conquest over high political powers, Jesus declared that the present day was the time for healing the downtrodden and preaching the gospel to the poor. It soon became clear to His followers that Jesus' healing and preaching to the poor was just the beginning of an engagement with spiritual evil and a proclamation of the gospel to the poor throughout the nations.

> Read Matthew 11:2-6 and consider what John expected. Ponder Christ's response and what it indicates about Christ's kingdom mission. Now read Matthew 12:17-21. It reveals what the disciples had come to discover about Jesus in the book of Isaiah. How was this prophecy fulfilled in Jesus' work? How is this prophecy still being fulfilled today? How will the nations be moved to hope?

B. The Surprise of the Servant. Jesus did not fulfill the general expectations of the people for a conquering ruler. Jesus knew that there was another model of the coming of the Messiah and the Kingdom. It is found in the passages of Isaiah which refer to the Servant. A key aspect of the vision of the Servant is that His work extends to all the nations over a prolonged period of time.

> Read the following passages in Isaiah. Which verses refer to the Servant figure fulfilling God's missionary purpose among many nations? Isaiah 42:1-12; 49:1-6; 52:13–53:12. How does this role align with Jesus' teaching about "the mystery of the Kingdom?"

C. The Son of Man. Jesus used this messianic title deliberately and frequently. He found it in Daniel who saw God inaugurating the rule of the Son of Man as king of all peoples and kingdoms. The global ramifications were clear to everyone of His day.

Read Goerner, "Jesus and the Gentiles," pp. 94-97a

Do the exercise below.

Designate the location of the following biblical phrases on the timeline to show when they were or will be fulfilled. Sometimes more than one correct answer is possible. From what we've seen of the disappointment of John the Baptist, which of these passages might he thought were very near? Place yourself on this timeline.

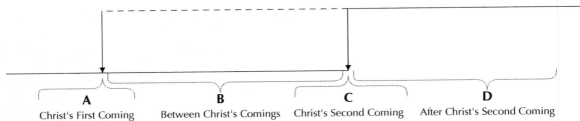

A	B	C	D
Christ's First Coming	Between Christ's Comings	Christ's Second Coming	After Christ's Second Coming

___ Daniel 2:44 "....the God of heaven will set up a kingdom which will....crush and put an end to all these kingdoms, but it will itself endure forever."

___ Isaiah 11:4 "He will strike the earth with the rod of his mouth; with the breath of his lips he will slay the wicked."

___ Isaiah 11:6 "And the wolf will dwell with the lamb, and the leopard will lie down with the kid....and a little boy will lead them."

___ Malachi 4:1 "....the day is coming, burning like a furnace; and all the arrogant and every evildoer will be chaff."

___ Malachi 4:5 "Behold, I am going to send you Elijah the prophet before the coming of the great and terrible day of the LORD."

___ Matthew 12:29 "Or how can anyone enter the strong man's house and carry off his property, unless he first binds the strong man?"

___ Matthew 12:18-21 "I will put My Spirit upon Him, And He shall proclaim justice to the Gentiles...Until He leads justice to victory. And in His name the Gentiles will hope."

___ Luke 11:20 "But if I cast out demons by the finger of God, then the kingdom of God has come upon you."

___ Matthew 28:18 "All authority has been given to Me in heaven and on earth."

___ Matthew 28:19 "Therefore go and make disciples of all nations...."

___ Matthew 28:20 "....until the end of the age."

___ Matthew 24:14 "....preached in the whole world for a witness to all the nations...."

___ Matthew 24:14 "....and then the end shall come."

___ John 12:31-32 "Now judgment is upon this world; now the ruler of this world shall be cast out. And I, if I be lifted up from the earth...."

___ John 12:32 "I....will draw all men to Myself."

___ 1 Thessalonians 1:9 "....you turned to God from idols to serve a living and true God...."

___ 1 Thessalonians 1:10 "....and to wait for His Son from heaven, whom He raised from the dead that is Jesus, who delivers us from the wrath to come."

D. God at War. Gregory Boyd helps us understand more about how Jesus acted in keeping with how the Jewish people of His day understood the Bible. This worldview was a thoroughly biblical outlook, enhanced by "apocalyptic" writers who emphasized that God was at war against a satanic insurrection. These angelic evil powers had been attempting to thwart God's purposes for Israel to become a blessing to the nations. In the apocalyptic view, this war was coming soon to a climactic finale. With this backdrop we can see Jesus on mission to overcome evil powers in order to liberate people. Further, we can see Christ's followers continuing this same mission.

1. Jesus as "the bringer of the kingdom of God." Notice Boyd's analysis of how Jesus understood the kingdom of God: "For Jesus, the kingdom of God means abolishing the kingdom of Satan." In this light the actions of Jesus can be seen as deliberate acts of mission to free people from the powers of darkness. Jesus aimed at nothing less than invading the present dark age to establish the enduring reign of God's peace.

Read Boyd, "God at War," p. 80a-81a, 82-84a

2. Continuing the work of God's war. Boyd describes how Jesus "commissioned, equipped, and empowered" not only His immediate followers, but the entire Church to continue His battle against evil by proclaiming and demonstrating Christ's kingdom. Boyd suggests how centuries ago, Western worldview assumptions may have turned the Church away from the mission of *fighting* evil to a practice of merely *explaining* evil. We are left with the question: Is it possible to carry out Christ's Great Commission without *in some way* fighting against evil?

Read Boyd, "God at War," p. 84b-85

VI. Strategic Prayer

John Robb presents prayer as a way to deal with supernatural evil in a forceful way. The purpose is to fulfill God's mandate for gospel proclamation as well as social transformation. He shows how truths about the kingdom of God have been put into practice in prayer, giving biblical as well as contemporary examples.

A. Socio-spiritual Forces. Two complexes, idolatry and strongholds, often hold the least evangelized settings so that gospel proclamation and even community development efforts have little reception. Idolatry usually enmeshes people into contracts with false gods. Strongholds are false patterns of thought which deny that Christ can be obeyed or, in some cases, that anything at all can change for the better. With idolatry locking up people's sense of allegiance, and with strongholds limiting people to a worldview of hopelessness, the work of prayer is important to prepare the way for the gospel.

B. Forceful Prayer is Not Magic. Prayer can be forceful because it invites God into the fray. The temptation is to see ourselves as intrinsically powerful because we are praying. Prayer should never be utilized as if it were a magic formula or a procedure guaranteed to work. Prayer does not so much work; God Himself is at work. Prayer is God's way of involving us with His work. With this balancing wisdom, it is important to pursue prayer in some situations as an act of spiritual violence.

C. Prayer for Unreached Peoples. Prayer is particularly significant for unreached peoples. Where Christ does not yet have a following, the strongholds which blind people to the possibility of obeying Christ have rarely been challenged. In such societies, where Christ-obeying churches do not exist, we should not be surprised to see that the worldview of the people is often impregnated with powerful patterns of thinking which resist the gospel. Prayer can be God's way of breaking these fatalistic, hopeless ways of thinking, preparing the way for many to follow Him. Prayer can present God opportunities to show Himself to be greater than other gods (sanctifying His name!), thus breaking patterns of allegiance with dark powers reinforced by idolatry. Prayer for laborers is another way that praying for unreached peoples is essential.

Read Robb, "Strategic Prayer," pp. 145-151, (all)

God's Purpose Summarized: For His glory in global worship, God purposes to redeem a people from every people, and to rule a kingdom over all kingdoms.

Now we can see better how the three parts of God's purpose work together.

- Concerning evil: We've emphasized how the kingdom of God advances His purpose against the Satanic counterfeit kingdom in order to rule a kingdom over all kingdoms.

- For the nations: The Kingdom victory opens the way for God to redeem people, bringing them into the blessing of Abraham under Christ's Lordship.

- Toward God: All of this takes place so that the nations will know and glorify God as King.

The mission that God gives to His Church is not a sideline affair. Christ gives us an enormous part to play to bring forth the fruit of His kingdom victory. In the next lesson we'll explore how Christ grounds the Great Commission on the full measure of authority and power of the Kingdom. In Lesson Six we'll explore how all of history after the New Testament times can still be characterized by the theme of the Kingdom striking back.

Conclusion of Certificate Level Readings for this lesson.

Credit Level Guide Notes continue...

After studying this section you should be able to:

- *Describe the apocalyptic background of the thinking in Jesus' day which show how His statements and deeds were understood to be an act of war against Satanic powers.*

- *Explain how Jesus' declaration of a time of mercy for the nations aroused the anger of the people of His hometown.*

- *Explain how the Western worldview may lead us to be more "truth-conscious" than "power-conscious." Explain the ramifications of such a worldview for ministry among many of the least-evangelized peoples today.*

VII. The Mission of God is a War against Evil

Gregory Boyd presents more about the background of Jesus' mission. A significant transformation of worldview took place during the "Intertestamental period." The Intertestamental period was the time between the final prophet that spoke to Israel (Malachi) and the precursor of Jesus (John the Baptist). Jewish teachers never changed their view of the magnificent supremacy of God at all, but they became convinced that a cosmic war was being fought between a Satanic counterfeit kingdom and the armies of the living God. This view had abundant grounding in the Scriptures (as Verkuyl has already pointed out to us, calling it the "motif of antagonism"). But the worldview was significantly developed during the Intertestamental period.

A. Cosmic War. Fallen angels were fighting against God. Had God "lost" or was He allowing a greater victory in the days to come? A middle tier of angelic powers were seen to be wreaking havoc with the complicity of people from many nations. Creation, at least during the "present evil age," was seen as a diabolical war zone. God would, of course, rise as Judge of all the earth at the fullness of time and bring complete defeat of His spiritual enemies. The day of God's climactic inbreaking power, which would inaugurate an era of great peace (Hebrew: "Shalom"), was referred to as "the Day of the Lord" and "the kingdom of God."

B. Jesus' Mission. Jesus is presented in the Gospels as overcoming Satan in a global struggle. At issue was the kingdoms of the world and their glory. Jesus' teaching and miracles were actually described with language that more than suggests that Jesus was boldly pressing forward a campaign to break Satan's power in order to free people. As you read Boyd's writings, take note of the careful balance that he injects. For example, Boyd notes that Jesus never endorses the apocalyptic tendency to speculate about hierarchies of angels. Being "saved" has the additional dimension of being delivered from the evil grasp of the enemy. Boyd is careful not to eliminate the meaning of spiritual regeneration from the idea of being saved. At times you'll need to refer to Boyd's footnotes (which are fascinating) to catch all the biblical references.

Read Boyd, "God at War," pp. 78-81

VIII. Attempted Murder for Mercy

Patrick Johnstone sheds important light on one of the opening acts of Jesus' ministry. Find it in Luke 4:14-30. Have your Bible open to this passage as well as Isaiah 61:1-2 as you read Johnstone's suggestions about how the original language could be translated. Ponder the possible meaning that could be attributed to Jesus' stopping abruptly in the middle of a line of Hebrew poetry. What was the popular idea of "the day of vengeance" concerning the nations? With the background we've examined about the apocalyptic war, and the expected outbreak of God's judgment on the nations, can you imagine what the townspeople were thinking about leaving things open-ended in mercy? Just when the people had begun to grasp what He meant by interrupting the reading, Jesus confirmed their thoughts by pronouncing, "Today, this scripture is fulfilled."

They understood that Jesus was opening a time of mercy. These were "the gracious words" that were coming from his lips. But Jesus did not just leave it to their imaginations to dream of God prolonging a time of kindness upon the nation of Israel. He made it abundantly clear that God's mercy was intended for the nations. It was this pronouncement that provoked them to kill Him.

Read Johnstone, "A Violent Reaction to Mercy," p. 106

X.   A Fresh Look at God's Supernatural

Much of what we have presented in this lesson may seem to be an argument for rowdy spiritual warfare. There are some who seem to present views on spiritual warfare which could be regarded as "vigilante warfare" in which Christians launch into attacks on spiritual powers without guidance from God or a sense of unity with others. Stereotypes of the extremes of spiritual warfare can only be exposed by a brighter, clearer vision of the Biblical ground. C. Peter Wagner, a leading missiologist and prayer leader, discusses some of the changes in evangelical mission circles regarding spiritual warfare and prayer. Wagner writes that he is not trying to persuade anyone to a Pentecostal or Charismatic view. In fact, he personally does not wish to identify with either of those streams. As an Evangelical, he respectfully invites fellow believers of any theological background to take a fresh look at matters of spiritual power and the kingdom of God.

A. A Sense of Powerlessness in the Face of Manifest Evil. Wagner recounts his own journey and the reports of many others who have had greater struggles with obvious encounters with horrific powers of spiritual darkness.

B. A Flawed Worldview. Wagner sums up the ideas of Paul Hiebert in a seminal article called "The Flaw of the Excluded Middle." We'll be reading this as part of Lesson 10. Western Christianity has not been neutral, but rather a very potent force for secularization, so that our own worldviews are skewed away from the biblical accounts.

C. A Fresh Examination of the Kingdom of God. Wagner's journey in understanding the kingdom of God may be similar to that of many evangelicals. Take the time to understand the progression of his thinking. His description of the overlap of the ages may be among the best in the Perspectives course. His articulation of the ramifications for missions is significant.

Read Wagner, "On the Cutting Edge," pp. 536d-540

4 Mandate for the Nations

Studying this lesson will help you:

- *Explain the strategic value of Jesus working with a few leaders to launch a movement to reach the entire world.*

- *Explain the strategic value of Jesus' focus on the Jewish people.*

- *Tell the story of how Jesus taught and modeled ministry to Gentiles.*

- *Explain the Great Commission, describing Christ's expectation of what is to be completed among all peoples.*

- *Describe the strategic value of focusing on people groups as it helps to complete the entire task of world evangelization.*

- *Explain how Jesus sends His followers on mission in the same way the Father sent Him on mission.*

- *Present the best biblical grounds for explaining the lostness of humankind in response to the ideas of universalism.*

- *Respond to the challenge of pluralism by presenting features of the uniqueness of Christ that mention His works, words, death and resurrection.*

We rightly exalt Jesus as personal Savior. But in seeking to honor Christ for the great worth of His death and resurrection we may have ignored much of the astounding accomplishment of His life. Jesus did far more than provide for salvation, He launched a movement that would actually bring that salvation to every part of the world. In this lesson we'll examine Jesus' life-work and His enduring mandate. He chose His followers and ordered His actions with strategic intent. He said to His Father at the end of His life, "I glorified You on the earth, having accomplished the work which You gave Me to do" (John 17:4).

Christ's mandate to us spells out our assignment to continue the work that He began during His life until it is complete in every people. It's obvious that we will miss the point of *our* mission if we fail to understand how He pursued *His* mission. For those who have embraced His purpose, no phrase becomes more precious than "As the Father has sent Me, I also send you" (John 20:21).

MANDATE To live under mandate is to be entrusted with a task of lasting significance. Mandates are not commands. By direct commands we assign small errands or daily chores. A mandate, on the other hand, releases authority and responsibility to pursue endeavors of historic importance. God has entrusted to Christ, and with Him to the Church, a mandate to fulfill His purpose for all of history.

I.   The Strategic Focus of Jesus

Jesus acted with strategic purpose. He not only modeled God's concern for world evangelization, He also prepared a dynamic, multiplying movement capable of evangelizing the world.

A. Jesus' Concentration on the Jewish People. God had prepared the Jewish people to receive and understand the gospel. Even so, when Jesus came, He faced vicious hostility from the first moments of public ministry. Though many Jews rejected Him, a substantial portion of the Jewish people eventually did receive Him as Messiah. God's desire to make the Hebrew people a light to the nations was indeed fulfilled. However it was not accomplished apart from a significant effort by Jesus to form His Jewish following into an mission movement.

He began to reveal God's mission heart to His followers by first sending the twelve to "the lost sheep of the house of Israel," adding that they were explicitly not to "go in the way of the Gentiles" (Matt 10:5-6). He then sent the seventy to "every city and place to which He Himself was going to come" (Luke 10:1). Because the number of nations, or peoples, in the mindset of Israel at that time was seventy, it's likely that Jesus was foreshadowing the eventual commission to evangelize every city and place and people throughout the earth.

Read Goerner, "Jesus and the Gentiles," pp. 97a-98a

B. Jesus' Concern for Gentiles. The Gospels report that Jesus was profoundly concerned for non-Jewish people. On dozens of occasions He modeled God's heart for all peoples by deliberate outreach to Gentiles, whom most Jewish people despised. Because His teaching throughout His ministry emphasized the global scale of God's heart, the Great Commission was not a last-minute add-on to His teaching. When we look at the entire record, everything Jesus did and said came to a crescendo in the Great Commission.

Read Goerner, "Jesus and the Gentiles," pp. 98a-99

Read Richardson, "A Man for All Peoples," pp. 104-107 (all)

C. Jesus' Focus on a Few. Robert Coleman, in his classic work, "*The Master Plan of Evangelism*" points out that Jesus selected a few people and developed them as leaders in a movement that would impact the entire earth. Jesus' strategy focused on:

1. Reproducing character. Jesus knew that people would have to be "imbued with His life" in order to reflect and reproduce His character. Thus, He focused on pouring His life into some who would continue to do the same with others.

2. Reproducing structure. Jesus knew that the only way to reach the world was to launch a movement that would reproduce itself. A multiplying church would continue to expand in "an ever enlarging circumference" until the multitudes of the earth had heard the gospel.

Coleman observes that for the disciples, the purpose of world evangelization was "progressively clarified in their thinking as they followed Him, and finally spelled out in no uncertain terms" in the Great Commission.

Read Coleman, "The Master's Plan," pp. 100-103 (all)

II. The Great Commission

It should be no surprise that each of the Gospels, as well as the Book of Acts, recount a direct expression of the mandate to complete world evangelization.

• Mark 16:15-16 is a direct imperative to communicate the gospel to every person in every place. The outcome described is either belief and salvation or disbelief and eternal loss.

• Luke 24:46-49 includes Jesus' summary of what Scripture promises will take place among all nations. He indicates that His followers are to be witnesses who will accomplish a proclamation of pardon for sin to all the nations.

• Acts 1:8 is more of a promise than a command, that the disciples would become His witnesses. But it nevertheless carries mandate force to live out the full intent of Christ that they would be His witnesses in every part of the world (more on acting as witnesses in Lesson 5).

• John 20:21-23 does not have a direct command concerning the nations. In the context however, Jesus imparts the Spirit of God and declares that they are sent in the same way and for the same purpose as He was sent.

• Matthew 28:18-20, commonly known as "the Great Commission" is the clearest expression of Christ's mandate for world evangelization.

Steve Hawthorne's description of Matthew 28 invites readers to place themselves alongside the eleven as they first heard the mandate. The word "all" is used four times in the text.

A. All Authority. The commission is based on a transaction of authority from the Father to the Son. What was this authority? When was it given to Jesus? How does this authority enable believers to carry out the mandate? Use what you have already learned about the kingdom of God to reflect on what Jesus meant by this authority transfer. Jesus was referring to the Father awarding Him spiritual authority to subdue every evil power beneath His feet as defeated enemies in order to bring people from every tribe and tongue under His headship as His devoted servants. This kind of authority is required for the mandate which follows. By "disciple," He means to enlist new followers as loyal, learning disciples. Christ expects more than an understanding of His message. He expects an obedience to the entirety of His commands. He mandates that people be trained to live under His Lordship.

Read Revelation 5:1-14, Daniel 7:9-14, and Psalm 110 (the most oft-quoted OT passage in the NT). How do these passages help you understand Matthew 28:18 better? What difference does it make for everyday obedience to the Great Commission to know that there is such an authority behind it all?

Read Hawthorne, "Mandate on the Mountain," pp. 108-109d

B. All the Peoples. The mandate to "disciple the peoples" does not refer to a particular ministry activity. Rather, discipling "all the peoples" must be understood as a once-for-all global goal. Nurturing and training individuals and small groups in basic discipleship skills who will pass it on to others is a wonderful and necessary activity. However, the original language used in Matthew 28 indicates that there will be a once-in-history achievement of establishing Christward movements within every people group. With this clarity, we can speak of finishing the task of world evangelization.

Christ's commission uses the Greek phrase, *panta ta ethne*, which in most English translations is translated vaguely as "all nations." The Greek phrase is more precisely understood in English as "all the peoples." Based on the way the full phrase *panta ta ethne* is used in the New Testament, we can rule out two possible interpretations and affirm a third:

1. **Countries?** Are the *ethne* nation-states or countries? This is probably the most common misimpression of our day. Jesus did not have politically-defined countries in mind. The Greek words in the Great Commission would not have been understood this way by those who heard it first.

2. **Gentiles in general?** Is Jesus referring to Gentiles in general? Another misimpression is that Jesus is simply sending the disciples beyond the bounds of Israel to non-Jewish persons. The way that the phrase *panta ta ethne* is used in other biblical passages will not sustain this view. The word ethnos in singular form is never used of Gentiles in general. It always refers to a people group. The plural use of the word can sometimes mean Gentiles, but the full phrase *panta ta ethne*, is always used to describe ethnicities defined by race, language or culture.

3. **People groups.** The interpretation of *panta ta ethne*, with the best support from New Testament usage, is that Jesus has in view the people groups of the world as they tend to understand and define *themselves*: by language, lineage or socio-cultural factors.

Read Hawthorne, "Mandate on the Mountain," pp. 109d-111a

C. All That I Commanded. Two activities, baptizing and teaching, define what it means to "disciple all the peoples." With John the Baptist's ministry as a backdrop to Jesus' command, baptism was to mark a loyalty change, a preparation for the Messiah's coming. Baptism forms a community of shared allegiance to God as He has fully revealed Himself by name—as the Father who sent His Son and gives His Spirit. In this context, "teaching" goes beyond merely educating people to know about Jesus commands. It refers to the work of training people to live in daily, vital obedience to Jesus. These two facets—proclaimed allegiance to the God of the Bible, and growing obedience to Christ as Lord—are the core of what it means to establish kingdom communities that we have come to call churches.

D. All the Days. This phrase clearly reveals that Jesus was issuing a mandate for the entire age and for every believer. It is not a command that any single person can accomplish. It is a mandate that can only be fulfilled collectively.

Read Hawthorne, "Mandate on the Mountain," pp. 111a-112

> How is it possible for you to respond to the Great Commission? Is it adequate to do all that you can do personally to share the gospel? Or does God expect us to co-labor with others in order to fulfill the entire task? How will you receive this mandate?

III. Focus on Finishing the Task

The Great Commission defines the task in terms of people groups. In our day, many have recognized that focusing on people groups is important. We need to be sure that we focus on reaching people groups for the best reason.

It may seem important to place priority on people groups because they are filled with lost people who have not yet heard the gospel. This consideration, while meaningful, is not nearly as significant as approaching people groups from the strategic viewpoint of fulfilling the task of evangelizing all of the world's people groups. Completing the total task will require that in every single one of the people groups, at some point in history, there be a movement of baptized and obedient disciples capable of evangelizing their entire people. Until there are such movements in every people, we have not completed the mandate Christ has given us. This means that it doesn't matter exactly how many individuals populate these people groups. If a people group numbers 10,000 or 10,000,000, the strategic priority is virtually the same with respect to finishing the entire global mandate. Completing the entire task, as Christ has given it to us, will compel us to make strategic decisions to labor among people groups which still lack such discipling movements until we have seen the essential beginning of a church planting movement in every people group.

Conclusion of Key Readings for this lesson.

IV. On Mission with Jesus

It may be more important to understand the *way* that Jesus sent His followers than it is to grasp *what* He sent them to do.

A. As the Father Sent Me. Consider one of the most powerful statements in all of Scripture: "As the Father has sent Me, I also send you" (John 20:21).

    1. The ways of God. We can understand this verse to read: "As the Father sent me, so also *in the same way* I am sending you." How did the Father send the Son? The Father loved and listened to the Son. The Son loved and watched for what the Father initiated. Jesus, in dynamic nearness to the Father, continued what God had been doing throughout history. Jesus sends in this same way.

    2. The purpose of God. The verse also means: "As the Father sent me, so also you are sent to accomplish *the same historic purpose* for which I was sent." This is more than mind-boggling. Jesus entrusted ordinary people with the same enormous matters which the Father entrusted to Him.

B. On Mission With God. Henry Blackaby and Avery Willis describe how God enlists people to be on mission with Him. Behind their statements are radical ideas! What Blackaby and Willis present is contrary to some high-pressure styles of mobilizing mission involvement. Such guilt-inducing tactics often backfire, causing many people to resent what seems to them to be an unbearable burden of saving billions of lost people. Notice how they give more detail to what Jesus meant by "As the Father sent Me" in John 20:21. Consider each of the seven points concerning God's ways. One of the last sentences of the article sums up much of God's ways of involving us in His will: "He calls every one of His followers to join Him in that relationship of *love, power and purpose*."

1. **Love.** God's way of sending is relational, rather than utilitarian. When God calls us to be on mission with Him, He always invites us to experience a more intimate love relationship with Him. He is much more focused on that love relationship than He is focused on getting certain jobs done. The tasks are indeed accomplished in God's ways, but in the power of a growing experience of close relationship.

2. **Power.** God's way of sending is empowering, rather than coercive. He extends invitation rather than obligating demands. He reveals first what He is doing rather than pointing out what is not being done. He speaks to us about His will as we listen. He enables us to respond in trust. He patiently works and waits for us to make adjustments to Him, so that we can do His will for our own good and His greater glory.

3. **Purpose.** God's way of sending is purposeful, rather than being oriented around us. As much as He loves us, He refuses to allow our lives be oriented around ourselves. God is focused on a historic fulfillment of His global mission. He is determined to honor us with the dignity of being on mission with Him fulfilling part of His historic purpose.

Read Blackaby/Willis, "On Mission with God." pp. 55-58 (all)

V.   To Seek and To Save The Lost: Dealing with Universalism

We've considered the primary focus of world evangelization God gaining worshipers for His greater glory. We've suggested that glorifying God is a more important focus of Scripture than saving people from eternal loss. But people do matter! Their eternal destiny must be our concern also. Jesus Himself said that He came "to seek and to save that which was lost" (Luke 19:10). What does it mean to be lost? Who are the lost? How shall we understand the plight of the people who have never heard of Jesus or those who have rejected Him? How can we carry this burden in the way God wants?

Universalism is a commonly held idea that God's salvation in Christ will be universally accepted or applied to all persons. Some models deriving from universalism—the so-called "wider hope" theories—assume that people are saved in a general way but damned only by rejecting the gospel. If this is true, then it might be better to keep the world ignorant of salvation in Jesus. But the Bible teaches clearly that people are not lost because they reject the truth, but rather because of sin that has warped them in their own evil.

Robertson McQuilkin affirms the biblical truth that there are two kinds of people: the saved and the lost. It may appear that universalism presents a more compassionate God. But only the biblical God is both loving *and* good. God does not mock His own goodness by declaring people to be good who have chosen evil. Instead, God honors an individual's choice of good or evil, always giving them enough spiritual light that they can choose God's way. God has appointed that people be saved in the light of Christ's name. Jesus Christ is the *only* agency of salvation.

What about those who have never heard? Based on the story of Cornelius in Acts, McQuilkin says that God brings greater light to any who respond positively to the light He has already given them. It is not possible to prove that people have never been saved by following all the light that they had. But neither is it possible to prove that anyone has been saved apart from Christ.

McQuilkin points out how universalism makes a mockery of the cross. If all are saved without hearing or responding to Christ, why did He die at all? It is this compelling thought that underlies his closing illustration of a bridge.

Read McQuilkin, "Lost," pp. 156-161 (all)

VI. The Uniqueness of Christ: Dealing with Pluralism

Another important consideration is not how restricted salvation may be, but the adequacy of other religions and ways of thought. Pluralism is a word which describes a philosophical assumption that it is not possible to recognize any one system of thought as absolute truth. Forms of pluralism are prevalent in many parts of the world.

Advocates of pluralism argue against the missionary enterprise in two ways. First there are some who declare that Christian missions are acts of intolerant bigotry. Secondly, there are those who dismiss the message of Christ because, in their view, it is virtually identical to other religions.

Ajith Fernando helps us respond to the pluralism we find in different parts of the world as well as the skepticism that may have already affected our own vision. He calls us to look to the uniqueness of Jesus, and therefore embrace a shameless, even joyous conviction that because Christ is unique, He is supreme. Fernando expands Jesus' own statement that He is the way, the truth, and the life.

A. Christ the Truth. Arguments for absolute truth must be grounded on the huge fact of the incarnation. Absolute truth can be known because the Absolute has become concrete in history in the person of Jesus. Jesus' words and works open people to an encounter which is not just a mental grasp of truths, but a personal encounter with the person who is Truth. What separates the gospel from all other religions is the joy of relationship with the person of Jesus and the completeness of His message.

Read Fernando, "The Supremacy of Christ," pp. 169-173

B. Christ the Way. Jesus meant by His statement in John 14:6 that He would become the way through His death.

1. The accomplishment of the cross. It is essential to understand what Jesus accomplished on the cross. We have already seen in the previous lesson how God used Christ's death to overcome evil. Fernando lists six more biblical ways of recognizing the uniqueness of Jesus' death. It's breathtaking to consider the global importance of each one.

2. The offense of the cross. People invariably attempt self-salvation. The cross shouts that this is impossible. This offense of the cross may explain some of the hostility of pluralists to the missionary movement.

The thief comes only to steal, and kill, and destroy;

I came that they might have life, and might have it abundantly.

I am the good shepherd;

the good shepherd lays down His life for the sheep.

I am the good shepherd;

and I know My own, and My own know Me,

even as the Father knows Me and I know the Father;

and I lay down My life for the sheep.

And I have other sheep, which are not of this fold;

I must bring them also, and they shall hear My voice;

and they shall become one flock with one shepherd.

— *John 10:10-11, 14-16*

Read Fernando, "The Supremacy of Christ," pp. 174-175d

C. Christ the Life. Jesus summons a people from every people. John 10:10 is commonly quoted to affirm Christ's intention to bring fullness of life. Fernando directs our attention further in this same passage (through verse 16), where Jesus is described as the singular life-giving Shepherd. By His life-giving power, Jesus is drawing together people from every people, so that there will be "one flock," that is, in Fernando's words a "new humanity with one Shepherd." This "Good Shepherd" passage is not about personal comfort through trying times, it is a declaration of Christ's global mission. Because the Shepherd figure lays down His life to defeat the marauding thief and to gather sheep from all over the world, there can be only one Shepherd. The Shepherd figure is necessarily unique. The resurrection makes it starkly clear that Jesus Christ is unique, and therefore, utterly supreme.

Read John 10:10-16. Why does this Shepherd give life? Reflect on the purpose of Jesus' words about "other sheep." How do they hear His voice? What is the significance of people being formed into "one flock?" Would this be possible without a single shepherd figure?

Read Fernando, "The Supremacy of Christ," pp. 175d-178

Conclusion of Certificate Level Readings for this lesson.

Credit Level Guide Notes continue...

VII. Discipling All Peoples

We've seen that the Greek word translated as "make disciples" requires a direct object in order to make sense. That part of the sentence is the phrase translated "all nations." John Piper helps examine the Greek meaning behind these words. He does this with such a methodical simplicity that you don't have to be a Greek scholar at all to grasp the incredible significance of the phrase *panta ta ethne*.

A. Comparing Singular with Plural Usages. The Greek word *ethnos* always means a people group defined by language or lineage when used in the singular. The plural usage rarely refers to Gentiles in general. The preponderance of the usages by far refer to people groups.

B. Old Testament Cross Reference. Of the five repetitions of the Abrahamic covenant, two of them (Gen 12:3 and 28:14) use the Hebrew phrase *kol mishpahot*. This phrase refers to even smaller groupings than the Greek word *ethnos*, such as clans or small tribes. The other three (Gen 18:18; 22:18; and 26:4) are translated in the Greek translation of the OT with the phrase *panta ta ethne*. These are the passages that Peter refers to in Acts 3:25.

Piper concludes that the Great Commission defines the task as discipling people groups defined by language, lineage or tribal boundaries. The weight of evidence excludes the ideas that Jesus was mandating an outreach to non-Jewish people in general, or an outreach to politically-defined countries.

This is an important distinction since the mandate is given to us as a task to be completed. To complete our mandate, we must understand what we are aiming to accomplish.

Read Piper, "Discipling All the Peoples," pp. 113-117 (all)

VIII. The Uniqueness of Christ

Charles Van Engen describes the pluralistic worldview of our day. To speak clearly and biblically about other religions today, we need to do something beyond proclaiming our opinion that Jesus is the one and only way. New categories may help us proclaim the astounding claims of Scripture in a relevant way. Without clarity on these issues, we can easily be made to feel that we are religious bigots, foisting our views on people in a religiously criminal way. Why would we ever feel that missions is this kind of insensitive operation? Because the standard categories force many, including some in the Church, to conclude that if someone believes that Jesus is unique (i.e. the only way to salvation) then they are offensively intolerant and should be asked to stop pushing their religion on others. The truth is that affirming Christ's uniqueness does not mean that someone is a mean-spirited exclusivist. There are other ways to understand and to proclaim the truth.

A. Three Standard Positions. There are three standard positions on the issue of the uniqueness of Christ and the adequacy of other religions: *Pluralist, Inclusivist,* and *Exclusivist.* Evangelizing Christians are usually placed in the exclusivist category. Confused Christians often drift toward a vague, unverbalized inclusivist position.

B. An Important Distinction: Faith Does Not Equal Culture. If faith were just another aspect of one's culture then faith might not be regarded as truth-based, but as an expression of one person's culture. However, Christian faith is based on the fact of the historic Jesus. The truth that is the basis of faith is not relative to different cultural environments.

C. A Fourth Position: Evangelist. To the three common positions: Van Engen adds another, the Evangelist. It is based on the historic Jesus as reported in the Bible. It is summed up in the core confession of the Church: Jesus Christ is Lord. The Evangelist position is:

1. **Faith-Particularist.** This is not a question of whether you are inside or outside any particular church boundaries. The particularist (having to do with that which is unique and distinctive) affirmation is the question of discipleship, "of one's proximity to, or distance from, Jesus the Lord."

2. **Culturally Pluralist.** If faith does not equal culture, then Christians can be eager pluralists regarding culture. This means that they can affirm the value and beauty of any culture. "Everything that does not contradict the biblical revelation concerning the historical Jesus Christ our Lord is open for consideration."

3. **Ecclesiologically Inclusivist.** "Ecclesiological" has to do with churches. The Evangelist position is so focused on Jesus as the Head of the Church that church membership is not seen as the dividing line between the saved and the unsaved. That distinction is left to Jesus Himself. The mission task is to gather people together under His Lordship. His Lordship over all requires a vision of His headship over the Church. This means that there is a diversity of churches which thrive under Christ's headship. The evangelist eagerly welcomes people into the Church because that is where Christ's Lordship is to be enjoyed.

Read Van Engen , "The Uniqueness of Christ," pp. 162-168 (all)

5 Unleashing the Gospel

Studying this lesson will help you:

- *Explain how God helped the early Church to be faithful to Christ's mandate to be witnesses.*

- *Describe the crucial importance of the Acts 15 council for understanding how to present the gospel to the nations without presenting cultural obstacles to following Christ.*

- *Explain why the mission purpose of God is fulfilled by planting churches more than any other activity.*

- *Describe both the apostolic and congregational structures of the Church using the terms modality and sodality.*

- *Explain how prayer can be strategically offered for people throughout a city in such a way that God's hand is revealed, allowing the gospel to move rapidly.*

- *Explain how Paul's strategy of suffering defeated evil powers with the weakness of Christ rather than the power of Christ.*

- *Explain the strategic value of suffering and martyrdom in terms of the triumph of truth, the defeat of evil, and the glory of God.*

- *Describe some of the biblical grounds for hope for a tremendous ingathering at the end of the age, in the midst of a time of great hostility to Christ.*

We have seen that whenever God's people have been unfaithful, God has remained persistent in His purpose. Through many generations God is the faithful One, unfolding His plan to bring light to the nations with steady continuity. All of history comes to a breakthrough moment in Jesus.

We have seen how Christ trained His followers. His death broke the power of sin in a decisive way. His resurrection meant the power of His life could be extended to all nations. He commissioned them with power and clear purpose. As Jesus departed, the entire purpose of God seemed to be in the hands of a few ordinary men and women with a spotty track record of faithfulness. What would happen? Would they fulfill God's purpose? Would God's purpose come to a standstill?

Some have judged that these early leaders failed for long years, delaying the advance of the gospel. The real matter to watch is not whether the disciples stopped the progress of missionaries going out to the nations. The wonderful thing to behold is that the nations were not hindered from following Christ. The Holy Spirit was at work, opening "a door of faith" for the peoples and helping the Apostles to hold it open. The crucial moment of unleashing of the gospel to advance throughout the nations was the Jerusalem council described in Acts 15.

In this lesson we will see how God launched the world Christian movement. We will discover the double structure of the Church movement that endures to this day. We will see how specific prayer for the felt needs of entire cities prepared the way for the rapid advance of the gospel throughout entire regions. We will see how ordinary people chose a strategy of suffering which they learned from Jesus. We will examine the biblical grounds of hope for an enormous ingathering at the end of age.

WITNESS A witness is what you *are* far more than it is something that you *do*. God arranges for His servants to display what they declare. By public testimony in the face of hostility, ordinary people accomplish far more than merely affirming the truth of Christ. Witnesses establish the value of following Christ. Their persuasive power is not only because their words match their life—their words and their life match those of Christ Himself. It is as if Christ Himself stands to testify before the world.

I. A Global Movement

Were the disciples slow to extend the gospel from Jerusalem? Hawthorne presents the idea that they were incredibly faithful, as God helped them to be obedient to what He had given them to do at that time.

A. Persistence in Big-Picture Vision. Jesus gave them orders by the Holy Spirit. The encounter on the Emmaus road prefigured how He continues to speak to His Church even though He may go unseen. At that time He recounted the entire biblical story of His glory and the Kingdom as a backdrop for the specific instructions they were to carry out. The specific assignment was to do a very strategic, and yet dangerous thing: stay in Jerusalem. It's a common misconception to imagine that instead of reaching out to the nations, the disciples stayed home. Jerusalem was not their home! In fact by staying, they subjected themselves to fatal dangers.

B. Boldness in Public Witness. The idea of "witnessing" in present day use is much different than the understanding in biblical days. To witness was to offer prolonged public testimony. The ordeal of public trial often established the value of following Christ, and thus confirmed the validity of the movement to the common people.

Read Hawthorne, "Acts of Obedience," pp. 121-123c

C. Faithfulness to Accelerate Gospel Breakthrough. One of the most crucial moments of the Book of Acts is certainly the Jerusalem council. The gospel could have very well evolved as a small splinter sect of Judaism. Instead, it became a movement of faith that centered on Jesus and extended the heritage of the Hebrew people. Yet it also encompasses the cultural expression and diversity of every race and language of the world. How God achieved this required a perceptive wisdom on the disciples part that we still need today. The issue amounted to this: Did God require non-Jewish people to become Jewish in cultural ways in order to follow Christ?

Read Thomas, "The Turning Point: Setting the Gospel Free," pp. 118-120 (all)

Read Hawthorne, "Acts of Obedience," pp. 123c-124

D. The Priority of Gospel Breakthrough. The Book of Acts highlights both the importance of declaring the Word of God and the greater priority of facilitating a movement of obedience to Christ. The issue of Acts 15 is alive today. Does God intend to divorce people from their home culture? If instead, God desires to draw many throughout an entire community to follow Jesus together, how does the account of the Book of Acts help us facilitate these movements today?

Simeon has related how God first concerned Himself about taking from among the Gentiles a people for His name. And with this the words of the Prophets agree, just as it is written,

"'After these things I will return,

And I will rebuild the tabernacle of David which has fallen,

And I will rebuild its ruins,

And I will restore it,

In order that the rest of mankind may seek the Lord,

And all the Gentiles who are called by My name,'

Says the Lord, who makes these things known from of old."

Therefore it is my judgment that we do not trouble those who are turning to God from among the Gentiles, but that we write to them that they abstain from things contaminated by idols and from fornication and from what is strangled and from blood. For Moses from ancient generations has in every city those who preach him.

— Acts 15:14-21

Read Acts 15:14-20 to review the statement of James at the Acts council. Observe how he called the council to base their decisions on the biblical vision of God drawing worshipers from the nations to a house of worship. Have you wondered about the strange-sounding restrictions about not eating strangled animals? Some scholars have suggested that the Acts council may have been going back to what God required of all humankind before the Jewish nation was formed and the law of Moses was given. Did James direct their attention all the way back to the way God was dealing with all people in the day of Noah? You decide. How do the restrictions of Genesis 9:1-4 and and the problems of Genesis 6:1-2 correspond to the desire of the Jerusalem council to offer as little hindrance as possible for people from all nations to follow Christ?

Read Hawthorne, "The Wall and The Canyon," pp. 125c

E. The Church Planting Mandate. Kenneth Mulholland points out that from the start, Christ intended to accomplish something far more than individual conversions. Christ intended that churches would be planted. The early chapters of Acts clarify the mandate to plant churches. Mulholland shows how fulfillment of the Great Commission needs to focus primarily on multiplying communities of people committed to obeying Christ.

Read Mulholland, "A Church For All Peoples," pp. 135-136 (all)

II.   Apostolic Passion

Floyd McClung defines the words "passion" and "apostolic" in a way that is a compelling invitation to be engaged in God's mission. Take note of McClung's observations of God as the source of passion. Watch how he says passion can be chosen and cultivated as if it were not a feeling but a fulfillment of life. McClung says that no one should assume that God does not want them to be directly involved in apostolic church planting. Instead of negotiating with God for a "safe" assignment, why not delight God by seeking to be directly involved in planting churches where Christ is not yet worshiped? Let God be the one who limits, who says, "Stay." Read the last three paragraphs to yourself out loud (Why not? Just do it!).

Read McClung, "Apostolic Passion," pp. 185-187 (all)

Is apostolic passion, as McClung describes it, an extraordinary sort of Christianity? Or is it for everyone? Do you agree that the beginnings of apostolic passion can be found in any worshiping Christian? How do you aspire to grow in apostolic prayer? In apostolic choices?

Conclusion of Key Readings for this lesson.

III. Apostolic Prayer

Ed Silvoso says that the gospel spread rapidly in Jerusalem because of the way that the Christian community prayed for people's felt needs beyond the walls of the synagogue and temple. When prayer for felt needs is offered in such a way that people know that they are being prayed for, eyes are opened to the reality and power of God. He calls this approach *prayer evangelism*. It can prepare entire cities to follow Jesus.

Read Silvoso, "Prayer Evangelism," pp. 152-155 (all)

IV. The Apostolic Band

The churches that were planted were, for the most part, light and lean "house churches" without a great deal of institutional trappings. Such house churches multiplied quickly throughout whole cities. But when God desired there to be a cross-cultural extension of the gospel, beyond the range of the existing churches, there came about another structure of the Church, what some have called "the apostolic band."

A. The Double Structure of the Church. Arthur Glasser describes the important emergence of the apostolic band. Such teams set their own membership, charted out their goals, were economically self-sufficient and were not expected to answer to a local church. They were a distinctive structure of the church in parallel with the congregational parish structure. Glasser argues that both congregational parish structure and the mobile missionary band structure should both be considered the "Church" since both express the life of the people of God.

B. The Strategy of Paul's Band. It is valuable to recognize that Jewish missionaries had preceded the Church throughout much of the world with the objective of strengthening scattered Jews in the Jewish faith, and proselytizing willing Gentiles (that is to make a proselyte, or someone who was circumcised and subscribed to all Jewish cultural practices). Paul's strategy was to reach to those, like Cornelius, who wanted to hear about the Hebrew God, but who were unwilling to become proselytes. Paul had great news for Gentiles: They could follow Christ without becoming Jewish! Thus house churches were formed after the pattern of synagogues as an initial structure of what later became the congregational parish church.

Read Glasser, "The Apostle Paul and the Missionary Task," pp. 127-131a

C. Modality and Sodality. Ralph Winter has applied some simple terms from the discipline of sociology to the double structure of the church. The two terms are *modality* and *sodality*.

- **Modality** refers to nurture-oriented congregational church structures.

- **Sodality** refers to task-oriented mission structures.

Read Winter, "The Two Structures of God's Redemptive Mission," pp. 220-222b, and pp. 223d beginning with "It is even..." to 224b

D. The Local Church on Mission. Paul did not at all regard the apostolic bands to be sufficient to fulfill God's work in the world. He fully expected God to work through the churches. The ministry of the churches was a matter of God's grace by spiritual gifts. Note how Glasser points out the likely aspiration to the higher gifts which were to extend the Word of God. A large part of the local church's fulfillment of its mission was by maintaining a fruitful symbiotic relationship with the apostolic bands. As you read this, consider the value of local churches today flourishing in relationship with mission structures. Take special note of why Paul wrote the book of Romans. It was not written as a treatise of doctrine so much as it was written to motivate the churches in Rome to become "a second Antioch."

Read Glasser, "Paul and the Missionary Task," pp. 131b-133c

V. Apostolic Suffering

Paul planted churches and suffered wherever he did so. Paul intentionally took the beating at Philippi, keeping his identity as a Roman citizen undisclosed. Why? It must have been purposeful. He would later tell the same church that they were "graced" by God, not only to believe, "but also to suffer, experiencing the same conflict *which you saw in me*, and now hear to be in me." (Phil 1:29-30) Paul must have known that the church he was planting in Philippi would need to stand boldly through a blast of hostility. His readiness to stand openly for the gospel, without using the privilege of citizenship to dodge the backlash prepared the church to enjoy "fellowship in the gospel" from that "first day," until "the day of Christ" (Phil 1:5-6). That fellowship in the gospel would always mean a fellowship in the sufferings of Christ Himself (Phil 3:10).

A. A Strategy of Suffering. Glasser points out what he calls a cardinal principle: that where the gospel is preached and people are gathered into congregations, there will always be people suffering for Christ in a way that fulfills what is lacking in Christ's afflictions. These afflictions do not bring atonement, as only Christ's death has done. These sufferings are however, a factor in overcoming the spiritual powers that blind people to the gospel.

Read Glasser, "Paul and the Missionary Task," pp. 133c-134

B. God's Purpose in Martyrdom. Josef Tson speaks about God's ways in suffering.

1. **Suffering for Christ** is never self-inflicted; but on the other hand, it is always voluntary.

2. **Martyrdom** is the function God gives some "to die for the sake of Christ and His gospel." What is God's purpose in martyrdom? Suffering and sacrifice are God's methods of overcoming rebellion and evil. Most notably, Christ has not changed His strategy of answering hell's hatred with suffering love. "His method is still the method of the cross."

Read Tson, "Suffering and Martyrdom: God's Strategy in the World," pp. 181-182c

C. Entering Suffering by Prayer. Brother Andrew's comments are rich with seasoned wisdom. Why have so many Christians been willing to suffer? The report of "the vanished church" today might parallel the report that Nehemiah heard in his day. Examine Nehemiah's response as an example for engaging in the work of the gospel in hostile environments.

Read Andrew, "If I Perish," pp. 179-180 (all)

VI. Apostolic Hope

Coleman starts at Pentecost, where this lesson began, to draw our attention to the global outpouring of God's Spirit in the midst of tumultuous days at the end of the age. In the midst of these days of great trouble, there will be a profound cleansing of the Church and the largest ingathering of people to the Church ever. Note that Coleman sees Christ's return coming after a global harvest of huge proportions so that "the nations of the earth shall come and worship before the Lord." Anticipating Christ's return is a summons to action to accomplish the central task of world evangelization. The hope of global revival becomes a call to advance the gospel, to unite in prayer, and to live in vibrant expectancy.

Read Coleman, "The Hope of a Coming World Revival," pp. 188-192 (all)

Conclusion of Certificate Level Readings for this lesson.

Credit Level Guide Notes continue...

After studying this section you should be able to:

- *Describe how the Church is formed by reconciliation and results in reconciliation.*

- *Define a church in biblical ways using the concepts of community and Christ's kingdom.*

- *Explain why describing the Church as a living thing is significant for mission activity.*

- *Draw the connection between God's global purpose for the nations and God's purpose for suffering as seen in Scripture.*

VII. God's Strategy in Apostolic Suffering

More people suffer persecution for Christ today than at any other time in history. Suffering is particularly intense in places where the gospel is advancing among unreached peoples. We only began reading Josef Tson's writing about suffering. Recall how he defines suffering: It is not self-inflicted suffering, but it is nonetheless voluntary. What is the purpose of suffering and martyrdom?

Earlier, we described God's purpose in this way: *For His glory in global worship, God purposes to redeem a people from every people, and to rule a kingdom over all kingdoms.* Tson says that suffering is part of God's way to defeat Satan and destabilize his kingdom. Tson says that suffering enables the truth to come to redemptive clarity so that God is recognized and glorified.

Suffering and martyrdom is in line with God's purpose at the end of the age. Then we should "think it not strange," as Peter puts it, that so many of our brothers and sisters in Christ are encountering phenomenal suffering. The best formulated strategies for advancing the gospel will take this factor into account. Tson sees three things achieved by this suffering. As you read, please look up the passages that he refers to. Some of them are passages that are not often brought to our attention.

A. The Triumph of God's Truth. When an ambassador speaks the truth in love and meets death with joy, eyes are opened to the gospel. Christ's own death had this effect on one of His executioners.

B. The Defeat of Satan. When martyrs meet their death without fear, they demonstrate that Satan's ability to control us by fear is broken. Tson suggests an important dimension to Satan's defeat and shame in the heavenlies was revealed in the account of Job. Paul echoes this purpose when he says that he was "a spectacle to the world, both to angels and to men" (1 Cor 4:9).

C. The Glory of God. In a powerful paradox, the shame of death brings about God's glory. Paul and Peter are both spoken of as having this destiny.

Read Tson, "Suffering and Martyrdom," pp. 182d-184

VIII. The Church in God's Plan

We have seen God's purpose unfolding throughout history coming to a mighty culmination as churches are planted in every people group. To many, this is not joyous news. Many have had disappointing or painful experiences with churches. These people are not going to eagerly support or even clearly understand mission efforts which talk about multiplying churches among unreached peoples. It's foundational to grasp what the Church is all about.

Howard Snyder guides us through a short study in the book of Ephesians to discover the purpose of God's brand new life form on the planet: the Church. Please keep your Bible open as you work throughout this article. Read the verses that come from Ephesians.

A. God's Purpose: Reconciliation Under the Son. Snyder proposes a very radical idea of reconciliation. He asserts that God's plan all along has not been to repair the earth or to simply rescue people from hell. God has been determined to bring about something better than what has ever come about before. God's purpose all along has been to enjoy a huge household. He is "the Father, from whom every family in heaven and on earth derives its name" (Eph 3:14-15). Bringing things together under Christ's headship is a double idea. It suggests a submission to Christ's magnificent lordship. It also opens the way for people to finally join together in joyous fellowship as a family. Reconciliation is not a sentimental affair of hand-holding and having nice feelings about one another. Reconciliation is the formation of something new far more than it is the restoration of that which was broken. Jew and Gentile were made to be "one new man" by Christ's reconciling power. Can you imagine what is on display in the heavenlies before the angelic enemies of God?

Every time a church is planted, there is another acceleration toward the grand finale of a Family of all peoples enjoying God's life in face-to-face glory. Never get used to the wonder of the Church!

B. The Biblical Vision: A Life and Love Affair With Christ. Different images are important to consider. Each of them helps church members and church planters grasp who they are and what they are a part of. Each of the images that Snyder mentions is a living thing. Even the temple is made of living stones. The Church is alive with the life of God. When we come to consider church planting, it matters greatly that we are basically tending a life form that can reproduce. Missionaries do not need to force or fake the Church. It is alive by resurrection power.

1. **Cosmic/historic perspective.** God has been working on His Church for millennia. The Church has a great honor from God. She has been placed at the center of all that God wants to do on the earth. That is no small thing. It wouldn't necessarily have to be that way.

2. **Charismatic, rather than institutional terms.** The Church exists by grace (Greek word, *charis*) and is build up with the gifts of grace (Greek word, *charismata*). This is why we must view churches as living organisms and relational communities instead of programmed marketing devices.

3. **Community of God's people.** The definition of the Church that lies at the heart of our mission is this: *the Church is the community of God's people.* Defining or organizing churches in any other way bogs down the work of evangelization as well as frustrates every other work of the Kingdom. This definition is the reason why the most effective missionaries are multiplying churches which are very simplified. They understand that they are God's household, so it's natural for them to meet in houses. They know themselves to be the Body of Christ, so it's natural for them to form churches as small cells. It really doesn't matter what external form the Church takes on, but the churches flourish when communal interdependency and the centrality of Christ's Lordship are emphasized. The Church is not the kingdom of God, but it expresses the King's will. It is the community of the King.

Read Snyder, "The Church in God's Plan," pp. 137-141

6 The Expansion of the World Christian Movement

Studying this lesson will help you:

- *Tell the "broad-stroke" story of how God's blessing has continued to extend to all peoples throughout 4,000 years of biblical history.*

- *Describe the progress of the gospel to different geographic areas and cultural basins in each of the five 400-year epochs since Christ.*

- *Explain how the gospel advanced even when God's people were disobedient. You will understand different "mechanisms" of mission: people "coming" or messengers "going," either voluntarily or involuntarily.*

- *Illustrate the idea that God's blessings are to be passed on, or they might be taken away.*

- *Describe some key mission leaders and movements in history and their strategic approaches.*

- *Describe the two functional structures of the Church through the centuries using the terms "modality" and "sodality."*

We have seen how the plot of the entire Bible unfolds steadily toward the fulfillment of God's global purpose. But what happened after Acts 28? Most of us have a vague idea of early believers enduring the catacombs as Rome burned around them. Then, in the popular understanding, the medieval dark ages blanketed the Christian movement with crusades and chaos until the Reformation. If this is really all that happened, then God's promises to bless the nations were more hype than hope. After the first century, did God get frustrated with His followers for long centuries and abandon His intention to see the gospel go to the ends of the earth? Has God only recently awakened to bright possibilities of missions in the modern world? Is God an opportunist, achieving great things when the situation seems ripe, but allowing eons of darkness to roll by without action?

The core question is this: Is there continuity to history? Many historians say no, explaining any apparent significant succession of events as only a mirage. Believers in Christ, however, have only to recall that Jesus Himself announced the kingdom of God by declaring, "the time is fulfilled!" (Mark 1:15). That statement alone should be enough to awaken us to the reality that there is a magnificent purpose in all of history. All of Scripture throbs with the steady pulse of God's purpose through the years. The kingdom of God has come and will come with even greater power. The God of all nations is the God of all generations. He can be fully followed by those who know Him as the God of all history.

Why delve into the archives? It's not a matter of memorizing the dates and names of past popes and rulers. It's a matter of tracing the hand of God as He fulfills His purpose. Those who follow history from God's perspective are not disappointed. They are the ones who can sort out the unfolding "plot" important from that which is popular but peripheral.

In this lesson we'll follow how God's blessing extended successively from one region and people to another. We'll see the drastic consequences for the Christian movement when the blessing of the gospel of God was not extended. We'll set the record straight about the wider impact and spread of the general blessings of the kingdom of God throughout the world.

MOMENTUM It's often hard to sense the accelerating pace of God's work in history. Many live encased in the present moment and tend to miss the momentum of the mighty God of the ages. But would God tell us so much of His story and His purposes without intending for us to follow Him through history? Those who know God's history can better lay hold of God's intended destiny.

I. The Drama Moving through All of History: The Kingdom Strikes Back

Human history could be summarized using one dominant theme. Ralph Winter finds the keynote theme in the Bible. He sees the theme of the kingdom of God as the primary drama throughout "a single ten-epoch 4,000-year unfolding story."

A. Ten Epochs through 4,000 Years. Dividing history into ten 400-year periods is a device to help us remember and follow the developing story. Even though fascinating patterns and recurrent themes do emerge, Winter does not mean to imply that history follows rigidly patterned 400-year cycles.

B. The Counterattack on Evil. In addition to the kingdom of God, another dominant theme is God's war against evil. God intervenes in the suffering of people under the domain and the devices of evil. History is God's invasion of the domain of Satan, undoing all of his works and freeing people to glorify His name. It is a costly war. Again and again in God's redemptive story, His servants suffer even as Christ suffered in the same struggle.

C. Redemption by Blessing. Winter's description of blessing is one of the best. He distinguishes between the common Western idea of *blessings* (plural) as material or social benefits, and the Hebrew idea of *blessing* (singular) as relational realities which confer responsibility and obligation as well as privilege. Blessing is a distinctively familial idea. By extending His blessing, God is establishing an enormous family, an array of households of faith which together display His Kingdom and His glory. This is the blessing that God's people were to become as well as pass on to others.

D. Four Mechanisms of Mission. Not every epoch is marked by God's people faithfully launching out in cross-cultural mission. During much of history there seems to be very little, if any, such obedience. Does this mean God's story slows down and stops? Not at all! Winter points out that God manages to see that the blessing continues to spread even when His people are unwilling to extend it. To see this wonderful continuity throughout history we need to recognize four mechanisms of mission. These concepts expand on the distinction of centripetal (coming) and centrifugal (going) mission explored in Lesson 2. These four mechanisms demonstrate how God presses His mission forward with or without the full cooperation of His chosen people:

1. **Voluntary Going**
2. **Involuntary Going** (without initial missionary intent)
3. **Voluntary Coming**
4. **Involuntary Coming** (occasions of forced settlement among God's people)

Read Winter, "The Kingdom Strikes Back," pp. 195-197d

MECHANISMS	OLD TESTAMENT	NEW TESTAMENT	EARLY CHURCH TO 1800	MODERN MISSIONARY ERA
Voluntary Go Centrifugal (Expansive)	• Abraham to Canaan • Minor Prophets preach to other nations near Israel • Pharisees sent out "over land and sea"	• Jesus in Samaria • Peter to Cornelius • Paul and Barnabas on their missionary journeys • Witness of other Christians in Babylon, Rome, Cyprus, etc.	• St. Patrick to Ireland • Celtic peregrini to England and Europe • Friars to China, India, Japan, America • Moravians to America	• William Carey and other missionaries of the 1st Era • Hudson Taylor and the 2nd Era missionaries • Third Era to present
Involuntary Go Centrifugal (Expansive)	• Joesph, sold into slavery in Egypt, witnesses to Pharaoh • Naomi witnesses to Ruth because of famine • Jonah—the reluctant missionary • Hebrew girl is taken off to Naaman's home • Captive Hebrews in Babylon witness to captors	• Persecution of Christians forces them out of Holy Land all over Roman empire and beyond	• Ulifas sold as slave to the Goths • Exiled Arian bishops go to Gothic areas • Christians captured by Vikings win them • Christian soldiers sent by Rome to England, Spain, etc. • Pilgrims and Puritans forced to the Americas and discover their mission to the Indians	• WWII Christian soldiers sent around the globe return to start 150 new mission agencies • Ugandan Christians flee to other parts of Africa • Korean Christians flee to less-Christian South, later sent to Saudi Arabia and Iran, etc. to work
Voluntary Come Centripetal (Attractive)	• Naaman the Syrian came to Elisha • Queen of Sheba came to Solomon's court • Ruth chose to go to Judah from Moab	• Greeks who sought out Jesus • Cornelius sends for Peter • Man of Macedonia calls to Paul	• Goths invade Christian Rome, learn more of the Christian faith • Vikings invade Christian Europe, are won to the faith eventually through that contact	• The influx of international visitors, students and businessmen into the Christian West
Involuntary Come Centripetal (Attractive)	• Gentiles settled in Israel by Cyrus the Great (2 Ki 17)	• Roman military occupation and infiltration of "Galilee of the Gentiles"	• Slaves brought from Africa to America	• Refugees from Communism • Boat people, Cubans forced out, etc.

II. The Second Half of the Story

Winter summarizes many of the events and themes of the last 2,000 years. As you read the following selection, take note of the names of the five most recent epochs on the timeline.

A. Advance Both Cultural and Geographic: Winter characterizes the advance of the gospel as an "invasion" of specific "cultural basins." A cultural basin is a large system of people groups, languages, cultures and political systems. Sometimes the advance of the gospel and the blessing of the gospel flow to, and then through, a specific cluster of peoples over many centuries, as with the Celtic peoples. In other cases the advance of the gospel can be described better by the geographic extent of Christianity's growing edge. Watch for both cultural and geographic expansion of the Christian movement.

Therefore I tell you that the kingdom of God will be taken away from you and given to a people who will produce its fruit.

—Matt 21:43

> **In light of what Winter says about the mission of Jesus, read Matthew 21:43. What does he mean that the Kingdom, or the mission of the Kingdom, will 97be given to someone else? How is God slowing or advancing His mission?**

B. Dismissing the BOBO Theory. A popular impression is that the Christian faith somehow "Blinked Out" after the apostles and then "Blinked On" (BOBO) again much later at the Reformation. The truth is that since the early Church, there have always been people of vibrant faith.

C. "Flourishings" or "Renaissances." Near the close of the epochs was often a time Winter calls "flourishings." These seasons of flourishing, or renaissance, were times when the gospel brought stability, abundance and strength to entire social structures. These times expressed part of the blessing of the kingdom of God.

III. Period One: Winning the Romans (A.D. 0-400)

A. Mechanism. The gospel advanced by all four mechanisms. The "voluntary-go" pattern was reflected by Paul's missionary band. The "involuntary-go" pattern was seen in the dispersion of Christians during times of persecution.

B. Advance. The gospel flowed along trade routes as well as throughout the social strata. During the early centuries Christianity was the one religion with no nationalistic political identity. As such, it appealed to many throughout the empire—and beyond. Once it became the official imperial religion, Christianity began to carry the political and cultural stigma of being Roman. This slowed down the advance which was already underway in areas beyond the Roman Empire, particularly where Rome was despised or feared. Winter suggests a new way to look at what might be regarded as heresy. There were different flavors of Christian faith that differed very slightly in the details but gave people a way to espouse their own brand of Christianity. Thus, areas hostile to the Roman empire were more likely to embrace what the Roman empire/church considered heresy, such as Arianism (even though Arian theology had been official in Rome for 60 years).

C. Flourishing. Winter mentions at a later point in the article a cultural "flourishing" of the peoples and lands which had become Christian. If Roman Christians had "used" some of the wealth and power of the A.D. 310 to A.D. 410 period, the fate of Roman society would have been much different and the gospel would have advanced more rapidly.

> **Read Winter, "The Kingdom Strikes Back," pp. 197d-202c**

IV. Period Two: Winning the Barbarians (A.D. 400-800)

A. Mechanism. The Barbarian tribes invaded the Roman Empire and became even more thoroughly evangelized. This period was an expression of the "voluntary-come" mechanism. Later in the period came the first establishment of monastic orders. Most of the monastic tradition should be recognized for sustaining and extending the faith in and around the monasteries. Some, however, became expressly missionary, following a "voluntary-go" pattern. Notable among these were the Celtic or Irish "peregrini" (wandering evangelists), and their Anglo-Saxon followers, among whom were Columban, Boniface and Patrick.

B. Advance. Barbarian tribes, such as the Goths, Visigoths, Vandals and Anglo-Saxons, invaded most of Western and Central Europe. Though Rome lost half its empire, the Barbarian world gained the Christian faith in the process.

C. Flourishing. Charlemagne, himself a descendant of a Germanic barbarian tribe, facilitated a rise of education and economic development that temporarily pulled Europe out of leaderless chaos. Under the strong influence of the monastic centers of his day, Charlemagne promoted the mission centers of monastic life that had spread and held the faith throughout Europe. Under his influence, the "Carolingian Renaissance" broke the medieval "Dark Ages" into two distinctive periods. As much as Charlemagne boosted the faith, his efforts to evangelize the attacking Vikings from the north were too little and too late.

Read Winter, "The Kingdom Strikes Back," pp. 202c-205

V.   Period Three: Winning the Vikings (A.D. 800-1200)

A. Mechanism. The Viking conquerors were themselves conquered by the faith of their captives. Once again, an "involuntary-go" pattern is observed.

B. Advance. The gospel spread to Scandinavia and other north European areas.

C. Flourishing. The Gregorian Reform was made strong by the Cluny, the Cistercian and allied spiritual movements. The expression of mission then went awry, as described in the next epoch.

Read Winter, "The Kingdom Strikes Back," pp. 206-208a

VI.   Period Four: Winning the Saracens? (A.D. 1200-1600)
This period differs in many ways from previous epochs.

A. Mechanism. Once the Vikings capitulated to "the counterattack of the gospel," they became leaders in the greatest perversion of mission in history: the Crusades. Using a deeply flawed "voluntary-go" pattern, they destroyed and conquered territory without any success in extending the blessing of the gospel to the Muslims, sometimes referred to as the Saracens. At the same time, a new type of monasticism arose which was truly missionary in nature. This resulted in the movement of Friars who traveled all over Europe with the gospel. However, just as it looked as if the Friars would bring blessing to lands beyond, the Black Plague struck. The Friars were especially hard hit. Winter theorizes that God employed Satan's intent of removing the messengers of the gospel as a judgment against those who chose not to hear.

B. Advance. The Crusades were an abortion of advance. The beginnings of colonial expansion brought some advance of Christian faith, but not of Protestant faith.

C. Flourishing. The Renaissance and the Reformation were times of flourishing. The Reformation created a drastic and dramatic decentralization of Christianity as it grew with vitality in many places. The Catholic, or Latin, variety of Christianity, with its growing monastic mission structures, developed alongside colonial expansion. The newly established Protestant movements were caught up in theological reformulation and remained virtually without mission structures that could reach beyond their own people.

Read Winter, "The Kingdom Strikes Back," pp. 208a-210c

VII. Period Five: To the Ends of the Earth (A.D. 1600-2000)

A. Mechanism. The Catholic expansion continued and then was suddenly wounded around 1800 with Napoleon's ransacking of Europe and the growing popularity of atheism (Voltaire, etc.), deism and humanism. At the same time, the "voluntary-go" mechanism of the Protestant mission movement finally became launched.

B. Advance. Protestant missionaries reached across the globe. The Protestant movement first advanced to the coastlands with or without colonial expansion. Then came another wave to the inland areas. Finally, the focus fell on reaching all the *peoples* of the earth.

C. Flourishing. Western civilization, with all of its wealth and corruption, may be the greatest flourishing of all. However, Winter poses the question: if we insist on keeping the blessing instead of sharing it, will God move so that we, like other nations before us, lose some of the material benefits of God's blessing in order that God's purpose to bless all the nations will be fulfilled?

Read Winter, "The Kingdom Strikes Back," pp. 210d-213

Conclusion of Key Readings for this lesson.

VIII. Mission Strategy

R. Pierce Beaver adds more color and depth to some of the historical figures we have mentioned. He explores different approaches to mission strategy in times preceding William Carey. As you read about each of the following figures and periods, watch for the different ways that missionaries handled these issues. The strategic issues described are still the crucial issues that we face today. There is a tendency to see our present generation as more radical and ready to develop innovative methods that will advance the gospel. This kind of historic prejudice—that later events and movements must be better or more advanced—is the most certain path to confusion and failure. We need to apprehend the seasoned wisdom of earlier experiments and advances. The sampler below highlights some important cross-cultural communication issues that we'll explore later in the course. Allow the accounts to whet your appetite to read beyond what the Perspectives course can provide. Pay particular attention to four broad areas of mission strategy:

- **Adaptation.** Ways that the local culture was respected, valued or the message adapted in gospel communication.

- **Civilizing.** Contextualization of the resulting movements. To what degree were the resulting churches allowed to reflect their local culture? Or were they instead brought into alignment with the missionary's culture?

- **Conquest.** Missionaries followed colonial or imperial powers. Did they intend to bring peoples under the political sway of their home countries? Were they perceived as facilitating control by foreign powers?

- **Development.** Missionaries often introduced significant ways of meeting basic human needs. At times these efforts were considered a civilizing service or possibly part of an economic conquest.

A. Boniface. Beaver characterizes this key figure of the monastic movement as exhibiting "a true sending mission." He went to convert tribes rather than extend a political domain. To encourage group conversions of entire tribes, he used what we have come to call "power encounter." An example would be when he cut down the sacred trees of other gods to expose their impotence, confronting them with the power of Christ. He established churches, monasteries and schools. Ultimately, however, he was perceived as an instrument of imperial expansion.

B. The Crusades. Tragically, the Crusades warped mission into conquest. The effect of the Crusades reverberates to this day in most of the Muslim world. The Crusades highlight two other notable monastic figures, Francis of Assisi and Ramon Lull, who sought to preach the gospel to Muslims instead of violent conquest.

C. Colonial Expansion. Portuguese, Dutch, Spanish, French and British imperial expansion was often linked with mission but in very different ways. Methods often hinged on whether to first "Christianize" or "civilize."

D. Strategists of the 17th Century. Jesuit mission strategy was innovative and important. The experiments and experiences of Jesuits have often determined the missiological climate that missionaries face today. The Jesuits not only encountered strong resistance in Japan, in spite of their innovative methods, they also affected modern Japanese resistance to the gospel. The approaches of Robert de Nobili and Matteo Ricci still challenge missionaries considering how to establish Christian movements.

E. New England Puritans. The American mission experience to reach the "Indians" began with what seemed to be an attempt to "civilize" them in special towns prior to "Christianizing" them. Evangelism by extracting converts from the larger tribal societies ended up forming a separated people who could not "pass on the contagion of personal faith." The "Praying Indian" towns may have been set up to protect the Christian Indians from both pagan Indians and pagan colonists. However, the "Praying Indian" towns were eventually burned down by unruly settlers from Europe. Notable figures in this chapter of mission effort were John Eliot and David Brainerd.

F. Danish-Halle Mission. An early, famous Protestant sending mission from Europe attempted some of the most innovative approaches to contextualize the message and assume effective roles to communicate the gospel. Two leaders stand out: Bartholomew Ziegenbalg and Frederick Schwartz.

G. Moravians. Beaver describes the Moravians' efforts to respect local cultures. They expected that the resulting movements would be different from their own. They taught new believers skills which established them economically.

Read Beaver, "The Hisory of Mission Strategy," pp. 241-246d

And after they had preached the gospel to that city and had made many disciples, they returned… strengthening the souls of the disciples, encouraging them to continue in the faith…. And when they had appointed elders for them in every church, having prayed with fasting, they commended them to the Lord in whom they had believed… and from there they sailed to Antioch, from which they had been commended to the grace of God for the work that they had accomplished. And when they had arrived and gathered the church together, they began to report all things that God had done with them and how He had opened a door of faith to the Gentiles. And they spent a long time with the disciples.

—Acts 14:21-28

IX. The Two Structures of God's Redemptive Mission

We'll now resume reading Winter's article "The Two Structures of God's Redemptive Mission" which we began studying in Lesson 5 (pp. 220-229). Winter states that the Church has grown and extended itself in mission by following forms found within the social structure of the day as well as forms found in the Bible. Throughout history, even though superficial details change, when we speak of the "Church" we see two fundamental structures: the congregational structure and the mission structure. Winter introduces the sociological terms "modality" and "sodality" to help identify these structures at different points of history.

- **Modality** structures are inclusive, nurture-oriented, structured fellowships (for example, a church congregation or a secular town).

- **Sodality** structures are second-decision, task-oriented, structured fellowships (for example, a mission society or a military force).

Both structures exist in civil and religious societies. Both are found in the Bible. Both are legitimate and necessary in God's redemptive mission. Sodality structures nourish and extend the church. Modality structures strengthen and support the mission band. They work together in an important symbiosis.

A. Redemptive Structures Prior to and During the First Century. The congregational structure followed the synagogue patterns of the day. The mission structures had precedent in the Jewish rabbinical mission efforts, but they soon became highly dynamic missionary bands, similar to Paul's small groups that traveled planting churches.

B. Early Development within Roman Culture. Local congregational structures recognized bishops with territorial jurisdiction, after the pattern of the Roman magisterial territories. The Roman term used for these territories was "diocese." The mission structures that emerged – the monastic movements – borrowed patterns from Roman military practice. Protestants generally have stereotyped impressions of monasteries as places where ascetic monks fled the world. In reality, the monastic movements were largely responsible for bringing the blessing of the gospel to the world.

C. The Medieval Synthesis. The survival of the parish church structures came to depend largely on the more committed devotion of the monastic movement. Several of the largest mission endeavors of Christian history arose from the monastic movement. As monastic movements became inadvertently wealthy, however, local rulers demanded and took control of their leadership, resulting in spiritual decline and decay.

Read Winter, "The Two Structures of God's Redemptive Mission," pp. 222b-226c

D. The Protestant Recovery. Earlier we asked why Protestants celebrated the gospel but failed dismally to extend it. For nearly 200 years there was virtually no mission outreach. Winter, along with Latourette and other scholars, points to what may be the greatest error of the Protestant movement: the Reformers abandoned sodality structures. Because monastic life was rejected, there was virtually no interest in preserving or extending the mission structures. William Carey called for Christians to "use means" to complete the commission of Christ. By "means" he meant organized mission structures. He called for the formation of mission societies. Once Protestants organized sodality structures, whether denominational or interdenominational, the numbers of Protestant missionaries exploded.

E. Contemporary Misunderstanding. Protestant missions were organized initially without denominational backing. Gradually, the once-independent structures became increasingly regulated and eventually were dominated by denominational leaders. This brought both health and problems to the mission expansion. As a result, there was launched a later wave of mission structures called the "faith missions," which was actually a second surge of non-denominational initiative (what we will call Second Era missions in Lesson 7). Some strong, highly regarded denominational leaders have recognized the value and importance of some mission structures which were not tied to any denomination. But on the whole there has been dubious support of mission structures. At times there has been critique and open doubt expressed concerning the legitimacy of sodality structures. The result on mission fields has predictably been a failure to encourage newly planted churches to form mission structures to send their own missionaries. The now vast phenomenon of "Third World" missionaries has grown up with little missionary or national church support.

How distinct was Paul's missionary band from the Antioch church? Examine the two aspects of the "sending" of Paul's missionary band in Acts 13. In verse 3, the English word for "they sent them away" has more to do with releasing and setting loose. The following verse, "being sent by the Holy Spirit," contains a forceful Greek word for sending that reflects something like military command. Was the missionary band commanded by the church, or commended to God's care and control? Note how the idea of commending appears in Acts 14:21-28 as an act of entrusting into another person's overriding care. How did their prayer and fasting play a part in recognizing new leaders for specific work under God's care in both Acts 13 and 14?

Read Winter, "The Two Structures of God's Redemptive Mission," pp. 226c-230

Reread the last sentence. What is particularly crucial about Winter's insistence that both structures are not only legitimate but necessary?

Now there were at Antioch, in the church that was there, prophets and teachers: Barnabas, and Simeon who was called Niger, and Lucius of Cyrene, and Manaen who had been brought up with Herod the tetrarch, and Saul. And while they were ministering to the Lord and fasting, the Holy Spirit said, "Set apart for Me Barnabas and Saul for the work to which I have called them." Then, when they had fasted and prayed and laid their hands on them, they sent them away. So, being sent out by the Holy Spirit, they went down to Seleucia and from there they sailed to Cyprus.

—Acts 13:1-5

Conclusion of Certificate Level Readings for this lesson.

Credit Level Guide Notes continue...

After studying this section you should be able to:

- *Describe how the strategic aims of Protestant missions have changed since the colonial era.*

- *Describe some of the features of social transformation that have resulted from mission efforts.*

A Note about Digging into the Story: Why would the average Perspectives student care about old strategies of the past? Why not get busy working on the realities of today's urgent needs? Some of God's servants have made strategic contributions toward the completion of His purpose while others have floundered, even with the best intentions. The history of strategy is bursting with practical significance for anyone who plays any part in the missionary enterprise. If your role in the Kingdom is to support frontline missionaries, your acquaintance with these issues will give you a wider panorama of vision, enhancing your decisions and encouragements. If you eventually head to the to mission field, even for a short term, an awareness of strategic breakthroughs and blunders can help you make a contribution of more lasting value.

X.   The Great Century of Protestant Missions

The 19th Century has been referred to as "the Great Century" because of the phenomenal advance of the gospel in every geographic area of the globe. We'll continue to read R. Pierce Beaver's summary of mission strategy which provides fascinating details about this period. These issues are very significant for the present era of mission. To help you follow the story through the first 18 centuries of mission strategy we pointed out a few themes—adaptation, "civilizing," conquest and development. Read Beaver's comments about the 19th Century, focusing on the following three themes:

- **Contextualization.** Because of a low view of the value of other cultures, the idea of "civilizing" the different societies to Western ideals was assumed.

- **Control**. Models of "conquest" were dismissed, partly because the colonial era had largely subjugated the unevangelized regions. Conquest was replaced by the far more subtle issue of control.

- **Transformation.** Development efforts multiplied. Beaver uses the term of "transformation."

A. Mission Structures. Operating mission structures was a new endeavor for Protestants. Confusion about control of the mission operation from the sending church structures dampened much of the early effectiveness. The issue of control from the European homelands was so great that mission structures were dominated by sending churches. William Carey's efforts were hindered by this confusion.

B. Mission Objectives. The general aim was individual conversions, church planting and social transformation.

- **Christianization or Civilization?** Local cultures were seen as primitive and superstitious. The approach of changing their culture as an initial effort to prepare the way for "Christianization" eventually gave way to the idea that the gospel itself would have a transforming power upon the culture. William Carey and the "Serampore Trio" provided a valuable pattern in pioneering the idea of independent churches and emphasizing the power of the gospel in transforming society.

- **Stations or Churches?** The mission station approach pressed converts into a social and economic dependency on missionaries. Carey had aimed at an educated and independent leadership and laity gathered in churches. Mission leaders Rufus Anderson and Henry Venn exerted great influence to break up the mission station structures and assumptions. They proposed the famous "three-self" formula to describe the independent churches that they wanted their missionaries to aim for. Venn and Anderson may not have been sufficiently influential enough in their day. Near the end of the 19th Century there was another emergence of colonial paternalism. This led to a hasty "evolution" of authority from the mission structures to the native churches at the earlier part of the 20th Century.

- **Transformation and Education.** William Carey had gone further than most of his counterparts would go in later generations in envisioning a highly educated leadership. Different views on transformation were related to different theological assumptions about the kingdom of God at the turn of the century. Missionaries worked industriously to establish medical and educational systems.

C. **Comity and Continuity.** The practice of "comity" exemplifies the long heritage of unity in mission efforts. Such recognition of diverse parts of the Church paved the way for national and international missionary conferences which have continued to this day.

D. **Transition to a New Age of Mission.** Beaver mentions Roland Allen's ideas as a radically different strategy. Compare his summary of this strategy to what Carey, Venn, and Anderson had been pressing toward. Allen may have simply been articulating a new level of simplicity of strategic intent that was devoid of colonial infrastructure. Note how Beaver describes the churches which result from Allen's theory as "spontaneously missionary." The very next paragraph mentions that several mission organizations were dissolved. Which dynamic was at work? The surging onward of mission? Or the dissolution of mission structures? This confusion is a telling example of two minds of Protestant mission at two very significant transitional periods. We'll examine these transitions in greater detail in Lesson 7. Beaver's assessment of a radical new strategy may actually be a simplification of church and mission structures, and a hope for tremendous transformation which was not dependent on Western colonial culture and power. Beaver's final statement of the "central task of the Church" refers to the mission calling of the Church in general. In Lesson 9 we'll identify an essential missionary task which can be completed, which opens the way for every kind of flourishing of the blessing of the kingdom of God.

Read Beaver, " The History of Mission Strategy," pp. 246d-252

XI. The Fruit of the Movement: Transformation

The key idea throughout this lesson is the continuity of history. God has been relentlessly unfolding His purposes throughout the generations and centuries. Not all times are equal. There are periods of decline and apparent inactivity. But God's mission purpose has never been fully dependent on human activity. We identified the nature of mission history as a prolonged struggle, virtually a spiritual war. We've seen how God has used different mechanisms and movements. We presented God's purpose as that of fulfilling His promise to bless the nations. Have the nations been blessed? Is God accomplishing His purpose? What has been the outcome? According to a popular view, Christianity has been a source of hindrance and damage to the best interests of societies all over the world. This view is not correct. Although there have been many disappointing and destructive things done in the name of Christ, the overall positive impact of the person of Jesus Christ on the societies of the world has been incalculable.

A. The Ideal and Goal of the Kingdom. According to the famous historian Kenneth Scott Latourette, the ideal and goal of the kingdom of God had vastly shaped history subsequent to Jesus. He documented the increase of the World Christian Movement in various bursts of increasing magnitude and frequency (see the chart on p. 211 which displays the "resurgences" and the "recessions"). In Latourette's view, the Christian movement entered its greatest expansion ever in this century. The movement has exploded just as he thought that it might. Latourette not only told the story of the ongoing movement of Christianity, he also summed up the fruit of the movement.

Consider this quotation from his two-volume work entitled *A History of Christianity*:

> From individuals who have been inspired by Christ and from the Church has issued movement after movement for attaining the Christian ideal. That ideal has centered around the kingdom of God, an order in which God's will is done. It sets infinite value upon the individual....Its goal for the individual cannot be completely attained this side of the grave, but is so breathtaking that within history only a beginning is possible. Nor can it be reached in isolation, but only in community. In Christ's teaching, love for God, as the duty and privilege of man, is inseparably joined with love for one's neighbor.

> The ideal and the goal have determined the character of the movements which have been the fruits of Christianity. Although men can use and often have used knowledge and education to the seeming defeat of the ideal, across the centuries Christianity has been the means of reducing more languages to writing than have all other factors combined. It has created more schools, more theories of education, and more systems than has any other one force. More than any other power in history it has impelled men to fight suffering, whether that suffering has come from disease, war, or natural disasters. It has built thousands of hospitals, inspired the emergence of nursing and medical professions, and furthered movements for public health and the relief and prevention of famine. Although explorations and conquests which were in part its outgrowth led to the enslavement of Africans for the plantations of the Americas, men and women whose consciences were awakened by Christianity and whose wills it served brought about the abolition of Negro slavery. Men and women similarly moved and sustained, wrote into the laws of Spain and Portugal provisions to alleviate the ruthless exploitation of the Indians of the New World. Wars have often been waged in the name of Christianity. They have attained their most colossal dimensions through weapons and large scale organization initiated in Christendom. Yet from no other source have there come as many and as strong movements to eliminate or regulate war and to ease the suffering brought by war. From its first centuries the Christian faith has caused many of its adherents to be uneasy about war. It has led minorities to refuse to have any part it it. It has

impelled others to seek to limit war by defining what, in their judgment, from the Christian standpoint is a "just war." In the turbulent middle ages of Europe it gave rise to the Truce of God and the Peace of God. In a later era it was the main impulse in the formulation of international law. But for it the League of Nations and the United Nations would not have been. By its name and symbol the most extensive organization ever created for the relief of the suffering caused by war, the Red Cross, bears witness to its Christian origin. The list might go on indefinitely. It includes many other humanitarian projects and movements, ideals in government, the reform of prisons and the emergence of criminology, great art and architecture, and outstanding literature. In geographic extent and potency the results were never as marked as in the nineteenth and twentieth Centuries.

Kenneth Scott Latourette. "A History of Christianity," (Peabody, MA: Prince Press, 1997) pp. 1470-1471

B. The History of Transformation. The fruit of changing society toward the peace and justice of God's kingdom was not a matter of passive hopes. The missionary movement has been an almost constant force for positive change. Paul Pierson tells the story.

1. **Monasticism.** Look again at the tremendous heritage of the monastic movement. The monastic movement, properly understood, has been salt and light in God's hand throughout many centuries.

2. **Forerunners.** It makes sense that the Church has had such tremendous impact on the nations when the core values of the gospel begin to bloom and bear fruit in later centuries. The Puritan, Pietistic, Moravian and Wesleyan movements each brought greater focus of biblical hope on the present day for transformed personal and community life. It's not surprising that a vision for evangelization went hand in hand with a vision for profound social transformation.

3. **A striking contrast of reality and false report.** William Carey is recognized as the father of modern mission. What is not often known is the phenomenal breadth of his endeavors and the incredible changes that are still continuing because of his work. In contrast is the stereotype of missionaries who ruin cultures. Pierson mentions some of the truth of the falsely maligned missionaries to Hawaii.

4. **A striking comparison.** Not every place that Christianity has touched has been transformed to the same degree. There are, of course, many factors contributing to the different impact that the gospel has in different places. One key factor is the vision and intentional labor of missionaries to include bringing local leaders about in a transformation of life.

> **Read "A Striking Comparison" (p. 266b-266d) carefully to imagine the dramatic differences in just one situation. On both sides of the river there had been a minimal influence of Catholic church. What factors were part of the difference between the different sides of the river? What does this suggest about the need for integrated community development?**

5. **The different routes toward fruit.** Missionaries have labored in education, health care, agriculture and ministries for oppressed people, particularly women and slaves. Pierson does not so much provide a summary as a sampler. He is offering just a few very specific examples of a huge movement. The impact of the Christian movement has been so pervasive that it may not be possible to ever trace the entire impact. But it's safe to say that there has never been a greater source of betterment of the human situation than the global Christian movement in terms of education, health care and the status of women and slaves.

Read Pierson, "A History of Transformation," pp. 262-268 (all)

7 Eras of Mission History

Studying this lesson will help you:

- *Recall the approximate dates, emphasis, leaders and student movement associated with each of the three eras of Protestant missions history.*

- *Explain the four stages of mission activity.*

- *Explain the tensions of the transitions between the eras.*

- *Describe a "people movement."*

- *Use the E-Scale to describe the cultural distance of missionaries from their intended hearers.*

- *Use the P-Scale to describe the comparative socio-cultural distance of existing churches from would-be followers of Christ.*

- *Describe the increase of the non-Western missionary force in recent years.*

- *Describe "people blindness."*

We have surveyed the expansion of the world Christian movement through the major epochs of the last two millennia, focusing on the steady growth from one cultural sphere to another. In this lesson we'll focus on how that steady expansion became an explosion during the last 200 years.

The pace of growth is accelerating so quickly that more people have followed Christ in the last 100 years than in all of the previous centuries combined. There are more people alive today who call themselves Christians than all the Christians of previous generations put together.

At times this phenomenal expansion has nearly brought itself to a halt. Whenever the harvest is great, the crowds of new Christians make new demands upon missionaries for nurture, training and discipling. This deflects the attention of missionaries away from other regions or peoples that have yet to hear. Were it not for the many determined leaders whose minds are set on finishing the entire task of world evangelization, the movement might have stalled long ago. We'll examine some key figures and features that have kept propelling wave after wave of workers to the least evangelized places.

Why dig into these episodes of history? The reason is because at this hour we stand at a critical moment. The entire world Christian movement is beginning again to penetrate the final frontiers. But legitimate demands of home and nearby churches can deter us from pushing forward with strategic wisdom to finish the remaining task.

Perhaps the most thrilling phenomenon today is that missionaries are not only *going to* every part of the world. They are *coming from* every part of the world. Church movements from Latin America, Asia and Africa are the fastest growing mission force. To keep up with this surging new vanguard of the Christian movement, we must get acquainted with these new "Third World" mission structures.

FINISHING Some set their hearts on finishing what God has begun. They are the ones who come to know the expanse of God, who is the Beginning and the End of all that lasts. It should be no surprise that these finishers are actually the ones who *begin* the things that matter. They order their steps with strategic simplicity, not hesitating nor hurrying, but tenaciously continuing to do whatever it takes to finish the task God has given them.

I.   The Stages of Protestant Expansion

During its first 200 years, the Protestant movement did nearly nothing to bring the gospel to the nations. After mission structures were launched and with years of painstaking effort, the first wave of Protestant missionaries began to see the fruit of their labors. Much of that original success ended up preoccupying missionaries with caring for new converts such that they were hindered from pushing on to lesser evangelized areas. For the first time Protestants began to deal with the reality and needs of younger churches of another culture in lands distant from the homes of the missionaries. By contrast, at two important times leadership arose which propelled the Protestant movement forward by recognizing new mission frontiers.

A. Four Stages. Most mission efforts pass through four stages of development in the relationship between the mission agencies and the national church they plant. Understanding these stages will help us recognize why churches and missions often pursue different mission priorities. Missionaries themselves struggle to prioritize allocation of limited resources. Crucial decisions rest on "identifying the maturity level" of the new church and weighing its demands against the priority of evangelizing the unreached.

1. **Pioneer stage**—First contact with a people group.

2. **Paternal stage**—Expatriates train national leadership.

3. **Partnership stage**—National leaders work as equals with expatriates.

4. **Participation stage**—Expatriates are no longer equal partners, but participate only by invitation.

Read Winter, "Four Men, Three Eras, Two Transitions: Modern Missions," pp. 253-254c

See "Mission-Church Relations: Four Stages of Development" chart p. 256

Recognizing the range of mission priorities is an important matter. For example, how would you respond if, while visiting a mission field, you heard one local Christian leader pleading for new missionaries from America; and then, an hour later in the same city, another respected national leader politely urged Americans to return home?

B. Three Eras. Winter describes three "bursts" of advance in Protestant mission activity. Each of them focused on finishing the entire task of world evangelization by calling attention to specific frontiers or unreached parts of the world.

1. **The First Era: to the coastlands.** This era was pioneered by William Carey, and was mobilized in part by a student movement associated with the Haystack Prayer Meeting. Mission structures were typically non-denominational mission boards. Two astounding features: Astonishing readiness to sacrifice, and bright insight into mission strategy.

2. The Second Era: to the inland areas. This era was pioneered by Hudson Taylor, and later mobilized largely by a student movement called The Student Volunteer Movement. Mission structures independent of any denomination were called "faith missions." The newer recruits sometimes ignored much of the developed missiological wisdom of the earlier era but eventually planted churches in almost every *geographic* area. By 1940, this accomplishment was celebrated as the "great new fact of our time." Churches were apparently established everywhere. To many, world evangelization appeared to be virtually finished. Some structures began to send missionaries home, presuming that the day of missions was over.

3. The Third Era: to the unreached peoples. This era was set in motion by Cameron Townsend and Donald McGavran. McGavran often declared that the present hour was the sunrise, and not the sunset of missions. It was mobilized in part by the InterVarsity-related Student Foreign Mission Fellowship and other mobilization ministries. Many new service and mobilization mission structures emerged. Non-western mission agencies are beginning to surpass the numbers and influence of earlier missions. Townsend focused attention on the linguistic groups lacking a Bible translation. McGavran pointed out bypassed social groupings. These two ways of distinguishing people groups helped clarify the people group concept. The two approaches were the ethnolinguistic ("horizontal" groupings viewed by linguistic or ethnic differences) and the sociocultural ("vertical" groupings taking into account the subtle cultural traditions and prejudices). Ralph Winter and others helped develop the term "unreached peoples."

C. Two Transitions Between Eras. Each of the explosions of Protestant mission vision for the frontiers has roughly proceeded through the four stages (pioneer, paternal, partnership, and participation). However, the overlap of these eras has resulted in confusion regarding the appropriate strategy. Because of the success of the previous era, many missionaries were recalled. At the same time, new frontiers were envisioned by others that demanded new workers. The pressing need in pioneer fields is for missionaries to complete their roles in the pioneer and paternal stages. After that point, many missionaries need to move on to other unreached peoples or strategically serve in the partnership and participation stages, encouraging the national church toward developing its own pioneer missions.

Two Transitions Between Protestant Mission Eras

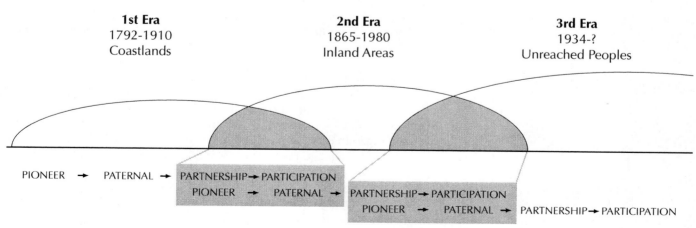

1st Era	2nd Era	3rd Era
1792-1910	1865-1980	1934-?
Coastlands	Inland Areas	Unreached Peoples

PIONEER → PATERNAL → PARTNERSHIP → PARTICIPATION
PIONEER → PATERNAL → PARTNERSHIP → PARTICIPATION
PIONEER → PATERNAL → PARTNERSHIP → PARTICIPATION

Periods of conflict and confusion of mission priorities during overlap of the Eras

Read Winter, "Four Men, Three Eras, Two Transitions: Modern Missions," pp. 254d-261c

D. One Movement. Winter points out that since the task has always been a global one, we can expect non-Western missions to play an increasingly major role in its completion. This could and should logically be the *final* era, in which the essential mission task, establishing a beachhead in every people group, is completed. This task is a once-in-history achievement. Never has the world Christian movement been so close to finishing that task.

Read Winter, "Four Men, Three Eras, Two Transitions: Modern Missions," pp. 261c-d ("Can We Do It?")

II. The New Macedonia

In 1974 Ralph D. Winter addressed the Lausanne Congress on World Evangelization in a way that brought much-needed light to the confusion of the second transition. By calling for a new thrust of mission to the bypassed people groups, Winter helped many recognize the malady which he called "people blindness." Winter later titled his paper "The New Macedonia" after the call for help in Acts 16:9. The influence of this address has been widespread and longstanding. Here you will read only a portion of it.

A. To Finish the Task. Winter identifies three different kinds of evangelism, distinguished by the cultural distance that the evangelist spans in communicating effectively with intended hearers.

1. The "E-Scale" has been a widely used reference tool for describing and comparing evangelistic difficulties and needs.

- **E-0** Evangelism of people who are part of Christian families and peoples. It is basically catechism and renewal. No real cultural barriers are crossed.

- **E-1** Evangelism of people outside the church but within one's culture. Only one barrier is crossed: the "stained-glass" membership boundaries of the church. This kind of evangelism is the "most powerful" because people are far more likely to understand what is being communicated in ways that they can pass on to others like themselves.

- **E-2** Evangelism of people of different but similar cultures. Two barriers are crossed: The "stained-glass" barrier and an additional cultural distance sufficient to require separate church fellowships.

- **E-3** Evangelism of people of radically different cultures. To emphasize the greater cultural distance of an evangelist attempting to communicate to a radically different and potentially hostile environment, it is supposed that evangelists attempt to cross at least three barriers in E-3 efforts. For example, working with Saharan nomads would require crossing the "stained-glass" barrier, a language barrier and a major lifestyle barrier. E-3 is the most difficult kind of evangelism.

2. Cultural rather than geographical distance. Winter uses Acts 1:8 as a rough parallel to the distinctions of the E-Scale. Geography does not matter nearly as much as the breakthrough to culturally different people groups.

E-Scale
Evangelist's Cultural Distance from Potential Convert

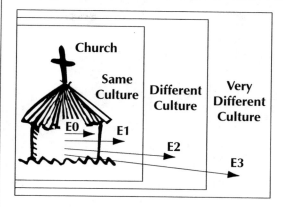

E0	Renewal evangelism of church members.
E1	Evangelism of non-Christians with no contact with the church.
E2	Evangelism of non-Christians in a similar but different culture.
E3	Evangelism in a completely different culture.

B. The Master Pattern of Evangelism according to Winter in 1974 was "first for special E-2 and E-3 efforts to cross cultural barriers to establish strong, ongoing vigorously evangelizing denominations, and then for that national church to carry the word forward on the really high-powered E-1 level."

C. People Blindness refers to a limited outlook that fails to notice the sub-groups within a country. The blindness is a significant barrier to developing effective mission strategy. Society should be seen, as McGavran suggested, as a complex mosaic of peoples. God loves and values each people group within the larger mosaic of society.

Read Winter, "The New Macedonia," pp. 339-346c

D. The "P-Scale" was also developed by Winter. Missionaries can better understand the overall task by looking at evangelization from the vantage point of unevangelized peoples. It evaluates the cultural distance that potential converts need to move in order to join the church most relevant to their own culture.

- **P-0** Identifies church members who need spiritual renewal. No distance lies between them and following Christ according to the customs of their church. It is more a matter of revival.

- **P-1** Identifies people who live in cultures which have a culturally-relevant local church movement capable of evangelizing them.

- **P-2** Identifies people who live in a culture that has no church relevant to their people group, but there is a church in a "near" culture. To follow Christ the potential convert would have to cross both a culture barrier as well as the "stained-glass" barrier by adopting the social and cultural values of a local church within a people other than their own.

- **P-3** Identifies people who also live in a culture without a relevant church. There are no nearby cultures similar to their own within which churches have been established. To follow Christ they would have to surmount significant cultural and social boundaries.

P-Scale:
People Groups' Cultural Distance from Nearest Church

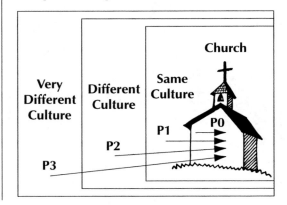

P0	People participating in a local culturally relevant church.
P1	A people whose culture contains a local church.
P2	People without a church whose culture is similar to a people with a church.
P3	People without a church whose culture is very different from that of the nearest group with a church.

Conclusion of Key Readings for this lesson.

III. The Bridges of God

Donald McGavran is one of the pioneers previously mentioned who set in motion the Third Era of Protestant missions as mentioned earlier. We will read an excerpt from his influential book *The Bridges of God.* His lasting contribution is the call to evangelize entire peoples who are culturally isolated from the gospel.

A. **Western Individualism.** McGavran says that Western individualism has long obscured the way that most people throughout history have ever become Christian. (In the full text of the book McGavran substantiates this point with examples from many parts of history.) Because peoples are not readily seen, people movements are often not recognized.

B. **Peoples and Multi-individual Decisions.** McGavran defines what is meant by a "people" and describes the dynamic of group decisions to follow Christ.

C. **People Movements.** These movements, marked by a group decision of a people-group to follow Christ but also to retain its identity and social relationships, should intentionally be sustained and nurtured to maturity. Achieving "a people movement to Christ" is McGavran's original phrase. This is another way to describe the essential missionary task as mentioned by Winter.

> **Read McGavran, "The Bridges of God," pp. 323-326a**

IV. Expecting a Great Harvest

Patrick Johnstone, author of the well-known prayer volume, *Operation World,* summarizes the phenomenal hope of completing world evangelization. He provides another look at the biblical basis for that hope, and then sums up the increase of the gospel over the centuries.

A. **The Spread of Christianity through History.** Note that the period of the most rapid expansion, from 1800 to the present, is the same 200-year period as the "Three Eras" above. In his graph, "The Spread of Christianity," Johnstone introduces David Barrett's model of Worlds A, B, and C as ways of looking at the world in terms of individuals being exposed to the gospel. "World A" is rapidly disappearing. This is what you would expect to see as evangelizing churches are planted within every people.

The chart below shows how the model of Worlds A, B, and C compares with Winter's E-Scale. Remember that Barrett recognizes many different factors in "exposure to the gospel," while Winter, following McGavran, regards the presence of an indigenous church movement as the only adequate evangelism.

B. Two Millennia of Evangelizing Peoples. Johnstone also gives us a similar view of the world in terms of ethnolinguistic peoples. Again the number and percentage of peoples that are unreached continues to shrink as missionaries of the Three Eras have "gone" to the "nations." Some day there will be no more P-2 or P-3 non-Christians who are beyond the reach of evangelizing churches (represented by the black area in the chart on page 217), this is what we mean by the term "world evangelization." On the other hand, the number of unreached peoples is constantly expanding as we discover that most "ethnolinguistic" peoples are actually clusters of smaller peoples!

Worlds: A, B and C (exposure to the gospel)	E-Scale (kind of evangelism required)
World C: all individuals who would identify themselves as Christians.	**E-0:** evangelism of those who would call themselves Christians or who are participating in a local church though not yet true believers.
World B: all non-Christians who live within societies where they have heard or are likely to hear the gospel during their lifetime.	**E-1:** evangelism of non-Christians within the same culture as the evangelist.
World A: all non-Christians who are "unevangelized" (not adequately exposed to the gospel) and are likely to remain so without a pioneering effort by Christians to bring the gospel to them.	**E-2:** evangelism of non-Christians within cultures that are similar to the culture of the missionary. **E-3:** evangelism of non-Christians within cultures that are very different to the culture of the missionary.

C. Discipling the World's Peoples. Johnstone shows a breakdown of the world's ethnolinguistic peoples according to those which are predominantly Christian, those which are not predominantly Christian but have had a "missiological breakthrough," and the people groups which are still "pioneer fields" requiring mission endeavor. Consider it well. Even though there are thousands of ethnolinguistic people yet to be evangelized, we can rejoice that work has already begun in more than half of them!

Read Johnstone, "The Church is Bigger Than You Think," pp. 214-218

Do you not say, 'There are yet four months, and then comes the harvest?'

Behold, I say to you, lift up your eyes, and look on the fields, that they are white for harvest.

Already he who reaps is receiving wages, and is gathering fruit for life eternal; that he who sows and he who reaps may rejoice together.

For in this case the saying is true, 'One sows, and another reaps.'

I sent you to reap that for which you have not labored; others have labored, and you have entered into their labor.

— John 4:35-38

VI. A Global Harvest Force

Larry Keyes presents the awesome reality that most of today's mission force comes from non-Western countries. He refers to them as "two-thirds world missionaries." Their numbers are already growing much faster than missionaries from America and Europe. In fact, their numbers are growing so rapidly that it is increasingly difficult to even keep track of estimates of non-Western missionaries. Overall we should be encouraged: never before has God raised for Himself a truly global force. It is a day of global partnership for a global harvest. While the evangelism of individuals will never cease, due to the thousands of children reaching the age of accountability every hour, at least the uniquely mission task of achieving a church movement within every unimax people group can be completed (more on the term "unimax people group" in Lesson 9).

Jesus took His followers on a training mission to Samaria. He wanted them to see the immensity of the harvest as well as the interdependency they would need to complete the task. Read Jesus' words in John 4:35-38. What does it mean to "enter the labor" of another person? Have you ever done this? Is it possible for you to take part in the huge harvest ahead without involving the partnership of other generations or cultures?

Read Keyes, "A Global Harvest Force," pp. 744-747 (all)

Conclusion of Certificate Level Readings for this lesson.

Credit Level Guide Notes continue...

VII. Farewell to "The Great Century"

We return to McGavran's assessment of the strategic approach of the first two eras of Protestant mission. We need to understand this pattern very well so that we do not inadvertently slip into an approach which fits the colonial era. Western individualism, when combined with a sense of cultural superiority, can sometimes divert well-intentioned missionaries into repeating a subtle form of the mission station approach. Many of the early workers of the Second Era ignored both the lessons to be gained from mistakes as well as the hard-won wisdom of First Era missionaries.

A. Across the Gulf of Separation: Exploratory Mission Station Approach. Missionaries encountered great cultural differences. The usual approach was to establish a mission station and draw converts in a "gathered colony" style. The pattern of conversion was extraction from family, culture and relationships. Evangelism was slow and often reached some of the least influential of the community. McGavran does not criticize missionaries for beginning their work in this way. In his view, it fit the colonial era as the best possible strategy.

B. The Fork in the Road: Mission Station or People Movement. McGavran describes this approach as a road on a flat plain which branches toward a steep high road of the People Movement Approach. Great hopes for large movements were often frustrated because of the vicious cycle of extracting converts out of their people. This led to a meager response, which in turn produced a mentality of abandoning the vision of large movements of people following Christ. In contrast, there were several significant occasions of people movements. These were usually not sought by the missionaries and in fact, were often resisted by them.

C. Resulting Churches Contrasted: Gathered Colony vs. Christward Movements. Gathered colony churches are dependent on missionaries. On page 330 McGavran describes how missionaries were often somewhat successful during the first and second eras, but came to be inundated by demands of pastoring and governing the institutionalized churches, schools and hospitals that were established. There was often a vested interest in the status quo, and little sustained effort to evangelize beyond the immediate vicinity of the mission station. In contrast, the Karen and the Chura case studies exemplify the dynamism of people movement churches. Take note that in both cases, an early convert from their people was far more influential than the foreign missionary. In both cases missionaries (even the notorious Adoniram Judson!) were doubtful of the value and appropriateness of these movements. God blessed the movements anyway. McGavran's point is that missionaries must now recognize the beginnings of such God-given movements and seek to enhance them.

Read McGavran, "The Bridges of God," 326b-336b

XI. Student Power in the Three Eras

The great waves of missionaries did not suddenly appear out of thin air. Many people served valiantly behind the scenes as mission mobilizers. Their work was always birthed and marked by sustained united prayer. David Howard finds an early example (around 1630) of students banding together in prayer and working together for the extension of the gospel. This dynamic of meeting for prayer occurs repeatedly. Understand Howard's analysis of the dynamics. Focus on three movements: the Haystack Prayer meeting, the Student Volunteer Movement, and the more recent emergence of Inter-Varsity with the Student Foreign Missions Fellowship. Be careful working through Howard's colorful summaries. Not every event is described in chronological sequence. Your awareness of the three eras will help you recognize the timing and the significance of these phenomenal mobilization movements. Howard writes to incite similar passion among young people today. Keep in mind how intergenerational the movements really were. Senior leaders were expected to participate. Leaders who were once students continued to mobilize students for decades.

A. **First Era Fuel: The Haystack Prayer Meeting.** Samuel Mills, impacted by the Great Awakening, joined other students in a gathering that met by a river, and during a storm, took refuge under a haystack. That particular meeting was the initial impulse for much of the early American missionary enterprise. They formed "The Society of the Brethren" with the goal of mobilizing others for missions.

B. **Second Era Fire: The Student Volunteer Movement.** Howard says that no single factor has wielded a greater influence in the worldwide outreach of the Church in modern times than the Student Volunteer Movement (SVM). Their watchword was "The evangelization of the world in this generation." Key leaders were John R. Mott, Robert Speer, Robert Wilder, Samuel Zwemer and A. T. Pierson. Howard describes the features of the decline of the SVM because of the potential for present-day movements of mission mobilization to repeat some of the same mistakes.

C. **Third Era Fusion: The Student Foreign Missions Fellowship and Inter-Varsity.** The SFMF was formed specifically to continue and extend the mission mobilization vision of the SVM. A few years later the SFMF became the Missionary Department of Inter-Varsity Christian Fellowship, widely known for the Urbana student missionary conventions. Along with the triennial conventions, the U.S. Center For World Mission (USCWM) and other mobilization structures continue mobilization of students, lay people, and local churches. Mobilization of missionaries in non-Western countries is being done by a multitude of diverse movements.

Read Howard, "Student Power in World Missions," pp. 277-286 (all)

8 Pioneers of the World Christian Movement

Here we will meet some of the key figures of the past 200 years. These people did not wait for someone else to be first; they opened the way for others. The only word that accurately describes them is "pioneers."

Why should we examine the lives and read the words of these pioneers? One reason is that they left us something to continue: a world almost evangelized—a nearly complete task. It would be foolish for us to respond to the needs of the world as if it had been our idea to evangelize it. God Himself began it all. He has had worthy people throughout the generations who have each finished their part. But some wise ones knew that they were laying down their lives so that others would complete what they began.

One notable pioneer, David Livingstone, said this to an assembly of people who had gathered to hear him tell of his ventures in Africa: "Do you carry out the work which I have begun. I leave it with you."

All of the people you will meet in this chapter were people of prayer. They prayed that others would join them. No doubt they prayed for those who followed them years later. Is it possible that you are the answer to their prayers?

In this lesson we'll listen to how one of the Second Era leaders specifically called his contemporaries to continue the task that earlier missionaries (from the First Era) left to them. We'll read the original writings of some of the key instigators of the three eras of Protestant mission history. We'll get acquainted with some of the women who have carried an enormous part of world evangelization. Pioneers are not solitary heroic figures. The Moravian movement is an exemplary pioneer fellowship.

FAITHFUL

Faithful people know they are being trusted. Zeal to fulfill that trust distinguishes the faithful from those who are merely dutiful. The dutiful perform what is required, and so they are sometimes daunted in the face of sacrifice. The faithful remain dedicated to the One who entrusts them despite high cost. Sacrifice is a light thing for them because they have already entered some of the joy of their Master, who commends them for being not only good, but also faithful.

I. A Case for Continuing

Samuel Zwemer was a leader in the the Student Volunteer Movement and worked for many years in the Muslim world. Discover what he means by "inverted homesickness," "apostolic ambition," "the pioneer spirit" and "the unoccupied fields." Learn the context for memorable statements, such as, "The prospects are as bright as are the promises of God," or "I never made a sacrifice."

> **Read Zwemer, "The Glory of the Impossible," pp. 311-316 (all)**

> **Zwemer challenged people in his day to consider "unoccupied fields." How does the call to labor among "unreached peoples" compare? Is this an identical challenge?**

II. Pioneers of the Movement

In the last lesson we read the words of Donald McGavran, one of the four key leaders mentioned by Winter as being largely responsible for spearheading the Three Eras of Protestant missions. We've selected some key writings of the other three leaders. As you read, take note of several common factors. First of all, each of them displays a confidence that world evangelization will be completed. They also call for others to be involved in specific parts of the world as a strategic step toward completing the entire task. Each of them displays an awareness of the demographic details. The efforts of each are grounded in Scripture, which they are convinced is the Word of God. Finally, each of them calls for prayer.

A. William Carey. Probably no piece of literature has motivated so many in such crucial ways as Carey's *Enquiry*. He offered a challenge to do at least as much as commercial ventures were doing to travel to distant lands in order to proclaim the gospel and to follow as far as commerce would go to reach distant lands. His exposition of the commission of Christ exposed the inadequate view that Matthew 28:18-20 pertained only to the first apostles and was no longer applicable.

> **Read Carey, "An Enquiry into the Obligation of Christians to Use Means for the Conversion of the Heathens," pp. 293-299 (all)**

> **Consider Carey's motto, "Expect great things from God. Attempt great things for God." At what points of your life have you chosen to follow God in this way? What happens when either half of the motto is followed without following the other? Is there any other way to experience great things?**

Conclusion of Key Readings for this lesson.

B. Hudson Taylor. In the following selection, Taylor recounts the development of his sense of calling to serve as a missionary. He describes how he pursued China as a field and how he prepared for that service. He radically simplified his lifestyle in hope of Christ's appearing and because it enhanced his ministry to the poor which was part of his preparation. He then describes how he began the China Inland Mission. The second reading, "China's Spiritual Need," reflects his passion for the Chinese. His specific vision and determination was to mobilize Christians to bring the gospel to every province of China.

> **Read Taylor, "The Call to Service," pp. 300-304 (all)**

> **Read Taylor, "China's Spiritual Need and Claims," pp. 305-308 (all)**

> **Consider Taylor's decisions to live simply and to give generously. How have you been challenged in similar ways? Take note of Taylor's confusion and anxiety about starting the mission structure. What can his experience teach you regarding obedience to God where there is need and opportunity?**

For the Son of Man has come to save that which was lost.

What do you think?

If any man has a hundred sheep, and one of them has gone astray, does he not leave the ninety-nine on the mountains and go and search for the one that is straying?

— Matthew 18:11-12

C. **Cameron Townsend** tells about the way several people argued against his vision to translate the Bible for the first tribal group of many thousands that would follow. He showed incredible resolve to launch a new kind of mission for an overlooked kind of people. Take note of the biblical grounds he found for establishing the mission and the biblical basis for his expectation that every tribe and tongue would be reached.

> **"Uncle Cam" Townsend found God's heart expressed in Matthew 18:11-12. He said, "That verse guided me." How might this same passage be God's way to guide you? Are there other verses about which you could say the same?**

> **Read Townsend, "Tribes, Tongues and Translators," pp. 309-310 (all)**

III. Women in Mission

Marguerite Kraft and Meg Crossman recount the tremendous record of women in missions. While the heritage is well worth celebrating, the women of earlier generations present us with more than marvelous examples to be admired. Kraft and Crossman tell the story in a way that effectively challenges faulty notions regarding the value and role of women in the mission enterprise. The patient leadership that women have offered in the past continues today. Women and men can find in this brief account many practical insights for how the entire Body of Christ can continue to work together to complete the task.

A. **Before the Protestant Reformation** women had always been a part of the mission efforts. The monastic tradition gave women a way to exert leadership in mission.

B. **The Beginning of the First Era.** A significant slowing down of women missionaries took place because of the typical Protestant policy that single women could not be sent alone, along with the assumption among Protestants that missionaries would be married. Still, the women went.

C. **The Beginning of the Second Era.** In the United States, women's participation in missions during the Second Era was spurred by the Civil War which wiped out a whole generation of men. Women, forced to emerge in leadership, began to organize their own mission boards. Gradually, however, the boards were absorbed into other mission structures and women lost the opportunity to direct the efforts.

D. **Women Excel.** There is no mission task that women have not, at some time, accomplished. Women are uniquely suited for several specific endeavors. In many tasks and roles they are essential.

E. A Mostly Female Force. For most of Protestant mission history as much as two-thirds of the mission force has been female. Recognizing the wide range of roles in which women are excelling may release an even greater number and enhance the effectiveness of women in mission.

Read Kraft and Crossman, "Women In Mission," pp. 269-273 (all)

What attitudes or expectations regarding women does this article reveal or challenge? What women do you know who are currently living out this heritage? What areas can you see for further involvement of women or partnership with women?

IV. Moravians: A Pioneer Movement

Colin Grant enables us to examine the Moravian movement in which we will recognize that mission obedience is not a matter of individual heroics. Pioneering is always accomplished by a movement working together.

A. Spontaneous Obedience, as Grant describes it, actually reflects the reality that the Moravians were the first clearly Protestant mission "order." They lived as a community of obedience. Such a shared sense of obedience to Jesus meant that not a few mission heroes were supported by people of lesser commitment. Everyone shared a ready eagerness to obey as directed by the Holy Spirit.

B. Passion for Christ. Singular devotion to Christ did not sideline Moravians into passive contemplation. Worshipful passion for Jesus moved them into powerful mission obedience.

C. Courage in the Face of Danger. Moravians articulated their mission motivation in this way: "That the Lamb who was slain would receive the reward of His suffering." Since Christ suffered and died, they did not think it was out of line for his servants to enter into difficult or painful situations.

D. Tenacity of Purpose. The perseverance of the Moravians may have been cultivated in their diligence in prayer. The movement sustained a 24-hour-a-day prayer meeting for over one hundred years seeking God's intervention for spiritual awakening and world evangelization.

E. Responsibility of the Church as a Whole. The approach of the Moravian Church may not be out of reach of many of our churches today. A sense of shared ownership filled the entire community.

Read Grant, " Europe's Moravians: A Pioneer Missionary Church," pp. 274-276 (all)

Describe one of the features of the Moravian community that is attractive to you. Has God surrounded you with some people who share your heart and mind for Christ and His mission? What features of Moravian life would you like to know more about?

Conclusion of Certificate Level Readings for this lesson.

Credit Level Guide Notes continue...

V. African Americans in World Missions

David Cornelius recounts the little-known history of African Americans in world mission. The relatively small number of African Americans in foreign missions may seem to suggest that this part of the Church has not been responsive to the Great Commission. The actual story reveals a substantial heritage of stalwart obedience.

A. Early Pioneers Before Emancipation. Just about every denominational stream of the African American church has a history of mission obedience. It was in the hearts of African Americans, even while they were slaves, to obey the Great Commission.

- **Freedom used for the Gospel.** Several of the pioneers of this period worked for decades to purchase their freedom, and then used that freedom to serve as missionaries.
- **Back to the Fatherland.** They were sent most often to Africa and other places where African Americans were enslaved, such as the Caribbean.
- **Another Pioneer named Carey.** One outstanding African American missionary was Lott Carey. He organized the African Baptist Foreign Missionary Society, the first organization established by African Americans for mission purpose.
- **Sacrifice and Partnership.** The mission ventures were funded with great sacrifice. There were requests for financial assistance from wealthier white Christians. Some were honored, others were turned down.

B. After Emancipation. African Americans suffered illness and death in Africa in the same way as did their white counterparts. The Baptist Foreign Mission Convention spearheaded many efforts. Decline came around the turn of the century as a result of hardships on the field and the diversion of attention to problems in America. Jim Crow laws mandating segregation and retarding the progress of African Americans toward economic and social prosperity made the struggle for human rights in America a high priority for many of the best leaders. For African Americans, the definition of missions came to include efforts for racial justice, hence the need for the "term international missions".

C. Recent Resurgence. There is a renewal of interest in international missions.

> **Read Cornelius, "A Historical Survey of African Americans in World Missions," pp. 287-292 (all)**

VI. World Mission Survey

Our tour through 40 centuries brings us to the present day which is probably the most exciting time of all. The most recent history is summed up by Ralph Winter and David Fraser. The world is surveyed in eight parts. The parts are basically geographical, but other factors come into the picture for this analysis. To make it easy to accurately but simply understand the remaining task, Ralph Winter introduced the idea of large "blocs" of unreached people groups: Muslim, Chinese, Hindu, Tribal and Buddhist peoples. By far, most of the world's least evangelized people live in these cultural basins. That same analysis is reflected in the breakdown of areas for this survey. Three of the areas are essentially continents: Europe, Latin America and Africa. The other five correspond to the five "blocs" of unreached peoples: Muslim, Chinese (China), Hindu (India), Tribal and Buddhist (Other Asian).

This survey will bring color and lively depth to the analysis of the remaining task which follows in Lesson 9. As you read allow your heart to marvel at God's hand. It's not just a survey, but an analysis of the dynamics of the progress of the Christian movement.

A. Europe. The surprising analysis is that Christianity was not so much snuffed out as disestablished by the tumult of events of the past century. Evangelistic ventures *to* Europe are still needed. There is much need for renewal and specific peoples are yet to be reached. Overall, there is more hope today than in the last few generations. Grass-roots movements are thriving in many parts. With regard to missions *from* Europe, the picture is bright. New student mobilization and cooperative partnerships have been formed.

B. Latin America. The gospel is exploding in Central and South America like few other areas of the world. The most thrilling aspect is that the revival is stirring sustained missions efforts from Latin America.

Read Winter and Fraser, "World Mission Survey," pp. 354-356d

C. Muslims. Muslim peoples have been regarded as resistant to the gospel. Winter suggests that many of them may not be resistant to the gospel itself, but rather resistant to a particular method or approach in evangelism. As such, we need to explore new strategic approaches. In the last few years, more Muslims have followed Christ than in all the years since Mohammed. Some of the experimental ideas will be explored in more depth in Lesson 14.

D. China (including the Chinese bloc of unreached peoples). This could be the most phenomenal Christian movement in history. The tens of millions of new believers in the last 20 years are continuing to multiply in both the "house church" structures, as well as the government-recognized "Three Self" churches. The huge growth presents challenges of nurturing and training leaders for what appears to be some of the largest people movements ever. The Christian movement is growing steadily among Chinese in other countries throughout the world. Mission efforts are sprouting with sophistication and effectiveness from many Chinese churches.

E. India (including the Hindu bloc of unreached peoples). The highlight of this section is the survey of the castes, and the analysis of the progress of the gospel among the castes. Strong mission efforts are emerging from the Indian churches. There are great challenges in India, but even greater hope.

Read Winter and Fraser, "World Mission Survey," pp. 356d-362

F. Tribes (including the Tribal bloc of unreached peoples). Be sure to grasp why tribal groups have proven more receptive to the gospel than Muslim or Hindu groups. Note the insights about the challenge of reading about the native tribes of North America.

G. Other Asians (including the Buddhist bloc of unreached peoples). This diverse region features an astounding range of high drama and great challenge. There are great breakthroughs and still never-evangelized peoples. Read this section with a map in hand. Winter and Fraser offer a five-point analysis:
- Christianized Asia
- Dynamic Christian Asia
- Christian Minorities—Sizable but Paralyzed
- Christian Minorities—Small but Stalled
- Precarious Beginnings

H. Africa. Sub-Saharan Africa has been the setting of some of the greatest sacrifices of missionaries in the past century. During the past few decades, there has been fantastic maturation and expansion of the churches. Many of these churches are growing, not only in numbers, but also in cross-cultural mission efforts within their countries. A large movement of "African Initiated Churches" has evidenced what many consider theological aberrations from the faith. Even so, there is vibrant allegiance to Christ that is bringing a stability and hope to regions and tribes experiencing great upheaval and change.

Read Winter and Fraser, "World Mission Survey," pp. 363-368

9 The Task Remaining

Studying this lesson will help you:

- *Differentiate between regular and frontier mission efforts using the E-Scale and the P-Scale.*

- *Define and use the terms people bloc, people group, unimax people group, socio-people, and unreached people group.*

- *Quote from memory the definition of a people group for evangelistic purposes.*

- *Explain the essential missionary task using and defining the term missiological breakthrough.*

- *Describe the rough percentages of the world's population who live in unreached peoples and in reached peoples.*

- *Recall roughly how many unimax groups there are in the four major cultural blocs of unreached peoples.*

- *Describe the imbalance of missionary allocation in today's world.*

- *Explain the biblical grounds for and strategic value of urban ministry.*

- *Explain how good mission strategy express both faith and faithfulness while allowing for the Lordship of the Holy Spirit in mission decisions.*

Just as mountains can be seen more clearly from a distance, the awesome strategic possibilities of our day can be seen with better clarity by stepping back to get a "big picture" viewpoint. Throughout this course we have stepped back, as it were, from the present day by tracing the progress of God's purposes from the time of Abraham until now.

We've seen the blessing of Abraham extended to the nations. The blessing spread at an uneven pace through history but, nevertheless, God has propelled His purpose forward with unrelenting passion. As we come to the present day we have to be stunned by the magnitude of the movement to Christ. Never before has Christ been named in so many languages and obeyed faithfully in such a myriad of cultural styles. Never before has Christ been so openly worshiped. Never before has Christ been so visciously hated or His servants so widely persecuted. Yet never before have so many people followed Christ. Could we now be seeing close-up what Abraham saw from a distance? Jesus said, "Abraham rejoiced to see My day, and he saw it and was glad" (John 8:56).

As we consider the realities of our day, we will understand even more clearly what it meant for God to promise blessing through Abraham to "all the families of the earth." This lesson focuses attention on the distinctive people groups of the earth. Once we master a few concepts and definitions regarding people groups, we can assess the remaining task.

Christ has given us a very narrowly defined task to finish. We are mandated to bring about a breakthrough of kingdom communities of obedient faith in every people group. But from that powerful beginning in every people group, God intends to bring forth some magnificent surprises that are samples of the fullness of His kingdom to come. God is waging His war against evil in many different ways. He is marshaling His people to fight with Him against evil of every kind in order to bring forth the abundant blessing promised through Abraham. We'll explore some of the wider vistas of spiritual war and God's mission to bring society-wide blessing in Christ's name.

STRATEGIC People pursuing a God-given vision live with strategic intent. The vision virtually captures them. They no longer dream about what *could* happen. They become convinced that certain things *must* happen. They make choices as if each day held abiding value. They are not driven by obligation. They live in the dignity and liberty of knowing they give their utmost for God's purposes.

I.   Finishing the Task

Ralph Winter and Bruce Koch describe the amazing threshold upon which we stand at this hour in history. The phenomenal progress in some parts of the world highlight the remaining task. It's crucial to comprehend the nature of the remaining task before we try to quantify it.

A. Amazing Progress. Amazing progress has been made in the fulfillment of God's promise to bless all the nations through descendants of Abraham. The sheer numerical increase is astounding. Biblical faith is growing and spreading as never before in history. There is at least one active Christian out of every ten people in the world.

B. Tragic Reality. Social and cultural realities greatly inhibit the progress of the gospel. The gospel readily "spreads" within peoples where it has been established, but it does not easily "jump" from one group to another because of prejudicial barriers between peoples. The result is that billions are left isolated from the gospel. They might be able to hear and understand the gospel, but may view Christian practices as alien or hostile to their culture. From their perspective, it is virtually impossible for them to follow Christ openly without abandoning their cultural identity and significant relationships.

Read Winter and Koch, "Finishing the Task: The Unreached Peoples Challenge," pp. 509-511b

C. Two Viewpoints on Evangelism Define Two Categories of Mission. The reason many do not follow Christ is not that evangelists can't get to them but that people can't find ways to belong to a church fellowship without losing their cultural identity.

1. E-Scale and P-Scale: Two viewpoints on the process of evangelization. We are reviewing these scales which were introduced in Lesson 7 to help us grasp the nature of the task before us. They represent two ways of looking at evangelism: from the evangelist's viewpoint or from the potential convert's viewpoint.

• **E-Scale -** Evangelist distance: the cultural distance between evangelists and potential hearers of the gospel.

• **P-Scale -** People distance: the cultural distance between potential converts and churches that may welcome them into fellowship.

2. What is a missionary? There is a tendency to define "missions" as any Christian work that takes place at a significant geographical distance. A missionary is then understood to be one who is on a foreign or distant "field." For clarity, it is better to understand a missionary to be *a worker laboring to reach people of a significantly different culture* (E2 or E3). By contrast, an evangelist is one who labors to reach others of their own culture (E0 or E1). The work of evangelism may have a great deal of missionary intent. However, to distinguish the different roles of evangelists and missionaries, it is best to reserve the term "missionary" for those doing, mobilizing for, or laboring in direct support of those doing *cross-cultural* work.

3. **Regular and frontier mission.** Almost every mission effort can be classified under one of two categories:

- **Regular mission:** cross-cultural Christian work that spreads the gospel within people groups where churches have already been established (P0-P1).

- **Frontier mission:** cross-cultural Christian work that seeks to establish churches within people groups where it does not yet exist (P2-P3).

The kind of mission effort required in the latter category is different enough to warrant different strategies, methods and workers. That's why the special category of "frontier mission" is needed to describe church planting efforts among unreached people groups. There is no value judgment implied in drawing the distinction between regular and frontier missions. Both are necessary. Frontier mission efforts, however, have a strategic priority in completing the overall task.

Example: An American missionary in Papua New Guinea teaches Christians from a jungle tribe to read the Bible in their own language. Their tribal church is thriving. Literacy will help them train pastors and lay leaders. The tribal culture is a very different culture (E3), but the missionary is working with Christians in their own culturally-relevant church (P0). This vital mission endeavor would come under the category of "regular mission."

On the other hand, people from the same American church as the above missionary might only have to cross the street from the American church to be categorized as missionaries. If they were to work with displaced Kurdish refugees from Iraq, where there is presently no thriving Kurdish church, their work, even though it takes place in an American city, would not only be cross-cultural work (E2 or E3), and therefore be considered missions, it would be among a people group lacking a church movement of their own, and therefore categorized as "frontier mission" (P2 or P3).

See charts, "E-Scale," "P-Scale," and "Regular Missions and Frontier Missions," pp. 510-511

Use the "Regular Missions and Frontier Missions" chart to classify the efforts of a recent short-term missionary with whom you are acquainted. Were they involved in regular or frontier missions? Does that distinction make them more or less valuable as a missionary? Now use the chart to identify maids from the Philippines working to evangelize their employers in Muslim Saudi Arabia. Compare their work to the short term missionary. Are the Filipino women more valuable as missionaries? Are they doing more strategic work?

And this gospel of the kingdom shall be preached in the whole world for a witness to all the nations, and then the end shall come.

—Matthew 24:14

D. **A Witness to All the Nations.** Matthew 24:14 helps us to understand what Christ expects us to have accomplished before He returns. Jesus states the goal of the Church in mission in terms of the "gospel of the kingdom" being proclaimed globally. There are two important qualifying expressions that have everything to do with the completion of the task: "as a witness" and "to every people." We can't be precisely sure what Jesus meant by either phrase, but they raise the right questions to envision the total task before us.

- **What is "a witness?"** Is there some kind of demonstration and declaration of the gospel of the kingdom that is a minimal achievement towards which we should aim? The rest of Scripture and God's work in history provide some powerful ways of understanding how the gospel of the kingdom is declared and displayed.

- **Who are "the peoples?"** Some translations render the Greek phrase *panta ta ethne* as "all nations," which brings to mind politically defined countries. As we've already explored in Lesson 4, this same phrase occurs in Matthew 28:19. It actually refers specifically to ethnic groups or people groups. Who are these people groups? How are they defined? How many are there?

Read Winter and Koch, "Finishing the Task: The Unreached Peoples Challenge," pp. 511b-512a

II. The Unreached Peoples Challenge

There are four main ways that the term "people group" is being used today. We need to become acquainted with each one and use them appropriately. When our thinking about people groups is fine-tuned, it will help us work together with strategic clarity.

A. Blocs. Blocs of people are summary categories which help us talk about all the unreached people groups on earth. There are two commonly used sets of blocs.

   1. Major cultural blocs. Tribal, Hindu, Chinese, Muslim and Buddhist. This set of blocs has been in use for over 20 years. Recent numbers still show it to represent the strong majority of unreached peoples.

   2. Affinity blocs. Johnstone and others have presented another way of grouping the peoples according to shared elements of language, history, culture, etc.

B. Ethnolinguistic Peoples. An ethnolinguistic people is an ethnic or racial group distinguished by its self-identity with traditions of common descent, history, customs and language. The value of the ethnolinguistic people approach is that it provides an easy way to identify peoples so as to mobilize prayer and stimulate initial planning. Since features of race and language are easily counted, lists of ethnolinguistic peoples tend to be stable. Ethnolinguistic peoples do not correspond to countries. A single country can have thousands of ethnolinguistic peoples. By the same token, a single ethnolinguistic people can be spread over a dozen different countries. Examine Nigeria as an example (see next page).

C. Sociopeoples. *A sociopeople is a relatively small association of peers who have an affinity for one another based upon a shared interest, activity or occupation.* Sociopeoples are not significant as groups which require a special church planting effort. They may require special evangelistic tactics, but not a full-blown church movement. On the other hand, they are very significant sets of people for preliminary evangelism as an intermediate bridge to long-range church planting goals. We can only estimate the number of sociopeoples since the different networks and social sets are virtually endless.

Political Boundaries: Nigeria and Surrounding Countries

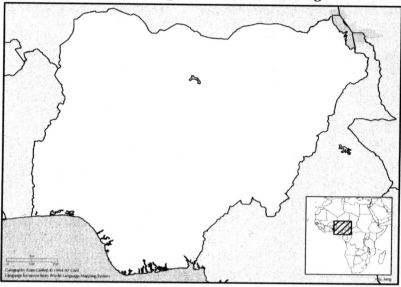

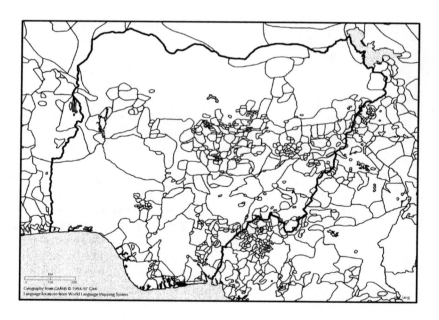

People groups do not equal countries. A standard map of Nigeria appears to be one country with 100 million people. In fact, Nigeria is one country with 427 ethnolinguistic peoples. The bottom map shows just some of the territories inhabited by some of the groups distinguished by language.

Mission Leaders Agree on Strategic Definitions

In March 1982 a group of mission leaders came together in Chicago for a meeting sponsored by the Lausanne Strategy Working Group. It was designed to help bring clarity and definition to the remaining missionary task. At no time before or since this meeting has as large or as representative a group gathered for two days to focus specifically upon the necessary definitions for a strategy to reach the unreached peoples. Two basic definitions came from this meeting:

1. **A People Group** is "a significantly large grouping of individuals who perceive themselves to have a common affinity for one another because of their shared language, religion, ethnicity, residence, occupation, class or caste, situation, etc., or combinations of these." *For evangelistic purposes it is "the largest group within which the gospel can spread as a church planting movement without encountering barriers of understanding or acceptance."*

2. **An *Unreached* People Group** is "a people group within which there is no indigenous community of believing Christians able to evangelize this people group."

D. Unimax Peoples. *A unimax people is the **max**imum sized group sufficiently **uni**fied to be the target of a single people movement to Christ.* The unimax approach helps identify the boundaries which hinder the flow of the gospel. At the same time, a unimax understanding helps indicate where dedicated Christians need to begin yet another effort of evangelization beyond boundaries of cultural prejudice. If widely applied, it will mean that no smaller group will be "hidden" from the view of missionaries in the midst of a larger ethnolinguistic group.

1. **An affirmed definition.** Memorize this definition of a people group: *"For evangelistic purposes a people group is the largest group within which the gospel can spread as a church planting movement without encountering barriers of understanding or acceptance."* There have been others who have suggested different definitions of peoples. This is the important 1982 definition, which not only carries the weight of broad affirmation at the time of its formation, but has proven useful for both field practitioners and sending churches to envision what should be the focus and the outcome of their work.

2. **Why are there different counts of unreached peoples?** Some mission leaders have chosen to count ethnolinguistic peoples. Others are estimating the number of unimax peoples.

3. **More unimax peoples than ethnolinguistic peoples.** The gospel "spreads" but does not easily "jump" over the barriers of hatred and fear that fragment the world's peoples. Even within language groups (an ethnolinguistic people), the social distinctions can prove to be daunting barriers for would-be converts. Instead of requiring such eager-to-believe people to divorce themselves from their own people in order to follow Christ, we should make every attempt to establish a movement of people following Christ within that group.

4. **Can they be counted?** The unimax peoples definition was never intended to precisely quantify the total task. Instead, it helps us recognize where the frontier mission task is finished and identify where that task has not yet begun.

E. Using all four definitions. Each of the understandings of people groups is helpful:

*   **To summarize** the total task, use the idea of *blocs* of unreached peoples, whether major cultural or affinity blocs.

*   **To mobilize** prayer, awareness or to initiate field action and partnerships, use *ethnolinguistic* distinctions.

- **To begin work evangelizing** an unreached people, start by identifying the *sociopeoples* which may serve as bridges to convey the gospel to the entire people group.

- **To plant churches** among an unreached people, use the *unimax* approach to identify the extent of the people you are reaching. New unimax peoples are discovered as we become aware of groups that will be bypassed by current efforts.

Read Winter and Koch, "Finishing the Task: The Unreached Peoples Challenge," pp. 512a-516c, and review chart on p. 515

III. The Essential Missionary Task

God has given us a mandate to accomplish. As we complete that mandate, it sets in motion all kinds of opportunities for God's people to co-work with God in bringing healing and hope to the nations. The blessing of Abraham only begins with the message of salvation. Entire societies to be transformed by God's work through the gospel, but only after a missiological breakthrough has occurred.

A. Missiological Breakthrough. The missionary task must never be understood as missionaries proclaiming the gospel to every person. Christ indeed wants every person to hear, but not from missionaries! The missionary task is to bring about a beginning of a gospel movement in every people, so that people of a given culture will eventually hear the gospel communicated by someone from their own people group.

1. The essential missionary task is to establish a *viable, indigenous church planting movement* within every people that carries the potential to renew whole extended families and transform whole societies.

- **Viable**—growing on its own.

- **Indigenous**—not seen as foreign.

- **Church planting movement**—continuing to reproduce intergenerational fellowships capable of evangelizing the rest of the people group.

2. Closure is a term usually referring to establishing a breakthrough in every people group on earth. Closure was expressed powerfully by the watchword for the frontier mission movement, "A Church For Every People by the Year 2000."

- **A church**—not "the" Church, but rather an indigenous, locally-relevant church; not just one congregation, but a multiplying movement.

- **For every people**—every one of the unimax people groups of earth,

- **By the Year 2000**—Some overemphasized the importance of the year 2000. The watchword, coined in 1979, used the millennial milestone to draw attention to the exciting possibility of bringing about closure in a relatively short period of time if the vast resources of the Church were mobilized. The year 2000 passed without establishing a church within *every* people, yet thousands of groups *were* reached. But possibly of greater significance is the fact that the watchword succeeded in convincing believers around the world that the goal of —A Church in Every People—must, can and will be completed.

3. Verifiable progress. We may not be able to precisely *quantify* the progress toward closure, but we can *verify* progress.

B. Beyond Breakthrough. We use the language of breakthrough because churches are established for the first time which express Christ's operative Lordship in the people group. These churches become communities of glad-hearted obedience and submission to His Lordship. The blessing of His kingship becomes observable and accessible to the community. The new church, with or without the participation of missionaries, becomes the primary agent of God's blessing, another manifestation of the seed of Abraham. The new churches provide a persuasive sign, we might even say a "testimony," of God's kingdom. Many mission endeavors aim at fighting evil and manifest the kingdom through relief and community development efforts. This is right and helpful, but an important strategic priority is the planting of a viable church, which is the beginning of all that will bear lasting fruit.

> **Read Winter and Koch, "Finishing the Task: The Unreached Peoples Challenge," pp. 516c-519a**

IV. Looking at the Task Graphically

The concepts we've learned will help us make sense of the status of the World Christian Movement and the crucial need of the hour.

A. The Status. A few statistics which you can easily remember:

- **Thirds.** Roughly one third of the world claims to be Christian in some way. Roughly one third are non-Christians living within reached peoples. The other third lives within unreached peoples.

- **How many unreached people groups?** Using the unimax definition, the best estimate is 10,000. Most are living in four blocs: Muslim (3,700 groups—a little less than 4,000), Hindu (2,700 groups—a little less than 3,000), Tribal (2,000), and Buddhist (1,000). (The figures above rounded to the nearest thousand: 4,000 Muslims, 3,000 Hindus, 2,000 Tribals, 1,000 Buddhists). Remember that there are unreached people groups in other sectors as well.

B. The Great Imbalance Chart. The same data is arrayed in a different way. A key comparison is the number of missionaries allocated to reached peoples and unreached peoples. Only 2.4% of the global foreign mission force is presently focusing on half of the world's non-Christians that are beyond the reach of the Church. Most non-Christians have never even met someone who follows Christ from their own culture. Two qualifying facts make this even more striking:

- **Consider the even greater imbalance of full-time workers.** The imbalance would be far more striking if we included all full-time Christian laborers such as music pastors and youth workers. The point is not that we need fewer pastors but that we need more missionaries.

  - **Consider the relative difficulty.** Evangelizing unreached peoples is far more difficult than working with unbelievers who live in cultures already saturated with the gospel. What kind of allocation would we like to see? We probably need to see the opposite proportion: three out of every four missionaries focusing attention on unreached peoples. How shall we move toward this goal? Rather than pulling effective missionaries away from reached people groups, why not mobilize many new missionaries from the rapidly expanding global Church?

"Shout for joy, O barren one, you who have borne no child;

Break forth into joyful shouting and cry aloud, you who have not travailed;

For the sons of the desolate one will be more numerous

Than the sons of the married woman," says the LORD.

"Enlarge the place of your tent;

Stretch out the curtains of your dwellings,

Spare not;

*Lengthen your cords,
And strengthen your pegs.*

For you will spread abroad to the right and to the left.

And your descendants will possess nations,

And they will resettle the desolate cities."

—Isaiah 54:1-3

Read Winter and Koch, "Finishing the Task: The Unreached Peoples Challenge," pp. 519a-524

V. The Challenge Before Us

The following excerpts come from an excellent book that every Perspectives student will want to acquire and read: *The Church is Bigger Than You Think* (published by Christian Focus Publications, available from William Carey Library). In the excerpt below Patrick Johnstone points out that Isaiah 54:1-3 promises the gospel will not only extend to every *people*, but that it will expand to every point of *geography* and to the *cities*.

A. The Geographic Challenge. Johnstone identifies what he calls a "Resistant Belt" and describes how this is equivalent to the "The 10/40 Window." Be sure you are aware of some of the stunning facts about this region of the world.

Examine what Patrick Johnstone says on page 214 about the woman described in Isaiah 54. What does this passage say about the strategic hope of completing the gospel? Is the woman supposed to rejoice before, during or after the global expansion of her family? Are you participating in this rejoicing? Meditate on the short command to "Spare not." In what way can you "Spare not" in your own life?

Read Johnstone, "Covering the Globe," pp. 541-543c

Conclusion of Key Readings for this lesson.

B. The People Challenge.

1. Affinity blocs and people clusters. Johnstone presents a list of 12 affinity blocs which encompass almost all of the unreached people groups (but not all peoples of the world). People Clusters subdivide the Affinity Blocs. Johnstone estimates the number of people groups within the Affinity Blocs to be 2,224. This is a count of ethnolinguistic peoples, not unimax peoples, as discussed above.

2. Prayer. Prayer has been focused on the peoples as never before by "Praying Through The Window" efforts.

3. Saturation church planting. There are about 3,000,000 churches in the world. To ensure that no people is overlooked, the DAWN Movement aims to see 7,000,000 more in order to saturate every city and place with churches.

C. The Urban Challenge. Johnstone states that "pioneer missions" in the coming century will be focused on "the great cities of the world—a more complex and multi-layered kaleidoscope of needs." Listen to the challenge and hope brought by two leaders with a track record in urban ministry and a passion for the kingdom of God breaking through in every city.

1. The cry of the urban poor. Viv Grigg describes the growth of cities and the incredible opportunity for a display of the kingdom of God in "slums of hope." He calls for a new force of missionaries returning to a biblical model of focusing on the poor and expressing ministry according to an "incarnational" model. (Incarnational ministry will be covered again in Lesson 11).

Read Johnstone, "Covering the Globe," pp. 543c-546c and 551c-552

and then,

Read Grigg, "The Urban Poor: Who Are We?" pp. 581-582b

2. **The future frontier of cities.** Roger Greenway gives more detail about the growth of cities in the near future. Despite great struggle and suffering in cities, there is tremendous opportunity for the gospel to flourish with a distinctive expression of the kingdom of God.

   • **Practical issues.** Greenway lists five challenges. How will they be met?

   • **God's Word.** Greenway lists seven substantial truths that shape all urban ministry. Which ones highlight or restate the concept of missiological breakthrough? Which of them restate the expression of a witness to the gospel of the kingdom? The concept of *Shalom* (the Hebrew word for peace) is strongly connected to a vision of the kingdom of God.

Read Greenway, "The Challenge of the Cities," pp. 553-558 (all)

VI. Attempt Great Things

Vishal and Ruth Mangalwadi present an astounding review of the activities of William Carey. Since you have read about William Carey in Lesson 8, you understand his determination to fulfill the mandate of Matthew 28 as the primary focus of his ministry. But while attempting that "great thing," look what other great things God was accomplishing through his efforts!

VII. The Mission of the Kingdom

Ralph Winter comments on the breadth of Carey's mission outreach. While the Bible never assigns the Church the task of engineering the arrival of the kingdom of God on earth, the Bible does enjoin the Church to fight evil with God. Is there any evil that is out of the range of Christ's cross and God's promise? While we labor to finish the Great Commission, God may give us assignments to join Him in resisting and overcoming social, spiritual, and even biological evil. It's easy to agree that it would be good for diseases to be eradicated. Winter poses the provocative idea that it might be God's will in overcoming evil to eradicate diseases. Could such triumphs over evil become part of the witness to every people of the gospel of the Kingdom? Winter does not move from his conviction that the mission of the Kingdom centers on and begins with planting churches among every people. He calls us to consider further frontiers beyond the beginnings that church-planting breakthroughs represent in every people.

Read Mangalwadi, "Who (Really) Was William Carey?" pp. 525-528 (all)

and then,

Read Winter, "The Mission of the Kingdom," pp. 529-530 (all)

VIII. The Place of Strategy

The idea of strategy strikes many in a negative way as though strategists might displace the Holy Spirit in initiating and guiding mission efforts to true fruitfulness. C. Peter Wagner describes how most mission strategists actually understand strategy as an expression of both faith and faithfulness. Take note of Wagner's understanding of faithfulness in light of the biblical truth of stewardship. Faithfulness, in this understanding, involves planning and working together toward success with a consecrated pragmatism. By consecrated pragmatism, Wagner means that while we should never change our doctrine or our ethical principles in order to do something that "works," we should remain flexible regarding methods. Strategy does not eliminate the Holy Spirit. Good strategies present the Holy Spirit with plans that He can change. Good strategies also provide human co-workers a common vision around which they can unite.

Read Wagner, "On the Cutting Edge of Mission Strategy," pp. 534b-535a

The rest of the lessons in this course will expand on this strategic perspective. First we will explore how to effectively communicate the gospel in the Cultural section of the course (Lessons 10 and 11). Then we will focus on development and further Strategic considerations as mission efforts touch the wide range of human need (Lesson 12). We will focus then on church planting (Lessons 13 and 14) before exploring strategic partnership on a local, global and field level (Lesson 15).

Conclusion of Certificate Level Readings for this lesson.

Credit Level Guide Notes continue...

After studying this section you should be able to:

• *Explain the importance of recognizing subtle social boundaries in order to plant churches among every people group.*

• *Describe the importance of "mother-tongue ministry" and "mother-tongue Scriptures" for establishing churches that multiply and endure.*

IX. Recognizing People Groups

We've made a distinction between ethnolinguistic people groups and unimax people groups. Both ways of delineating people groups are valid and useful. But the two definitions lead to different tallies of how many people groups remain to be evangelized. Ethnolinguistic estimates can seem to be more reliable because they are based on observable features of race, language, geography and culture. Unimax peoples are usually shaped by social boundaries. People have understandings of who they are and who they are not which are not always based on physical or linguistic features. Often people groups sort themselves out by fears or prejudices. These dynamics are not usually apparent to those distant from the situation. The only features that can be seen from a distance are language, racial lineage and geography. The more subtle, but very powerful dynamics of attitudes and assumptions of social gaps between peoples can only be discerned by living among the people. The key point is that unimax people groups are defined by *how the people themselves distinguish themselves* from other peoples.

When counting people groups, unimax people groups can only be estimated. When actually planting vibrant churches, it will always be essential to recognize the reality of unimax people groups.

A case study will help illustrate the point. Larry Walker's experience among the Tzutujil (tsoo-too-heel) people of Guatemala is a classic case where one ethnolinguistic people actually turned out to be two different people groups. Walker came to recognize that there were subtle differences of dialect which were laden with issues of pride and resistance to being identified with the other group. An existing translation was understandable but not regarded as valuable. It sounded "foreign" to their ears even though they knew that the "foreign", even offensive, group was the people who lived one mountain valley away from them. When specialized efforts were made to bring Scripture in their dialect, the initial interest in the things of Christ was strengthened and maintained as "an indigenous people movement."

This case study actually deals with a linguistic distinction of dialect. There are many thousands of other unimax people groups that differentiate themselves by social distinctions such as caste, class, or historical animosity. Recognizing these differences helps in two ways: first, to direct new church planting efforts to reach every group, and then eventually, to advance God's work as the Holy Spirit brings about reconciliation and new relationships of honor, service and unity between the churches of the different people groups.

> **Read Walker, "How Many People Groups are There?" pp. 562-563 (all)**

X. The Missiological Breakthrough: Mother-Tongue Churches

Barbara Grimes highlights the value of pursuing "mother-tongue ministry" in order to bring about "mother-tongue disciples" and churches that impact their entire society. The key point concerns the decision over which language to use in mission work. Too often the choice of language is based on what is expedient for the communicators instead of what is valuable for the hearers. Grimes stretches our vision beyond the question of which language will be adequate as a medium of exposure toward which language will be best for facilitating a people movement. The vision should always be more than merely bringing the message to every language. Instead, our vision needs to focus on what can happen *from* every language: worship toward God and witness to the society.

A. The Best Outcome: "Mother-Tongue" Churches. The prime value of using the local vernacular is seen in terms of enduring, fruitful churches.

B. The Expedient Distractions. Grimes points out two ways that appear to offer short-cuts through the difficulties of language-learning and translation.

- **Multilingual Populations.** Beware of attempting to use a trade language that only some members of a society may understand. Consider the perceptions and attitudes about what is foreign and what is credible. Realistically consider the number of people in that society who may lack fluency in the second language.

- **Bilingual Brokers.** Another temptation is to work through an interpreter. Leadership development is severely diminished.

Read Grimes, "From Every Language," pp. 559-561 (all)

XI. By Every Means

One of the key distinctions of this lesson is the very nature of evangelism. Is the task which Christ gave us a matter of bringing about an exposure to the gospel? Or are we mandated to bring about a response to the gospel? The Great Commission seems to call for ongoing labor that is eventually fruitful among every people group. The focus on bringing about a beginning of an indigenous movement of obedient faith in every people requires a wide array of means to communicate the gospel.

Patrick Johnstone surveys some of the phenomenal ways that the gospel is being conveyed among the peoples of the world. Recognize the explosion of gospel communication and how the world is being evangelized as never before. None of the different media will automatically evangelize the world. Each of these media require face-to-face ministry and leadership training to establish ongoing movements.

A. Scripture Translation. Scripture translation, as Barbara Grimes points out, is not merely a matter of exposing people to the gospel. The indigenous church movements that we are hoping to see as a response to the gospel will usually need a mother-tongue translation and an effective literacy to use it.

B. Literature. Every Home For Christ (EHC) is an example of how literature ministry can be done well with a focus on new churches being planted among unevangelized people groups. EHC aims to plant "Christ Groups" in areas where there are no churches.

C. Tape and Film Media. Gospel Recordings works to produce evangelistic materials in every language. In doing so, they have often identified several unimax people groups that distinguish themselves by their accent, but can still use the same Bible translation. Once again, there are more unimax people groups than there are ethnolinguistic peoples. The medium of taped messages includes the phenomenal *Jesus Film* and videos.

D. Broadcast Media. Some of the most powerful radio broadcasting mechanisms on earth are missionary radio broadcasts. One of the best cooperative partnerships in world evangelization is the collaboration of missionary radio networks. Fantastic opportunities are opening up with satellite communications.

Read Johnstone, Covering the Globe pp. 546c-551b

10 How Shall They Hear?

We have already seen that the gospel cannot be *discovered* by people, it must be *disclosed* to people. If the gospel were merely information, then perhaps God's plan would have been to let sincere seekers ransack the created order and piece together ideas about Him. But the gospel is not just *information*. It is essentially an *invitation* to relationship. That's why God wants everyone to get a chance to hear His invitation. He sends messengers to convey that message.

If the messengers are not sensitive as they convey the message across cultural barriers, then the message becomes only so much intercultural noise. One stereotype of a missionary is that of an arrogant, imperious bigot who imposes Western beliefs on innocent cultures. No one wants to be involved in this kind of religious propaganda. Happily, the stereotype is largely false. Most missionaries work at great length to adapt their message to the heart of another culture. In this lesson, we'll explore what missionaries have learned from Scripture and experience about how to communicate so that all may hear.

The complexity of culture explains why the gospel "spreads" powerfully within a culture, but does not "jump" easily across cultural boundaries. In this lesson we'll explore what culture is and how we can better make the jump across the cultural boundaries that have long obstructed the advance of the gospel among the least evangelized.

We'll also explore how to communicate within a culture at a deep level, and why it's important to look for keys God may have provided to communicate His truth in unique ways. Then we'll consider the cultural dimensions of the response to the gospel. What is true conversion? How does God change people without tearing them out of their culture? God wants more than a message conveyed. He wants a movement of obedience to Christ to flourish. How can new churches *redeem* instead of *reject* their home culture?

HEARING We make ourselves heard every-day. To make God Himself heard is not a feat of speaking, but an act of assisted hearing. It is a marvel of heaven's power.

I.   Experiencing Cultural Differences

Our world is an increasingly multicultural place. People of different cultures live in close proximity. Even though we are used to being around people of different cultures, we may still be unprepared for the disorientation which occurs when we are immersed for an extended time in a different culture.

> **Read Hiebert, "Cultural Differences and the Communication of the Gospel," pp. 373-374b**

> **Think about the chart on page 373. Have you experienced this curve of wanting to stay or leave a foreign culture? Hiebert says that the term "culture shock" describes the experience of people who realize that the new culture will be their life and their home. What most tourists experience is not true culture shock but what Hiebert calls "culture stress." With this distinction, is it possible for short-term missionaries to experience genuine culture shock?**

A. **The Concept of Culture.** Paul Hiebert defines culture as "the more or less integrated systems of *beliefs, feelings and values,* and their associated symbols, patterns of behavior and products shared by a group of people." The thing to remember as Hiebert unpacks this definition is that people's behavior is guided in large part by an underlying mental map. We sometimes refer to this mental map as *worldview.*

The Dimensions of Culture

Figure: EXPERIENCES → (triangle) Beliefs / WORLD-VIEW / Values / Feelings → Decisions → BEHAVIOR PRODUCTS; EXPERIENCES →

1. **Behavior.** The first thing we encounter in another culture is the different behavior. Entering another culture can be like being thrust into the middle of a game that you have never played. What are the rules? Culture functions like a set of rules that lets everyone know how to interact. Underlying this set of rules is a mental map of assumptions. Those who approach other cultures can learn the new rules of behavior better by understanding the mental map of fundamental assumptions.

2. **Worldview.** At the heart of culture is people's mental map of their world. This map is highly dynamic because it involves three dimensions which are shaped by experience: beliefs, feelings and values. All three are vitally important in intercultural communication of the gospel.

- **Beliefs** (cognitive) reflect shared understandings concerning the nature of reality. Effective gospel communication must recognize these assumptions about what is real and what is true.

- **Feelings** (affective) are experienced, treasured, avoided and shared differently in different cultures.

- **Values and allegiances** (evaluative) are assumptions about relationships and loyalties that guide how people judge what is right and wrong, worthy or threatening.

Read the report of Phil Elkins to learn how drastically a worldview can differ from your own. Can you imagine living as one of the Tonga people? How does this "mental map" portray powerful assumptions about what is real and what people are expected to feel? What kind of apprehension and fear had people grown so used to feeling that it became part of their worldview? Can you guess how Elkins' team presented the gospel so that the message was relevant to their worldview? Read Elkins on pages 669d-670d (ending with "an area of *felt need*.") Use the diagram to understand the Tonga worldview.

B. Cultural Differences. Examining these three dimensions of worldview is the most helpful way for cross-cultural messengers of the gospel to be effective. Since the gospel invites a response of every part of life, gospel communicators need to achieve more than a cognitive understanding of the message. We need to overcome confusion in the emotional and evaluative areas as well.

1. **Misunderstandings: differences of beliefs.** If our impression of another culture is that it "makes no sense," then we can be sure that we are not making sense to them either. The solution is to become a learner.

2. **Ethnocentrism: differences of feelings.** Early in life we grow up as the center of our world. We are egocentric. We also grow up in a culture and assume that its ways are the right ways to do things. Ethnocentrism involves both the evaluative and affective dimensions of culture. Ethnocentrism is based on our natural tendency to judge the behavior of people in other cultures by the values and assumptions of our own. The solution is empathy.

3. **Premature judgments: differences of values.** Early reaction to the difference of other cultures can result in a negative assessment. Is cultural relativism the best alternative? Is every culture as good as any other? Every culture can be recognized for its value and integrity. But convictions about the nature of truth and righteousness require us to hold all cultures, including our own, under the judgment of biblical norms, affirming the good of human creativity, but condemning the evil.

- **Evaluating culture.** Missionaries are therefore faced with the necessity of evaluating culture. We must work to do two things: first, *recognize our biases* when interpreting Scripture so that our biases are challenged by God's revelation; and second, *receive the help of Christians of other cultures* to detect our blind spots.

- **Submitting our views to supracultural truth.** Dialogue with Christians of other cultures guards us from exporting vital Christianity in ways which result in "legalism" in other cultures. This kind of exported "legalism" results from imposing foreign behaviors or beliefs directly without working to bring the truth in its simplest biblical essence. While the gospel is "supracultural" (above every culture), its message is embedded in the cultures of biblical events and writings. We cannot ever detach ourselves from our culture. However, the process of cross-cultural interaction and vigorous investigation into the Scriptures may be the best way to develop more culture-free views of God's truth as revealed in the Bible.

- **Becoming global people.** By learning to live deeply in another culture we can become what Hiebert calls "global people" who move from assumptions of uniformity to an outlook which values cultural variety.

Read Hiebert, "Cultural Differences and the Communication of the Gospel," pp. 374b-380d

Read the report from James Gustafson about Thai villagers presenting the gospel with sensitivity to Thai culture. Their approach was designed to "create a way for Jesus to come alive to the Northeast Thai." As you read the story, can you imagine doing the job of the people who specialized in the arts? Why was their work necessary to engage the feelings dimension of the people's worldview? How did this effort produce "Christ-honoring and culture-affirming churches?" Read the first two full paragraphs on pp. 677d-678b (starting with "The ministry has one..." and ending with "...to be understood by them.")

II. Communicating the Gospel in Culture
Reaching people for Christ means gathering them into Christ-honoring and culture-affirming churches. Charles Kraft revisits the crucial matter of worldview. Like Hiebert, he regards worldview as a structured set of underlying assumptions. It is the deepest level of presuppositions upon which people base their lives.

A. **Contextualization.** To "contextualize" means to present something with regard to the cultural context. It means adapting ourselves and our presentation of God's message to the culture of the receiving people.

B. **Worldview** works like a river with surface behavior fairly easy to observe, but dynamically affected by the undercurrent of the assumptions by which people govern their behavior. The term "deep-level culture" refers to worldview. We need to communicate the gospel with a biblical critique of people's culture and worldview, but with profound respect for the only way of life that they have known.

C. **Subsystems of Culture.** There are subsystems of culture which are greatly affected by the worldview. It's tempting to present the gospel so that the religious parts of our home culture replace the religious parts of the local culture. This approach can only lead to a superficial expression of Christianity. Instead, the message must be directed so that the worldview is affected by the truth of the gospel. When the gospel affects the worldview level, then it can powerfully influence every part of that society.

Read Kraft, "Culture, Worldview and Contextualization," pp. 384-388a

III. Cross-Cultural Communication

Two basic barriers hinder cross-cultural communication of the gospel:
- The message is perceived as a threat to the recipient culture and society.
- The message is presented in alien cultural forms.

Both of these problems are real. In a sense, the gospel is truly alien. No one could have figured out this plan of salvation; it is a supracultural message from God. The gospel does challenge and change aspects of every culture and society that it touches. But both barriers can be minimized. It is our responsibility to see that the gospel is understood and to see that obstacles are not needlessly thrown before peoples needing to respond to the gospel. The Willowbank report urges us to contextualize the gospel with *faithfulness* to the original biblical presentation and with *relevance* to the new cultural situation. This usually means finding a unique way to present the gospel in every setting. There is no standard, universal way to express the gospel which is equally sensitive to every culture. God entrusts us with the responsibility to find the best ways to communicate His message.

Sensitive cross-cultural communicators do not arrive in their sphere of service with a prepackaged message. Effective communication involves:
- active, loving engagement,
- thinking in their thought patterns,
- listening to their questions,
- feeling their burdens and
- depending on the Holy Spirit.

Read The Lausanne Committee's "The Willowbank Report," pp. 489c-490c

Dean Hubbard tells the story of Bhimrao, an Indian believer who found sensitive ways to present the gospel in ways that were understandable and relevant. Consider how Bhimrao's team was able to overcome both of the barriers mentioned in the reading above. Was the message perceived as a threat? How did Bhimrao avoid presenting the gospel in alien cultural forms? Would a blonde missionary from Scandinavia have been as effective as Bhimrao, who was from that region of India? Read Hubbard on pp. 698b-699a ("A Key Leader").

IV. Redemptive Analogy

Messengers of the gospel need to carefully learn the culture and history of the people group they are approaching in order to find ways that the message can be understood and received. Such sensitive messengers look for ways that God prepared the people of a culture to hear and understand the gospel. God often preserves a concept or sense of yearning in a people's culture which can be fulfilled by the gospel.

Read Richardson, "Redemptive Analogy," pp. 397-403 (all)

Conclusion of Key Readings for this lesson.

V. Contextualization and Culture Change

Messengers of the gospel should not aim merely to convey the meaning of the gospel. They should aim to serve a movement of the gospel. What will the resulting movements look like to the local receiving community? How will they appear to the missionaries and those who have sent them?

A. For Missionaries: Sort Out Gospel and Culture. We must diligently labor to sort out the biblical message and our own cultural preferences. One Indian leader gave this challenge to Western missionaries: "Do not bring us the gospel as a potted plant. Bring us the seed of the gospel and plant it in our soil."

B. For New Church Leaders: Reject or Redeem Cultural Forms. Missionaries should remain helpful, but it is the new church leaders who must make important decisions about traditional customs, beliefs and practices which appear to be in conflict with biblical teachings. Careless contextualization can result in syncretism (a blend of surface-level Christian traditions with an underlying non-Christian worldview and practice).

C. For Missionaries: Responsibility and Reliance on God. Missionaries need to realize that intercultural communication is so complex that there can be unforeseen side-effects in changes that the gospel brings. It is their responsibility to anticipate when response to the gospel results in breakdown of culture. At the same time, they must ultimately be guided by the Holy Spirit who alone brings about any significant change. God is already at work in all the cultures of the world. Missionaries accompany and extend, rather than begin God's work among the cultures of the world.

Read Hiebert, "Cultural Differences and the Communication of the Gospel," pp. 381b-383

Read Ernest Boehr's report about how workers among the Hakka people substituted a Christ-honoring practice in place of a Buddhist practice Can you imagine the powerful impact in a culture which has a longstanding practice of worshiping ancestors? What would you have done at the funeral if you had been in charge? Find Boehr on page 674 ("A Funeral Takes New Meaning").

VI. Worldview and Culture Change

The gospel has already been likened to a seed which must be planted in the soil as opposed to a potted plant to be transported. Kraft extends the illustration to help us understand how the churches which result from effective gospel communication almost always seem different from the churches of the home culture of the missionary. He says indigenous churches can be likened to trees that bear similar fruit, but appear much different from the "trees" of the home culture of missionaries. What is the responsibility of missionaries in the process of God transforming cultures by the power of the gospel?

A. Warped Meaning. God intends to bring about good changes in cultures by the power of the gospel. One common mistake occurs when missionaries bring a surface-level change and fail to recognize that an alternate deep-level meaning has been applied to the change. The message of the gospel can be significantly warped. The better way to communicate the gospel is to bring understanding at the level of worldview assumptions. Missionaries can then work with local believers to find how God may be changing their surface-level culture of behavior.

Give particular attention to the analogy of the gospel sprouting and growing as a tree which on the surface may look different than the home church of the missionary, but can be a beautiful expression of the same spiritual life. The term "dynamic equivalent church" refers to a church movement that has different surface-level characteristics, but expresses the meaning of the biblical message.

B. Syncretism. Whenever missionaries bring a change in meaning in order to bring about a change in practice, there is a risk of syncretism. Syncretism usually refers to the situation in which foreign religious practices have been adopted, but the deep-level worldview has not changed. Syncretism is a constant risk of mission work. It is better to meet the risk than to try to avoid it. Meet the risk of syncretism by helping believers use the Scriptures themselves in order to walk with the Holy Spirit as God brings about the changes He desires.

Read Kraft, "Culture, Worldview and Contextualization," pp. 388b-391a

Ironically, trying to avoid syncretism can sometimes be the reason that foreign ideas come to be mixed with the gospel message. Read Brian Hogan's report from Mongolia. At issue is the word used for God. Should they use a foreign fabricated word that was empty so that they could fill it with meaning? Or should they use the standard word for God and work to fill it with new gospel meaning? The gospel began to move rapidly after these leaders made their decision. Whose responsibility is it to guard against syncretism—the missionary or new church leaders? What happened in Hogan's case? Read page 695 (*"Breakthrough of understanding"*).

VII. Turning to God: Allegiance and Power

Communicating the gospel is not merely a task of getting the message across. The gospel is not merely *information to know about God.* It is an *invitation to follow God.* In our pluralistic age the idea of conversion has been made to seem like the aftermath of an oppressive religious conquest. The truth is that God is even less interested than we are in pushing for superficial conversion. God is drawing people to Himself. It's the real thing. It's what people really want. But it doesn't happen unless there is a new allegiance established under Christ's lordship. The kingdom of God comes and His will is done on earth by people who openly serve Him.

A. A Radical Turning. Conversion is best seen as a death and new beginning of life. It is grounded in the fact of Jesus' death and resurrection.

B. Lordship Brings Transformation. Conversion should bring revolutionary change in three ways: worldview, behavior and relationships. (These three areas correspond to the three areas of encounter explored by Kraft below). Conversion should never "de-culturize" a convert.

C. Liberating Power. Power encounters refer to dramatic actions of God that attract people's attention and free them from the grip of the spiritual powers of darkness.

Read The Lausanne Committee's "The Willowbank Report," pp. 494c-496c

VIII. Full Encounter

Charles Kraft outlines three encounters necessary to communicate the gospel. Most Christians recognize the need for "truth encounter" in gospel communication at the cognitive level. But there are other dimensions of encounter by which the gospel brings about change throughout an entire people. Kraft identifies three encounters. He first indicates how Jesus was involved in all three. Then he describes how they can be balanced and work together.

A. **Truth Encounter** deals with understanding. The vehicle of action concerning this encounter is teaching.

B. **Allegiance Encounter** deals with relationship. The vehicle of action here is witness.

C. **Power Encounter** deals with freedom. The vehicle is spiritual warfare.

These three encounters may unfold in different sequences. Usually all three are a part of gospel efforts that bear fruit. Conversion is often a process. Encounters of all three sorts should be viewed as part of that process. Kraft suggests three stages to illustrate the almost endless possibilities of the way God works to bring forth the transformation of mind, loyalty and liberty that He intends.

"... I am sending you, to open their eyes so that they may turn from darkness to light and from the dominion of Satan to God,

in order that they may receive forgiveness of sins and an inheritance among those who have been sanctified by faith in Me."

— Acts 26:17-18

Read Kraft, "Three Encounters in Christian Witness," pp. 408-413 (all)

What is effective communication of the gospel? Read Acts 26:18 to find three ideas about the outcome of gospel communication: opening, turning, and receiving. Is this sequence significant? How are people's eyes opened by the gospel? Or by prayer? How do the phrases about "turning" compare with evangelism as you have seen it practiced? What does the idea of inheritance have to do with the outcome of evangelism?

Read the thrilling account John Robb tells of a classic power encounter. Would you have dared to pray as they did? What other options were there for the missionary team besides the course of action they took? Find the story on p. 145 (end at "The Spiritual Nature of Social Problems").

IX. Conversion: A Process for a People

People in North America and other Western nations have a tendency to assume (perhaps this is part of your own worldview!) that they are essentially individuals. Most of the world's people have a much more communal or corporate views of themselves. Conversion in the Bible and throughout most of history has been a family affair.

A. **Group Conversion.** We should desire and work for group conversions.

B. **Process Conversion.** We should recognize that conversion is a process.

Read "The Willowbank Report," pp. 496c-497a

Conclusion of Certificate Level Readings for this lesson.

Credit Level Guide Notes continue...

X.   Communicating Faithfully Between Cultures

Cultural barriers are not insurmountable. The message can get through. The proof is your own faith! You have come to understand the message of Christ and His kingdom in such a way that you, and many of those from your own people group, have entrusted your lives to Him. You have entered an eternal relationship with God. Do you have a perfect grasp of the truth? No. What you do understand is adequate though not perfectly accurate. Do you have a sufficient grasp of the truth to pass on the gospel to people of another culture? You likely have much more to learn, not just about abstract theological ideas. We can be more confident of passing on the gospel in an effective and faithful way if we work to understand three worldviews: our own worldview, the worldview of the culture of Bible times, and the worldview of our hearers.

David Hesselgrave describes the exciting process of communicating the gospel in a faithful and fruitful way. He presents the three-culture model popularized by Eugene Nida. The main idea is to communicate as much as possible of the biblical message with as little intrusion from influences of our own culture as possible. Because worldview operates at such a deep level of assumptions, we are usually blind to our own worldview assumptions. We can safely presume that our own grasp of the gospel is adequate but cluttered and flawed by our own cultural assumptions.

To minimize the distortion in our presentation of God's truth, we need to "decode" the message from the "Bible culture" and "encode" the message to people of the respondent culture. Be sure to understand the diagram on page 393.

A. Back to the Bible. The first challenge of the missionary is to *decode* the truth in accordance with the most likely intended meaning of the authors. The human authors of Scripture always conveyed the truth in the dress of their culture. There are actually several different cultures and worldview elements represented in the books of the Bible. Basic humility requires us to delve into the cultural background of the stories and statements of Scripture. Then we can more accurately grasp and give the message to others. This process of Bible study is called "exegesis" (after the Greek word *exegeomai,* which means to explain fully). The process of interpretation is called "hermeneutics" (after the Greek word *hermenia,* which means interpretation).

B. Finding the Best Expression. The second challenge of the missionary is to *encode* the truth in the respondent culture. The goal is to strip away as much as possible the extraneous ideas and distortions which may have come from the missionary's culture. Take note of the real purpose: to equip communicators in the respondent culture. As much as possible, missionaries should equip church leaders of the respondent culture to go directly to the "Bible Culture" themselves to go through the same process.

Read Hesselgrave, "The Role of Culture in Communication," pp. 392-396 (all)

XI. A Case Study on Communicating at a Worldview Level

Phil Elkins tells how a team of missionaries found a way to communicate the gospel in keeping with the worldview of the Tonga people. Take special notice of two aspects of their efforts to grasp the Tonga worldview.

A. Understand Different Elements of Worldview. The missionaries worked to discover elements of the Tonga worldview that were foreign to their own. They did not immediately try to *correct* the worldview, but instead sought to *connect* with the worldview at a point of felt need.

B. Understand Their Story. A common feature of the worldview of most cultures is an underlying, defining story or collection of stories. The story can be a mythical drama or a portion of a historical saga. The story often recounts how the people group came to its present experience. For the Tonga, their defining story organized their belief that a Creator God had lived with them at one time, but had left them. Gospel communication, as we shall see, can be powerfully effective when the biblical story is linked to the worldview story of the people.

> **Read Elkins, "A Pioneer Team in Zambia, Africa," pp. 668-672 (all)**

XII. The Flaw of the Excluded Middle

Paul Hiebert describes his journey in discovering a particular worldview dimension in an Indian village. Worldview assumptions of other cultures can differ greatly from Western ideas, and yet correlate quite closely with biblical assumptions. Hiebert describes the problem as he and other Western missionaries have encountered it. He offers an analytical framework. From this framework he asserts that Westerners simply omit an entire tier of power and spiritual beings present in many worldviews. Thus, they fail to see or meet the people's felt needs and miss the drama by which the people frame their self-understanding.

A. An Analytical Framework. The framework that Hiebert suggests is a matrix.

- **Organic-Mechanical.** From left to right is the Organic-Mechanical Continuum. "Organic" refers to explanations based on the view that things are living entities, seen or unseen. The "Mechanical"end of the spectrum offers explanations based on impersonal forces such as luck and karma or what Westerners regard as "natural" forces. Mechanical analogies are basically amoral, whereas organic analogies have an ethical dimension since one being's actions always affect other beings.

- **Seen-Unseen.** From top to bottom are different realms or categories classified by how readily they can be observed.

> **To understand Hiebert's analytical matrix better, review the Tonga worldview on pages 669d-671d. At which level of the grid was *Leza*? At which level would you place the *isaku* spirits?**

B. The Excluded Middle. Western worldviews have usually ignored the middle tier of beings and forces, dismissing them as "not real." What is "real" is precisely the issue of worldview. When missionaries have denied the middle tier and explained things only by what is empirically observable, they have in effect denied the reality or pertinence of the top level; thus missionaries have inadvertently been a major force in "secularizing" many societies while trying to evangelize them. Use care when you read Hiebert's analysis of the concerns and questions of the middle level (on pages 418b-419). It can be easy for Westerners, even eager Perspectives students, to disregard these concerns as being of lesser importance. However, these are often the most critical needs and concerns of many of the peoples of the world.

C. Implications for Missions. We need to form holistic theologies that have a complete triple-layered "bandwidth" of history. Western theology is severely impoverished compared to the wealth of clear biblical revelation if we only have room for the upper level of cosmic history (God confined to heaven awaiting disembodied souls) and the lower level of natural history (the created order running autonomously according to scientific laws). Biblical revelation is full of references to supernatural beings and supernatural powers intertwined with the affairs of man. Without a clear theology of the middle level, the relevancy and effectiveness of our gospel message for victorious living is diminished.

There are two dangerous extremes to be avoided in forming a theology which includes the middle level and a third way beyond them both:

1. **Secularism.** Denying realities of the spiritual realm in the events of human life can result in a form of syncretism where high theology about God is adopted from missionaries, but in times of crisis, middle level dealings with sickness and demonic powers are continued from folk religious practices.

2. **Christianized animism.** Spiritual dynamics can be over used to explain everything. The subtle danger is a form of Christian magic where prayer formulas are used to counter every problem as if they were all caused by spiritual powers. Magic, as Hiebert described in the opening of the article, is a way for humans to control unseen forces through rituals of some sort. Could it be that some of the "spiritual warfare" prayers express a bid for control, but lack a fundamental focus on the centrality and supremacy of God? Read these paragraphs carefully. Hiebert acknowledges that much of our struggle is against Satan and fallen angels. There is a place for spiritual warfare accomplished in part by prayers of God's people.

3. **God and His acts.** The emphasis in Scripture is on God and His acts. The story of what God has done and will do is paramount. The point of prayer is not fundamentally a way to make things happen, but rather to bring God glory. The point of mission is not to teach how to control God by prayer, but rather to bring about a relationship of worship.

> **Read Hiebert, "The Flaw of the Excluded Middle," pp. 414-421 (all)**

XIII. Communicating Through Stories

Tom Steffan relates how he integrated stories into his evangelistic efforts. Storytelling can be one of the most effective ways to communicate the gospel on a worldview level. The story of what Christ has finished and will yet finish can be connected to the unfinished story of the hearers. Storytelling can become a practiced skill of gospel communicators. It's powerful and practical for everyone. Once again, notice the emphasis on the *ongoing* communication of the gospel beyond what missionaries themselves might convey. Storytelling not only conveys the message in a profound way, it makes it memorable and repeatable.

> **Read Steffan, "Why Communicate the Gospel Through Stories?" pp. 404-407**

11 Building Bridges of Love

Studying this lesson will help you:

- *Explain how the incarnation of Christ serves as a primary model for communicating the gospel with a grasp of both His renunciation and identification.*

- *Describe the importance of understandable and credible roles for missionaries in a new culture in order to become viable gospel communicators.*

- *Describe how a missionary can begin to establish a sense of belonging in a new culture.*

- *Contrast the way the gospel flows in the different social structures found in urban, peasant and tribal societies.*

- *Explain the necessity of "bi-cultural bridges."*

Missionaries can only make their message clear if they are recognized as credible messengers. How can missionaries from foreign cultures be received as trustworthy?

Ever since Paul's day missionaries have been learning about effective relationships that span the gap between cultures. Forming friendships is essential to conveying the message in other cultures. This lesson explores how to form and extend those important friendships within different social structures.

Christ is our model. His incarnation is a tremendous pattern of identifying with human condition and culture. Foreigners may be tolerated, but not trusted, unless they are accepted in some way as "belongers" with some understandable role in the society. How much of a "belonger" can outsiders become? Is it possible to so thoroughly identify with a new culture that people perceive the missionary as one of them? We'll find that identification has its limits. With Christ-like attitudes, however, missionaries have been learning how to humble themselves as "learners" before they assert themselves as communicators.

We'll see that the most effective communicators in any society are not missionaries, but local people who were born in the culture. Not every person communicates with equal power to others of their own society. We'll examine the fascinating possibilities of initiating gospel communication with the people who have the highest potential to lead many others of their people to believe and obey Christ.

Ultimately, missionaries are not successful because they recognize intricate sociological structures or because they have mastered the local language. It is their love that opens the way for their speech. That love becomes the authentication of Christ's love. The heart of mission work is building bridges of love.

RECEIVED Jesus framed the first mission very simply: "The one who receives you receives Me." It was more critical that His messengers were received than that they were believed. The gospel has always been more than a message; it is an introduction to life under Christ's lordship. When His messengers have connected with others in significant relationships, Christ can be introduced in powerful ways.

For though I am free from all men, I have made myself a slave to all, that I might win the more.

And to the Jews I became as a Jew, that I might win Jews;

to those who are under the Law, as under the Law, though not being myself under the Law, that I might win those who are under the Law;

to those who are without law, as without law, though not being without the law of God but under the law of Christ, that I might win those who are without law.

To the weak I became weak, that I might win the weak;

I have become all things to all men, that I may by all means save some.

And I do all things for the sake of the gospel, that I may become a fellow partaker of it.

— 1 Corinthians 9:19-23

I.   A Biblical Model: Incarnation

The writers of the Willowbank Report have summarized the core issues of missionary humility and identity around the life and ongoing ministry of Jesus. When Jesus said, "As the Father has sent Me, I also send you" (John 20:21), He was not only expressing that we would be sent with the same purpose, or that the ways of God mandating and guiding us would be similar, He was also saying that we should look to fulfill our ministry in the same way that Jesus accomplished His. How can we follow Jesus in His marvelous humility?

A. An Analysis of Missionary Humility. When considering cross-cultural communication, there are five aspects of humility worth considering:

1. **Challenged by the task.** Humility seeks to admit that the task is difficult.

2. **Need to understand.** Humility seeks to understand the cultures to which we go.

3. **Start where people are.** Humility seeks to begin communication with "felt needs."

4. **Recognize locals.** Humility seeks to recognize the superior potential of local Christians to communicate in their culture.

5. **Trust the spirit.** Humility seeks to trust the Holy Spirit to do what we can never do: open the eyes of the blind and reveal Jesus.

B. Incarnation as a Model. With the source and model of humility found in Christ Himself, we are open to considering two large areas: sacrifice (renunciation) and service (identification). Meditate carefully on these crucial matters. Would it be possible to advance the gospel without emulating these features of our Lord?

1. **Renunciation.** Jesus renounced status, independence and immunity.

2. **Identification.** Jesus took on our full situation. His example challenges our lifestyles and attitudes. The incarnation teaches identification without loss of identity.

In 1 Corinthians 9:19-23, Paul expresses his determination to live in vital, persuasive relevance with the people he was seeking to reach. Does it appear from this passage that Paul was experienced in communicating the gospel in different cultural settings? What indication is there that he did not concede any essential truths of the Bible when adapting his lifestyle to fit within different cultures? What does it mean to be a " fellow partaker of the gospel?"

Read The Lausanne Committee's "The Willowbank Report," pp. 491d-494b

II. Building the Bi-Cultural Bridge

Communication across cultures requires relationships that span the gap between cultures. The necessary relationship between a missionary and the national counterpart is called a bi-cultural bridge. The bi-cultural bridge is a blending of features from both cultures, which actually results in a third sub-culture with newly defined rules and shared assumptions. This is why missionaries can never truly "go native" and become a member of the host culture.

Paul Hiebert introduces two key aspects of how missionaries have developed effective relationships for cross-cultural communication. The two related issues are *roles* and *identification*.

A. Roles. Before local people can consider the message, they must have an understanding of the messenger. Even before the question "*Who* are you?" comes the question, "*What* are you?"

1. Roles in the culture. If missionaries fail to present themselves in appropriate roles, the people of the local culture still place them in some role intelligible to them. Sometimes those roles are not helpful for encouraging close personal friendships that enhance communication of the gospel.

2. Roles in the church. Role relationships also to be examined in terms of how the missionary relates to national Christians whom he seeks to carry significant leadership responsibilities in the national churches. Instead of assuming the roles of parent or authoritarian empire builder, missionaries interact as siblings and servants according to the biblical model.

B. Identification. It's not very difficult for missionaries to observe a few superficial features of lifestyle, what we might call a formal identification which emphasizes an external, formal equivalence of lifestyle. What proves most challenging is an authentic attitude of respect. The mark of such identification is always a sense of mutual reciprocity in relationships.

> Read 1 Thessalonians 2:7-12. How do you see Paul expressing readiness to extend more than a message, but to communicate the gospel in relationship with the people? What did Paul do to build trust? What kind of relationships were formed? Did Paul express superiority when he says that he addressed them as his own children? How does his vision of them walking after God's call make a difference in this apparent expression of paternalism?

> Read Hiebert, "Social Structure and Chruch Growth," pp. 422-425c

III. Viable Roles

Donald Larson says the gap between missionary and community members can widen or narrow depending on whether or not missionaries take on appropriate roles. Larson says that missionaries need to find "viable roles" in their adopted communities. The word "viable" means "capable of success or continuing effectiveness." Can missionaries even guess how they are being perceived? There are three interpretive backdrops operating in most cultures: schoolhouse, market and courtroom.

But we proved to be gentle among you, as a nursing mother tenderly cares for her own children.

Having thus a fond affection for you, we were well-pleased to impart to you not only the gospel of God but also our own lives, because you had become very dear to us.

For you recall, brethren, our labor and hardship, how working night and day so as not to be a burden to any of you, we proclaimed to you the gospel of God.

You are witnesses, and so is God, how devoutly and uprightly and blamelessly we behaved toward you believers;

just as you know how we were exhorting and encouraging and imploring each one of you as a father would his own children,

so that you may walk in a manner worthy of the God who calls you into His own kingdom and glory.

—1 Thessalonians 2:7-12

A. Encounter Models. Local community members often assume that foreigners have come as teachers (schoolhouse), sellers (market) and accusers (courtroom). How can missionaries avoid being seen in this light?

B. Entry Models. If missionaries understand how schoolhouse, market and courtroom roles are ascribed and take care in the way they present themselves in the adopted community, they are more likely to succeed in being regarded as learners, traders and story tellers. While we may not be used to thinking of missionaries in these roles, effective missionaries have not been those who barge into a culture with demands to be heard, accepted or valued. Those who "back in" find greater receptivity to their message.

Read Larson, "The Viable Missionary: Learner, Trader, Story Teller," pp. 438-443 (all)

Role relationships can be complex. Read the story of two women in a Chinese village on pages 613-614 in Case study 1 and Case study 2 until the line "...they were regarded as family breakers." Compare the efforts of these missionaries in effective role relationships with the two women who went to another village in Asia as found in the first three paragraphs of "Women in Mission" on page 269, ending at "...Jesus as Lord of the Balangao." There is one key distinction between the stories. Jo Shetler either accepted, or sought out, a father figure. Because of this father figure, role relationships could unfold in a socially acceptable way. How was this different from or lacking in the Chinese example?

IV. The Limits of Identification

William Reyburn explores the limits of missionary identification. An important part of the missionary task is to search for a point of connection or contact. Without establishing such a point of relational contact, missionaries have not assumed responsibility for communication. There are significant limits formed in deeply ingrained habits and attitudes.

A. Unknown Habits and Known Origins. Difficulties in identification can arise from our unconscious, habitual way of doing things—such as the way we walk. The greatest barriers of identification are the perceptions and categories of the new community. Most cultures have a distinctive category for those who have been born into the culture.

B. Attitudes. Deeply rooted attitudes, such as private ownership or what food we are willing to stomach, can be overcome by willing missionaries who are pursuing an authentic expression of love.

Read Reyburn, "Identification in the Missionary Task," pp. 449-454c

Read a story of an attempt at identification that went awry. What went wrong with this attempt at taking on the role of a "learner"? Was this a case of trying to "go native"? What could the missionary have done that would have enhanced future ministry? Read on page 657 (starting with the second paragraph) "In my former country of ministry..." until "...leave that village immediately and never return." (near the bottom of the first column).

V. Bonding

Tom and Betty Sue Brewster present some practical ideas to illustrate the possibility of becoming a "belonger" in another culture. Watch for the ways that missionaries intentionally work to identify with the new culture and to enter appropriate roles. The idea of "bonding" illustrates the practicalities of newcoming missionaries immediately immersing themselves in language and cross-cultural relationships. Pay special attention to the way the Brewsters refer to language learning. Many Americans consider themselves failures as language *students*. The Brewsters encourage us to consider the far more feasible role of becoming language *learners*, while deeply immersed in relationships in a new culture.

Read Brewster, "The Difference Bonding Makes," pp. 444-448 (all)

VI. Communication in Social Settings

Communication across cultures involves multiple steps. We've seen how effective missionaries initially seek to learn language and culture in relationships with local people. We've seen how those relationships are enhanced when missionaries present themselves in socially recognized roles that are appropriate and acceptable. When missionaries fail to interact with respect for matters of social structure, such as roles and status, their words may be intelligible, but will not likely be received as credible. But there is an even more important matter of communication flowing in powerful ways throughout the society beyond the initial communication of the missionary. The focus of gospel communication should always be to enable local people to become effective, reproducing communicators of the life of following Jesus. Not every person within a society has the same potential for extending the gospel in effective ways. Eugene Nida explains how communication flows within social structure.

A. Avoid Creating a Christian Sub-Culture. Missionaries have sometimes erred by attempting to protect converts in a "hothouse" environment isolated from the larger culture. This almost always frustrates ongoing communication.

B. Communicating Within Social Structure. Almost all societies can be diagrammed with different tiers or layers of classes. Two basic directions of communication within or between these layers of society can be observed:

   1. Horizontal tends to be reciprocal. People communicate more with people of their own class. Truly effective communication is almost always of this kind.

   2. Vertical tends to be unidirectional. People are often affected by communication from higher or more prestigious classes. This communication is not necessarily more powerful in the long run.

Read Nida, "Communication and Social Structure," pp. 429-432c

C. Types of Structures. Nida identifies two basic types of social structure: urban (metropolitan) societies, and rural (face-to-face) societies. Hiebert gives them different names and presents a third: the peasant society. The gospel flows in different ways in each of these structures. Do as Hiebert suggests while you read, try to imagine yourself as part of these kinds of societies. You will appreciate how important it is to set in motion the right kind of gospel communication.

1. **Tribal or face-to-face societies.** Tribal decisions are made by a limited number of elders. Most people movements have flourished in these kinds of social structures. Note how missionaries need to *evaluate* and *understand* the group decision-making process. According to the diagram of the society, to whom should the gospel be addressed? How will most people hear and decide to follow Jesus?

2. **Peasant or folk societies.** Kinship is less dominant. Leadership is exerted by a powerful elite. Caste groupings are common but not the only kind of societal group found in peasant societies. It is important to recognize that these kinds of societies abound in urban environments. Just because another category of social structure is called "urban" does not mean that peasant societies are not found in cities. In the mix of distinct socio-cultural groupings, we can see horizontal communication flowing easily while vertical influence almost exclusively flows from the upper to the lower ranges. People movements take place in these social groupings. Hiebert expresses some concerns that many have about people movements within groupings that are socially defined. Ponder the way that he frames the issues surrounding such movements.

3. **Urban or metropolitan societies.** Individual decision-making patterns are dominant. Organizations are voluntary. Communication flows rapidly, but not necessarily powerfully along social networks. No clear-cut strategy has emerged. But family and kinship ties are still an important factor.

Read Hiebert, "Social Structure and Chruch Growth," pp. 425c-428

It's exhilarating to see the gospel move rapidly along social networks and surge forward in bursts through different social settings. Americans are often blind to these dynamics having experienced primarily Western, urban individualistic settings. Read the case of the gospel moving among Mongolian people. Which two of the three types of social structures mentioned above do you see at work in this movement? Read Hogan on page 695 starting with "Breakthrough into the mainstream..." subhead and going to "...ranks of our provisional elders."

Another hybrid of two social structures can be seen in the story of the Bansari caste. How does the Bansari society function according to features of both the peasant and the urban models? How present was the foreign missionary in this case? What kinds of people turned out to be the best multipliers of the gospel? Read last paragraph of Hubbard on page 700b "The Bansari number in the millions..." and then go to "...they began visiting their villages."

Conclusion of Certificate Level Readings for this lesson.

VII. Communication and Social Structure

Effective missionaries aim to see most of the gospel communication accomplished by ordinary believers evangelizing through the normal dynamics of social interaction. Insights from cultural anthropology help missionaries convey the message with relevance and clarity. Insights drawn from sociology can help missionaries initiate movements. We return to Eugene Nida for insights about social structure.

A. Face-to-Face Societies. Hiebert and Nida both use the term "face-to-face society." There are two different types, which are both described with interchangeable terms.

1. Folk or peasant. In these societal structures, there is a dependency on and interaction with other societies or urban centers.

2. Primitive or tribal. In these societal structures, there is an independence from outside influences.

B. Communication Approach in Face-to-Face Societies. The four principles that Nida outlines are highly significant for other social structures as well. How might these four concepts prove helpful in an urban setting?

1. Personal friendship. The relationships foster a connection with the entire community, in what Nida describes as a sort of sponsorship dynamic. How much more meaningful would a message be if it was introduced by a trusted sponsor?

2. Effective communicators. The most important of the four principles is to make the initial approach to those who are able to effectively pass on the communication.

3. Allow time. Group decisions take time, often weeks and months. Individuals who are perceived to have made a decision which threatens group solidarity often bring about a larger negative response.

4. Address decision makers. Present the challenge of change of belief to key people who are socially instrumental in making such a decision.

> Read Nida, "Communication and Social Structure," pp. 434a-437

VIII. Practical Identification

"Bonding" and cultivating role relationships, as we have discussed earlier in this lesson, are costly endeavors. Phil Parshall describes four areas of practical lifestyle choices that require reflection and principled decisions.

A. Finances. Six useful ideas center on the idea of living as closely as possible to the lifestyle of the receiving culture without adverse effects on the missionary team or family.

B. Housing. Avoid the isolation of mission compounds and their equivalents. It leads to a "foray" approach to ministry whereby the missionaries make occasional ventures to the local community from their safe island of Western wealth. Live among the people if at all possible.

C. Intellectual Life. Immersion in the new culture does not mean detachment from the flow of ideas and inspiration from colleagues, senders and the larger mission industry. Keep channels of communication open. Most of all, consider training to be a lifelong process.

D. Ministry. Many missionaries are vague about how long they will stay to get the job done. Ironically, a "whatever-it-takes" attitude can backfire if the missionary does not have it firmly in mind to entrust leadership to trained local Christians at a time that is invariably sooner than is comfortable. If this kind of determination is not made ahead of time, most missionaries end up staying too long. There are two common outcomes of over-staying. First, missionaries tend to develop a more lavish lifestyle than they might otherwise, neutralizing much of their effectiveness. Second, a dependency on the missionary begins to form, which is debilitating for the national churches and a burden on the missionary.

Read Parshall, "God's Messenger," pp. 456-459 (all)

12 Christian Community Development

Studying this lesson will help you:

- *Describe some of the most critical dimensions of global human need and comprehend the nature of global poverty.*

- *List and evaluate four approaches to meeting global human need.*

- *Compare and contrast Christian Relief ministry with Transformational Development.*

- *Explain why and how Christian Community Development offers the greatest hope and promise for reaching people suffering from spiritual and physical hunger and is the most effective long-term approach to integrating evangelism and church planting with community development efforts.*

- *Explain how the gospel offers the best hope of significant transformation for the poor and unreached peoples of the world when church planting movements are underway.*

- *Answer the charge that Christian missionaries destroy culture.*

- *Describe the difference between absolute poverty and relative poverty.*

- *Describe ways that cross-cultural workers have been encouraging reconciliation between people groups.*

It might seem from Jesus' words "The poor you always have with you" (Mark 14:7), that God doesn't intend to change the plight of the poor. The truth is that God has chosen to bring forth outposts of His coming kingdom in the poorest communities of the earth. Remember how John the Baptist was confused by the way Jesus conducted His mission? Jesus was expected to launch a campaign of God's judgment amidst the echelons of wealth and power. In Matthew 11:2-6 we read Jesus' response. He was healing broken lives and communicating the gospel amidst the poor. Christ's mission to the poor began the mission that He would later turn toward the people of all nations. The outcome is promised to be a triumph of God's justice in which the nations will hope (Matthew 12:18-21).

Such biblical hope frees us to be fully aware of the needs of poor. We often turn our attention away from despair. We cannot make ourselves gaze for long at what seems like an unceasing holocaust of hurt throughout the earth. A closer inspection of what God is doing actually reveals that there is, in fact, no "God-forsaken" place on earth. God sees and anguishes with every moment of suffering. God is sending emissaries of His kingdom in significant numbers to bring healing and help in Christ's name. This lesson focuses on what those servants are doing. It's not really about needs and opportunities. Christian community development is all about hope.

Anticipating the progress of the gospel should rivet our attention even more upon the poor and broken of the world. Crowded into the "10/40 Window" region is the greatest concentration of unreached peoples and the largest concentration of physical and social needs. In this lesson veterans of community development tell their stories and distill their experience into valuable principles.

Hope is never without controversy. We'll examine the charge that missionaries destroy cultures as they try to serve them. We'll survey the nature of urban poverty and the potential for significant change. We'll see how missionaries are working to establish Christ's peace in the midst of ethnic hatred.

TRANSFORMATION

One of the final statements in the Bible is "Behold, I am making all things new!" That sums up what God has always been doing: making the entire world new. The gospel begins the re-creation by transforming people from the inside out. But the transformation doesn't stop until a sample of God's new kingdom is on display throughout whole communities. Transformation is God making people truly new, and doing it now.

I.   A World of Need

Jesus' words in Matthew 25 reveal the mind of our Lord with respect to suffering. What follows is a brief survey of world need viewed in the same six categories Jesus used. Our understanding of the needs will shape our response. The following report warns that a sense of powerlessness to deal with the needs of the entire world can lull us into complete inactivity. We should refuse to view the world with a despair that assumes that nothing can be done. The fact is biblically clear that God is not finished. He has always been pleased to multiply seemingly small efforts of His servants into lifegiving ministry which often brings lasting change.

Hope means that we can strive to understand the problems of the world for what they really are. The suffering of the poor and needy is rarely an unexplainable happenstance. Close examination of most human suffering reveals that societies are often mired in structural injustice. That injustice results in great devastation. Even worse, the poor lose hope that anything will ever change.

Take special note of the analysis of these problems. Hunger, for instance, is not really caused by a shortfall of food supplies. It is caused by a complex of problems, the chief of which is distribution. The entire approach to illness has been primarily oriented around treatment of disease. We stand at a threshold of hope that many diseases can be eradicated. Many others are manageable by simple efforts of bringing primary health care and education to the fourth of the world's population which lacks any access to minimal health services.

Read World Relief, "State of World Need," pp. 569-574 (all)

In light of this world of need, what should the Church's response be? Evaluate how complete and relevant Jesus' description of human poverty is for the Church today. Reflect on the immediate implications for missions seeking to penetrate the still unreached peoples.

II.   Hope and Holism

Christian ministry to whole persons—body, mind and soul—as they live in whole communities, is called "holistic mission." The truth of the Kingdom presents a comprehensive vision of God's purpose to redeem and to rule. No person and no portion of the communities of earth are beyond God's concern. This comprehensive vision enables Christians to seek God's ways and timing to touch the entire range of human need. The vision of the kingdom of God motivates and integrates mission efforts.

A. **Fulfilled at the End, Furthered by the Church Until Then.** God's inbreaking Kingdom is characterized by righteousness, justice and peace. The gospel of the Kingdom declares that sin, disease, and oppression are never the last word. Where Jesus is King, He brings forgiveness, healing and liberation. God alone will bring it to fulfillment at the end, when Christ comes again. But until then, God is always working to display tangible signs of the governing love of His Kingdom. The primary agent of the Kingdom is the Church, the redeemed community of the King.

B. Hope Integrates and Motivates. The hope of the Kingdom fuses together what may appear to be a double motivation.

1. **Jesus' commission** to disciple the nations holds before us a vision of Christ the King being followed by believers in each of the peoples of earth.

2. **Jesus' compassion** to bring help and healing signaled to all that there is no need which the kingdom of God will not touch. Such hope fuels the lasting compassion that stirred in the heart of Jesus. He did not pity the poor; He saw instead the worth of each person. In that hope He exhibited a focused and sustained compassion. He saw God's destiny of blessing for the poor as well as the rich (Luke 18:35-19:10).

Read "The Lausanne Covenant," pp. 760d-761a

C. Beyond Mere Balance. Meeting basic human needs is inextricably linked with the gospel, just as it was in Jesus' ministry. Sometimes social concern is a consequence of evangelism; sometimes it is a bridge to evangelism; and sometimes social action accompanies evangelism and church planting as an integrated activity.

1. **Which comes first?** A word of dynamic balance in holistic mission comes from missiologist Stephen Hoke:

> Asking, "Which is more important, evangelism or social action?" is a misleading question. Over the last generation it has led Westerners to spend fruitless years trying to analyze and rank which is more important. A more biblical approach, derived from studying the life of Jesus, would be to ask, "What comes first, evangelism or social action?" In Jesus day, the question would have been phrased, "What did Jesus do first, evangelize or minister to physical needs?"
>
> And the obvious answer is "Both" or "It depends." Sometimes Jesus healed the sick; sometimes He preached the gospel of the Kingdom. We usually see Him doing both. With the vision of complete personal and community transformation in view, Jesus did what the situation demanded. He always dealt directly with the presenting problem, be it physical or spiritual. When the sick asked for help, Jesus healed them. When people engaged Him in spiritual conversation, Jesus led them to make a decision about who He was. He never skirted the issue. He never changed the subject to move to more spiritual matters.
>
> So, in response to the question, "What did Jesus do first?" we can only respond, "It depends on the situation." Similarly today, in response to the question, "Which comes first, evangelism or social action?" we must respond with humility and honesty, "It depends on what the situation demands." When among unreached peoples a Christian is asked about Jesus, he or she may find it appropriate to share the gospel story in the context of their personal experience. There are many situations among unreached peoples that the only door open to Christians is to offer hope in the form of emergency relief or long-term community development. We can step eagerly and lovingly through these doors to establish a bridge for future relationship and hopefully effective evangelism.
>
> Because God is in control and engineers the opening and closing of cultural and political doors, we can feel free and confident to respond as Jesus would, without having to worry about which is more important. They both are. The real issue is timing and appropriate communication. So we follow Jesus' lead and respond as He would.

2. **The leading partner.** Veteran missionary and scholar Samuel Moffett helps reshape our understanding of what evangelism is and what it is not. In a kingdom context, he suggests that evangelism is not the only priority, but must be held in partnership with social action. Moffett says that confusing evangelism and social action in definition and separating them in practice hinders us from seeing churches planted among unreached peoples. They belong together, not just balanced but in dynamic partnership. In Moffett's view, evangelism needs to be the leading partner. We must continue to be concerned with both hungers—the spiritual as well as the physical—as we seek to reach the two billion who live among unreached peoples. Though the numbers may change slightly from year to year, the idea of biblical balance remains unchanged.

Read Moffett, "Evangelism: The Leading Partner," pp. 575-577 (all)

III. Approaching a World of Need

When Christian missionaries encounter poverty and human needs, it isn't hard to see the problems. What's difficult is knowing just what approach to take which will both address the numerous needs and accomplish evangelism and church planting.

A. **Four Approaches to Human Need.** Four strategies have been used in recent history for meeting basic human needs. Identify what is valid about each strategy, as well as its strengths and weaknesses. Be sure to grasp the significance of the matrix. Two of the approaches look to *local resources* and leadership, expressed by the words, "Help From Within." The others may set up an increased reliance on *resources coming from outside.* Another helpful angle to consider when evaluating human needs is whether meeting the immediate needs outweighs dealing with underlying causes. To what extent should missionaries and/ or local Christians be involved in any or all of these approaches?

1. **Economic growth** often focuses upon macro-statistics and issues of a country instead of micro-economic factors such as adequate food, fuel and health for each family.

2. **Political liberation** often focuses upon oppressive regimes, violations of human rights and exploitative commercial structures which widen the gap between the "haves" and "have-nots."

3. **Relief** aims at providing basic necessities for survival for victims of war, natural disaster and prolonged injustice.

4. **Community/transformational development** focuses on both adequate assessment and the use of personal and community abilities and resources with the goal of basic needs being met with local leadership and resources.

B. **Limitations and Promises.** Each approach has limitations and promises. While a lengthy consideration of Economic Growth and Political Liberation is beyond the scope of this course, note the following evaluations:

1. **Economic growth** has not proven to bring lasting help to the poor except when it is accomplished by means of Community Development.

2. **Political liberation** is best done by and for insiders, rather than outsiders. It holds little promise without Community Development.

*The Spirit of the Lord GOD is
    upon me,
    Because the LORD has
    anointed me
    To bring good news to the
    afflicted;*

*He has sent me to bind up the
    brokenhearted,
    To proclaim liberty to captives,
    And freedom to prisoners;*

*To proclaim the favorable year of
    the LORD,
    And the day of vengeance of
    our God....*

*Then they will rebuild the
    ancient ruins,
    They will raise up the former
    devastations,
    And they will repair the ruined
    cities,
    The desolations of many
    generations....*

*But you will be called the priests
    of the LORD; You will be
    spoken of as ministers of our
    God.*

*You will eat the wealth of
    nations,
    And in their riches you will
    boast....*

*For I, the LORD, love justice,
    I hate robbery in the burnt
    offering;*

*And I will faithfully give them
    their recompense,
    And I will make an everlasting
    covenant with them.*

*Then their offspring will be
    known among the nations,
    And their descendants in the
    midst of the peoples.*

*All who see them will recognize
    them
    Because they are the offspring
    whom the LORD has blessed....*

*For as the earth brings forth its
    sprouts,
    And as a garden causes the
    things sown in it to spring up,*

*So the Lord GOD will cause
    righteousness and praise
    To spring up before all the
    nations.*

—Isaiah 61:1-2, 4, 6, 8-9, 11

3. **Relief** aims at short-term survival. Unless a long-term plan is initiated from the start, relief efforts can produce the "rice Christian" syndrome. "Rice Christian" refers to the stereotype, almost never true, that people have converted to Christianity because a staple food, such as rice, was offered to them as an inducement.

4. **Community development** aims at enabling a community to meet its own basic needs. Unfortunately, even Community Development efforts flounder without a foundational shift in values within the community. Therefore, there is a need for Christian Transformational Development which aims to bring about a new expression of church life exhibiting and multiplying the values of the kingdom of God.

Read Isaiah 61. Underline the phrases that express the mission of God. What does God indicate about His people bringing healing and hope to the suffering of the world? How will this compassion result in God's glory? How will God's blessing become known among the nations? How can it be that the same passage which describes compassion for the brokenhearted also describes God's desire for His people to be noticed for His exceptional blessing upon them? The last verse views the earth as a garden growing two important things: righteousness (which should be understood to be justice lived out without being enforced) and praise (which should be understood to be explicit worship of God). How does the mission described in the first few lines of the chapter result in the fruit of the final lines?

Read Voorhies, "Transformational Development: God at Work Changing People and Their Communities," pp. 588b-590c

IV. Christian Community Development

Relief efforts are crucial to preserve life. While relief work and appeals for funding often get a higher profile, mission leaders have been focusing their efforts on development. Different leaders may use slightly different terminology to describe their work, but their work basically aims toward the same vision of bringing enduring transformation in Christ's name and by His power. Five different terms are commonly used to describe this approach:

- **Community Development.** Community developers aim to enable local people to mobilize local resources to meet basic needs in an enduring way throughout an entire community.

- **Christian.** Development workers seek to ground the changes on the values of the kingdom of God. When people are changed and begin to emulate Christ's own character and concerns, many others throughout the community have before them examples and encouragement to participate in selfless service, trust and industrious hope. When Christian missionaries seek to do development work, they usually aim to plant new churches or renew existing churches as the basis of the crucial worldview and value shifts which are needed for lasting change.

- **Transformational.** The aim is for people and entire communities to be changed, not merely impacted in a passing way. Christian community developers do not view the sought after changes as being accomplished by an exercise in social engineering. Christ Himself is seen as the source of significant transformation.

- **Holistic.** The entire range of human need is addressed.

- **Integrated.** All aspects of the ministry are tied together, linking diverse endeavors such as training in literacy, digging wells or enabling indigenous worship leaders.

A. God at Work. Changing People and Their Communities. Sam Voorhies tells the story of fruitful development effort. Don't miss the first step, identifying the resources, after which the problems are considered. Would you have first listed the problems or the resources? As Voorhies describes the outcome, ask yourself how each of the different needs was met. Observe how much better it was to deal with the needs together on a community-wide basis. How was worldview changed? What was the basis for the change in worldview? What was the place of the new church and its worship in the transformation? Examine the list of principles. Notice the ones which describe how people and communities are valued. Which ones describe how change takes place and which ones describe foundational changes which enable others? How does Voorhies view the respective roles of local people, God, and missionaries?

> **Read Voorhies, "Transformational Development: God at Work Changing People and Their Communities," pp. 586-588b & 590c-591**

B. "Enabling Jesus Christ to be Born into Northeastern Thai Culture." James Gustafson presents a case study which highlights the place of local churches in providing a foundation for "true transformation of society." The developers have gone to great lengths to plant churches that are remarkably in tune with the Thai Issaan culture. Why does the cultural relevance of the new churches help them deal with other community needs? What does he mean when he says that "development must serve, not lead?" How does this emphasis prevent the "rice Christian" syndrome as described above? Gustafson describes an example of the "microcredit" system mentioned above in the World Mission Survey article. Gustafson refers to this system of offering small non-monetary loans to a "cooperative project." It is important to understand how this approach differs from relief efforts that give away resources. How does Gustafson's team operate in the reality of hope? Which items on Gustafson's list of principles match items on the list that Voorhies provided?

> **Read Gustafson, "Pigs, Ponds and the Gospel," pp. 677-680 (all)**

Conclusion of Key Readings for this lesson.

V.   Transforming or Destroying?

Do the changes that missionaries bring sometimes destroy the culture? So goes the stereotype of missionaries as cultural imperialists. Is this perception based on historical fact or is it a myth perpetuated by critics and writers antagonistic to Christianity? Is the seemingly enlightened policy of "Leave the innocents alone" a realistic option in today's world? As modernity and technology press global change at a breathtaking pace, negative change will take place if Christians do not intervene in positive ways. Look for principles of appropriate culture change in these case studies that can guide missionary work in tribal cultures.

> **Read Richardson, "Do Missionaries Destroy Cultures?," pp. 460-468 (all)**

VI. The Urban Frontier of Change and Hope

Pioneer urban missionary Viv Grigg describes the crying need for development efforts in the cities of the world.

A. The Nature of Poverty. Grigg helps us understand the nature of urban poverty. There are key distinctions between first and third world poverty. Another way to understand this distinction is to see the difference between "absolute poverty" and "relative poverty."

1. Absolute poverty describes situations in which people have an absolute insufficiency to meet their basic needs.

2. Relative poverty describes situations in which people are on the margins of society. A person's standard of living is compared in relation to others in the community or nation. A family may be regarded as poor if they do not have a telephone or a car in North America. Another family lacking a telephone or a car in India may not be considered impoverished at all. If neither family is suffering from an absolute lack of food, shelter or clothing, then their poverty is a relative poverty.

> **Compare some of the poorest communities of North America with the poorest parts of Calcutta. How would you categorize most of the poverty of North America? Is it absolute poverty or relative poverty? Why does the distinction matter?**

B. Reachable Communities. Why is the distinction of "slums of hope" and "slums of despair" important when dealing with the huge complex of needs of the city? Is the city too large a community in which to accomplish development? Grigg says the challenge is "how to generate movements of disciples among the poor and subsequently among the rich." How does this statement display Grigg's hope-based approach to the city? Why does he propose the strategy of bringing the gospel to the city from the economic underside of the city? From the small excerpt of Grigg's writing which appears below, what community development principles can you see Grigg applying in an urban context?

> **Read Grigg, "The Urban Poor: Who Are We?" pp. 582b-585**

VII. The New Frontier of Hope

John Dawson describes how Christians are finding creative and powerful ways to pursue the reconciliation of peoples. We are mandated to establish a movement of discipleship under Christ's Lordship *within* every people. At this hour God is energizing hope that the wounds *between* the peoples can be healed in substantial ways.

A. Business as Usual? The human heart is bent toward envy, fear and contention. Racial strife is increasing. Many of these struggles are outgrowths of ancient conflicts. Reconciliation leaders have identified 14 general categories of deep-rooted, systematic alienation between peoples and elements of a society. How shall we respond to such deep-seated hostility? Does God want us to respond?

B. Seeing Jesus Beyond Church Walls. Only Christians can act in the humility and the power of Christ's forgiveness to introduce the power of the Cross. As Christians lead the way in modeling humility and forgiveness, there is almost limitless potential for Christ to be glorified and for some of the wounds of the world to be significantly healed. Cross-cultural workers are finding creative ways to bring healing throughout communities long troubled by racial and economic discord.

Read Dawson, "Healing the Wounds of the World," pp. 564-568 (all)

Conclusion of Certificate Level Readings for this lesson.

Credit Level Guide Notes continue...

VIII. Poverty and the Power of the Gospel

How we view the world's needs will shape our response. Bryant Myers challenges us to take another look at poverty.

A. The Standard View: Poverty as Deficit. While it is obvious that poverty is a lack of basic necessities, it may be misleading to view poverty a problem that can be eradicated by economic solutions.

B. A Better View of Poverty. Poverty is more than deficit. Understanding the causes of the deficit helps us know how the gospel can bring about sustainable change. Watch for features of worldview that are being described.

   1. Broken relationships. The Bible suggests that broken relationships are at the root of the ills and grief of the poor. It leads us to understand the history of the impoverished and see the complexity of their predicament.

   2. Misused power. There has been controversy over the idea that people are poor because they have somehow suffered an abuse of power. And yet an examination of the plight of most poor communities usually reveals some kind of exploitation.

   3. Fear. Prolonged severance from blessing and safety sets in motion structures of fear which often invite a debilitating servitude to idolatry.

C. The Gospel as Truth and Power. Poverty is essentially a spiritual issue. Only the gospel—all of it—contains the hope that the poor will be enabled to live in communities where relationships are restored, abusive power is broken and fears are allayed.

> **Read Myers, "What is Poverty Anyway?" pp. 578-580**

IX. Transformation: The Missionary's Role

We earlier examined the four basic approaches to bringing about benefit for a community: Economic Growth, Political Liberation, Relief and Community Development. As much as missionaries want to be of help, direct aid such as relief and economic growth programs can be debilitating if there is not a transformation at the grass-roots level. We've seen some of the basic approaches missionaries have taken in community development. It's important to recognize that lasting change takes place only when local leaders act as the agents of change. When those local leaders bring about changes with a local church at the center of the changes, there is a life-giving continuity to the changes.

Dale Kietzman and William Smalley explore the role of missionaries in bringing about cultural or societal change of any kind. Their comments pertain to the role of missionaries in changing the way communities work to meet basic human needs.

We've already touched on the issue of missionaries bringing about unwanted change. Don Richardson asserts that missionaries are most often involved in what has been called "directed change" which helps tribal groups deal with inevitable transitions in the modern world. This kind of change rarely destroy cultures. But sometimes missionaries can bring about desired changes that are not sustainable. At the center of lasting transformation are new communities. In this approach to societal change, the missionary's role is to be a catalyst and a source of new ideas and information. This approach seems to take more time and leave more up to the Holy Spirit. But it is the only way to bring about changes which are not dependent on the presence or advocacy of outsiders.

Read Kietzman and Smalley, "The Missionary's Role in Culture Change," pp. 480-482 (all)

13 The Spontaneous Multiplication of Churches

Studying this lesson will help you:

- *Explain why aiming to evangelize whole families is the best way to plant churches that will evangelize throughout a people group.*

- *Describe the four ways that churches grow.*

- *Explain why it is important to view the Church as a new creation of God.*

- *Distinguish between New Testament commands, apostolic practices and human customs. Describe the value of this distinction for church planting.*

- *Explain the value of emphasizing obedience to Christ in evangelism, church planting and in training leaders.*

- *Describe the process of how a mother church reproduces churches by extension chains.*

- *Describe what makes a church truly indigenous.*

- *Explain the value of saturation church planting.*

- *Recognize the similarities of people movements and multiplying reproducing chains of churches.*

- *Explain what is meant by "spontaneous" multiplication of churches when missionaries work very hard behind the scenes.*

We have seen the biblical mandate for reaching every people. We've examined the historical record to see the exciting story of how the gospel moved through huge geographic areas and ethnolinguistic basins. Most of us have not seen the kind of multiplying church movements that sweep through large areas or peoples. Of course, we've all seen churches, but perhaps few of us have experienced the kind of church movement that is crucially needed among unreached peoples.

Not just any church will do. We've borrowed words from botany to describe the kind of churches that are needed among unreached peoples: viable, indigenous churches. *Viable* refers to the capability of living things to survive and reproduce. Viable churches thrive and multiply. *Indigenous* describes living things that are native to or have originated from a particular environment. The term "indigenous church" refers to a church that arises from the soil of its own society. It is native to the culture, abidingly relevant and powerful, influencing entire communities with the life of the kingdom of God.

This lesson again explores the concept of people movements for the purpose of fully comprehending the potential of multiplying churches throughout cities and societies. Veteran church planters will explain how missionaries serve such reproducing movements. We'll discover some surprising features of truly indigenous churches. We'll consider how many more churches are needed in order to fill the earth with Christ's glory. Strategically saturating every place with churches is yet another way to see a church for every people.

Lessons 12 through 15 are arranged in strategic reverse sequence. The outcome is portrayed first, followed by the necessary stages to achieve that end in reverse order. Lesson 12 describes the fruit of the gospel's transforming power. Lesson 13 describes life-giving church movements which bear these fruits of social change and thriving evangelistic efforts. Lesson 14 addresses the challenge of how these movements are launched in entirely unreached peoples. Lesson 15 will conclude by considering the partnership and discipleship required to send, support and sustain the needed mission force.

MULTIPLY Only living things multiply. God has formed the Church, as a living thing, to represent His Son's character and to reproduce His Spirit's fruit in every part of the world. As God announced from the very beginning, the way to fill the earth is to multiply.

I. **Unvalued Pearls: The Value of People Movements**

In his classic work *The Bridges of God,* Donald McGavran surveys the growth of the world Christian movement since Pentecost. He shows that throughout history most of the people who had ever followed Christ have done so as part of what he called "people movements." The term "people movement" is used here to describe a wave of group decisions to follow Christ by people who share culture and kinship, while retaining their identity and relationships within their people. These people movements, which McGavran often called "people movements to Christ" or "Christward movements," can and should be recognized, nurtured and sustained. One outstanding feature which is almost always part of sustained people movements is multiplying networks of simple and powerful churches. McGavran describes five advantages of people movements. Notice how each of them actually describes the kind of churches that become the multiplying infrastructure of the people movement.

A. **Enduring Churches.** McGavran describes these churches as being "rooted in the soil of hundreds of thousands of villages." They are independent of Western dominance and tested by local persecution. If anything could have made them collapse, they would have been gone long ago.

B. **Indigenous Churches.** Earlier in his writing McGavran has distinguished the "mission station approach" churches from "people movement" churches. The mission station approach is the pattern of missionaries inviting converts to become part of highly Westernized congregations on mission stations. People movement churches, on the other hand, remain immersed in their own cultures.

C. **Spontaneously Expanding Churches.** McGavran refers to an important piece of mission strategy written by Roland Allen called "The Spontaneous Expansion of the Church" (from which this lesson title is derived). Allen declared that if new churches were fully equipped and released by missionaries to multiply themselves, they would indeed do so without any direct help from missionaries. Such an idea, written in a colonial era, was disturbing to many, but nonetheless true. Even today, the tendency is to plant churches that are dependent on missionary care. Such churches do not grow. In the midst of people movements there are usually too many converts for missionaries to care for. Independent churches, however, have a chance to multiply without missionary interference.

D. **Enormous Potential for Growth.** People movement churches have great potential for ingathering within the people group. "The group movements are fringed with exterior growing points among their own peoples." There are windows of opportunity to be recognized and, on rare occasions, there are bridges reaching beyond their own people group to another people group. Looking for and using these bridges is the primary activity of what we call pioneer church planting (to be discussed in greater depth in Lesson 14).

E. **Displaying Christ's Power.** The churches are so lightly institutionalized and so devoid of foreign influence that what is outwardly manifested is a "change in inner character made possible by the power of God." The churches do not lean on outside funding or base their success on buildings. Instead, the people themselves are the spectacle. They become known as "people with churches, who worship God."

Read McGavran, "The Bridges of God," pp. 335d-338

But about midnight Paul and Silas were praying and singing hymns of praise to God, and the prisoners were listening to them; and suddenly there came a great earthquake.... And when the jailer had been roused out of sleep and had seen the prison doors opened, he drew his sword and was about to kill himself, supposing that the prisoners had escaped.

But Paul cried out with a loud voice, saying, "Do yourself no harm, for we are all here!" And the jailer called for lights and rushed in and, trembling with fear, he fell down before Paul and Silas, and after he brought them out, he said, "Sirs, what must I do to be saved?"

And they said, "Believe in the Lord Jesus, and you shall be saved, you and your household."

And they spoke the word of the Lord to him together with all who were in his house.

And he took them that very hour of the night and washed their wounds, and immediately he was baptized, he and all his household.

And he brought them into his house and set food before them, and rejoiced greatly, having believed in God with his whole household.

—Acts 16:25-34

II. Evangelizing Whole Families

One of the features of growing churches is that they generally aim to evangelize whole families. Chua Wee Hian contrasts Western missionaries who failed on two counts. First, they did not present themselves as respectable members of any family and thus they had no appropriate role or status in the eyes of the Chinese village. Second, they did not aim to reach whole families, attempting instead to win individuals to the faith. Thus the missionaries were considered to be "family-breakers." The individuals did not have as much power to make decisions as the missionaries had thought. Their experience is contrasted with the evangelistic efforts of an indigenous movement of multiplying churches called the Little Flock Assembly. This movement not only sent out whole families as the evangelizing force, but they also aimed carefully to draw entire families to Christ.

A. Different Social Assumptions. Evangelizing whole families is appropriate in most cultures of the world. Hian mentions a few cultures as examples. He points out the philosophical roots of Western individualism in the statement "I think, therefore I am." Because of this, a Westerner usually assumes that he can think out and decide matters of faith for himself. Most non-Western social and family structures are built on the assumption that "I participate, therefore I am."

B. The Biblical Data. Families were both recipients and agents of salvation blessing.

> In Acts 16:25-34, you'll notice that the jailer's household is mentioned four times. What people might have been part of this man's household? Did the different members believe for themselves or were they another captive audience of the jailer? What does this say about households being a primary focus of evangelization?

> Read Chua Wee Hian, "Evangelization of Whole Families," pp. 613-616 (all)

III. The Avenues of Church Growth

How do churches grow? The Church is a living organism, expanding with a growth that comes from God (I Cor. 3:6-7). A church can and should grow in four ways:

- **Internal**—Maturity and internal strength.
- **Expansion**—Continually adding new believers from the immediate neighborhood.
- **Extension**—Multiplying itself, producing daughter churches.
- **Bridging**—Extending its witness and church planting efforts beyond its own culture.

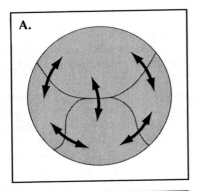

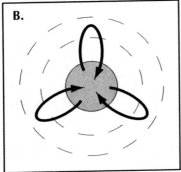

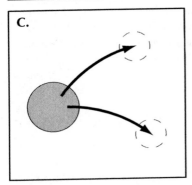

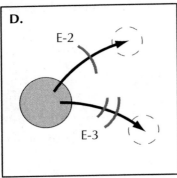

A. Internal Growth. Internal growth includes three quite different processes:

1. **Structural growth**—Growth of internal structure, such as the formation of youth groups, choirs or schools.

2. **Spiritual or "qualitative" growth**—Growth of the church community in faith, hope and love.

3. **E-0 conversion growth**—Conversion of nominal church members to genuine faith.

B. Expansion Growth. Through expansion growth the church grows numerically in several well-defined ways:

1. **Biological growth**—Children of church members also become church members as they reach adulthood.

2. **Transfer growth**—Members of other churches transfer to a specific church. Transfer growth certainly indicates an attractive church, but the unbelieving community may remain untouched.

3. **Conversion growth**—A truly healthy church will reach out to the non-believing community to win people to the Lord and to its membership; this is E-1 growth.

C. Extension Growth. Extension growth takes place as local churches plant new churches. Few pastors have a vision for extension, and in certain spheres it is almost a lost art. It requires a very different set of church planting skills in addition to those needed for internal growth and expansion growth. Studies have shown that a church movement that relies on expansion growth, and is unable or unwilling to plant new congregations, is a movement whose growth rate will rapidly taper off.

D. Bridging Growth. Bridging growth plants churches in different cultures. E-2 or E-3 evangelism requires cross-cultural communication of the gospel. The concept of "bridging growth" applies to church planting efforts among another people group whether the people group is technically "reached" or not.

The sequence of growth patterns is important. A church can hardly extend itself without growing sufficiently in maturity. But timing is every bit as crucial as sequence. If a church is not encouraged to evangelize people throughout its community immediately, a stagnation usually occurs. The church may remain focused on growing in spiritual and structural ways, relying on biological and transfer growth and never acting to multiply by extension growth. Churches need not be large or exceptionally mature in order to plant daughter churches.

IV. The Spontaneous Multiplication of Churches

George Patterson has been training people to multiply churches in many parts of the world. In the article below he tells the story of how he began in Latin America. His summary of key principles illustrates the kind of healthy, multiplying movements of churches that can bring the gospel to people throughout a region or people. He describes spontaneous multiplication of churches as the Holy Spirit moving churches to reproduce without the immediate presence of outsiders. But missionaries can help serve and facilitate the process of multiplying churches.

1. **A Basic Assumption.** The final paragraphs of the article reveal Patterson's fundamental assumption that the Church is *a living creation of God,* alive with a life from God that will reproduce.

2. **A Definition.** Patterson defines a church as *a group of believers in Christ dedicated to obey His commands.*

3. **Two Principles.** Patterson says that a missionary should never aim merely to plant a church. He says missionaries should aim to plant a church that will be able to plant many other churches. He learned to infuse the vision of extension growth into the leaders he was training from the very earliest days. The churches he planted were always born to reproduce. Churches multiply when two conditions are met:

   - **Following Christ.** First, churches multiply if people are following Christ, not just hearing and circulating religious words. There is an emphasis on *obeying Christ.*
   - **Forming Leaders.** Second, churches multiply if leadership is encouraged and trained. There is an emphasis on *leadership development.*

Patterson presents the practical outworkings of his approach with four principles which expand the two principles mentioned above.

A. **Know and Love the People You Disciple.** Patterson's approach is very intentional. Movements of reproducing churches may be spontaneous, but they are rarely accidental. The preliminary steps invariably shape everything that follows. At the beachhead stage it's crucial to think through how the church will be "of the people" and be led by the people. The most successful church planters avoid public preaching of the gospel. They work from the very earliest stage to train and to coach local leaders to communicate the gospel, primarily by way of family ties in small home settings rather than formal preaching venues. New churches are formed in the simplest of ways so that the people can see the church being born as part of the essence of their community. Since Patterson defines a church as a group of believers committed to obeying Christ together, it follows that a list of initial steps focuses on obedience to Christ in order to build (or edify) leaders.

B. **Mobilize Your Disciples Immediately to Edify Those They Are Discipling.** Patterson sees the church planting missionary as essentially a trainer. The training must be carried out in relationship. Missionaries should never merely train a student; they should always train leaders on the job. For the missionary, the best focus is to aim at building up, or edifying, the new church through the leader being trained. The discipling relationship between missionary and leader becomes a model for new church leaders to follow. The Lord's Supper should be the center of the church gatherings rather than the preaching of missionary or even local leaders. When preaching and extensive public teaching is minimized, pastors-in-training learn to focus on nurturing their flock in relational ways instead of dominating them from a platform. New leaders are encouraged to disciple others more readily. When discipling ties are promoted among all members, the idea of multiplication has already begun.

Read Patterson, "The Spontaneous Multiplication of Churches," pp. 595-600d

C. Teach and Practice Obedience to Jesus' Commands in Love, Above and Before All Else. Probably the most important idea of multiplying churches is to promote the core reality of people obeying Jesus Christ. This cannot be overlooked.

1. **Begin with loving obedience to Jesus' basic commands.** Whenever an obedience orientation is sidelined, problems arise: institutional ideas begin to dominate; nominal Christians come to be tolerated; foreign traditions can be misunderstood as essential; and of course, the churches stop multiplying. Patterson sees a simple list of seven commands of Christ to be helpful.

2. **Design evangelism and theological training in terms of obedience.** Don't seek "decisions" for Christ; seek to bring about repentance and faith throughout entire families. The emphasis needs to be the Lordship of Christ. Offers of going to heaven as a free gift are less likely to bring about this kind of relationship. Important doctrines need to be taught, but in connection with a point of obedience or with a problem that needs a solution in the church. Patterson suggests having a "training menu" of many important topics. When problems emerge, that particular item can be selected from the menu.

3. **Orient teaching to loving obedience.** Teach every leader to help his or her people make important distinctions between:

   - **New Testament commands.** These are primary, carrying the authority of heaven. They are at the heart of obeying Christ.
   - **Apostolic practices.** These are not commanded. They may have value, but they are not expected to be part of every believer's practice.
   - **Human customs.** These are practices not mentioned in the New Testament. They are often Christian traditions developed in Western countries and are foreign to the people. They may be valuable, but they are not necessarily looked on as an authoritative source for life and church practice. Distinguishing human customs from Christ's commands rescues young, maturing churches from most problems with legalism and syncretism.

D. Build Loving, Edifying Accountability Relationships between Disciples and Churches in Order to Reproduce Churches.

1. **A vision for "great-granddaughter" churches.** Help churches reproduce by giving them a vision that they are intended to be a "grandmother" church. Encourage them to pray and plan for "great-granddaughter" churches. A "hub" strategy does not work. A "chain" approach will be flexible and endlessly reproducible.

2. **Train believers to evangelize.** Show believers how to evangelize neighbors and relatives. As they follow the natural connections of family and social ties, new churches will spring up in different locations.

3. **Train church leaders and pastors to train other pastors and leaders.** Simple patterns of training are the most reproducible. If training in the "grandmother" church was kept simple, it will be reproducible for many generations to come.

4. **Keep missionaries and funds out of the way.** Beware the missionary's greatest error: controlling national churches. Instead, keep missionaries out of the way. Insist that missionaries and others who are planting new churches are seeking to swiftly commend new churches to the Holy Spirit's power and care. Beware of stifling churches by providing outside funds. Mobilize local resources. Help the new believers to learn generosity and dependence on God. Outside funding almost always freezes church multiplication.

Read Patterson, "The Spontaneous Multiplication of Churches," pp. 600d-605

Is this pattern of church planting effective only in Latin America? Would it be effective in other parts of the world which have little or no awareness of the truth of Christ? Take a quick look at a church planting effort beginning to multiply in Mongolia. Evaluate the missionaries' vision to bring about a movement that would disciple the Mongols "as a people." Is this a realistic vision? What has already taken place that suggests that God may honor their efforts with success? What difficulties should they anticipate? Read the subsection titled, "The Beginning of a Church Planting Movement" in Hogan on page 697b.

Conclusion of Key Readings for this lesson.

V.   Truly Indigenous Churches

We continue to consider the kind of churches that will multiply. Everyone would agree with Charles Kraft that churches should be both "Christ-honoring and culture-affirming." But what is a truly indigenous church? William Smalley challenges the early formula of what constitutes indigeneity in churches. The early formula, "self-governing, self-supporting, and self-propagating," seems to be an easy diagnostic tool for deciding if a church is indigenous, but that assumption deserves examination.

A. **Three "Selfs" Reflect Institutional Features.** Upon careful scrutiny, the three "selfs" each reflect an assumption that churches are essentially institutional realities. These aspects–government, funding and expansion–are the very areas foreign influence can most easily dominate. We still want to see these features of independence. But churches can often be thoroughly independent of direct foreign control and yet alien to the local culture.

1. **Misinterpretation of self-government.** Western patterns of government are borrowed as if they were biblically mandated. Many churches are structured with slavish imitation of Western governmental ideas, such as voting for leaders, or organizing sub-committees.

2. **Misapplication of self-support.** The very indigenous church in Jerusalem accepted outside funding. What matters most is not the source of the income, but how the funds are handled.

3. **Misunderstanding of self-propagation.** At times it is precisely the foreignness of a church that is the reason why it grows. Just because a church appears to be increasing without outside help does not mean that it is indigenous.

B. The Nature of an Indigenous Church. An indigenous church is *a group of believers who live out their life, including their socialized Christian activity, in the patterns of the local society, and for whom any transformation of that society comes out of their felt needs under the guidance of the Holy Spirit and the Scriptures.* Smalley points out that churches are social entities and, as such, borrow patterns of life and thinking from their society. He points out that the Holy Spirit brings changes in keeping with the culture.

C. Missionaries Often Do Not Like Them. Indigenous churches are usually sufficiently distant from the missionaries' culture that they often offend or bother missionaries. Missionaries have been the primary force thwarting the emergence of contextualized churches.

D. Missionaries Can Serve Them. The missionary task is to communicate the truth of Jesus Christ and help people follow Him in culturally appropriate ways which are faithful to the Scriptures as guided by the Holy Spirit. Technically, missionaries cannot "found" an indigenous church. It must be planted and emerge with a life of its own. Once again, the illustration of the gospel as a seed sprouting in the soil of the society is used. Because missionaries do not often work to enable local movements in this way, most indigenous churches get their start apart from missionaries. This does not have to remain true. It's time for missionaries to expect and desire that the Church will have different cultural manifestations in different settings.

> **Read Smalley, "Cultural Implications of an Indigenous Church," pp. 474-479 (all)**

> **Read the story of an indigenous movement in India. How has this movement presented itself to the surrounding communities? Is it authentically in touch with the society, or is it seen as "a new Christian caste" which would be disregarded as foreign? Why would worship that centers around "the Lord's Meal" be seen to have such a powerful relevance? What indicators are there that this movement is "self-governing?" What do you see that would persuade you that it was "self-propagating?" Read section entitled "Following Christ Without Betraying Family" starting on p. 700 and ending on p. 701.**

VI. His Glory Made Visible

Jim Montgomery tells the story of how God guided him to formulate a vision for planting churches in every place in order to be sure to reach every people, and eventually, every person. He has come to call the strategy "Saturation Church Planting," or SCP. The SCP strategy is the heart of the vision referred to as "Discipling A Whole Nation," or DAWN.

A. The Purpose of God's Glory. The vision highlights the fantastic value of bringing Christ's glory in every people group. Montgomery finds the idea of establishing Christ's glory throughout the Bible, and planting churches as the best way of revealing Christ's glory.

B. Aiming at Converts or Churches? SCP planners deliberately frame goals around how many new *churches* must be planted instead of aiming at numbers of *converts*. Studies show that when leaders aim to multiply churches, great numbers of new disciples are made. If goals are framed around the numbers of new converts, there are much smaller results.

C. Church in Every People or Throughout Every Nation? Even though Montgomery is aware that the biblical usage of the term "nation" refers to people groups, he has chosen to use the word in the acronym DAWN as a way of mobilizing churches throughout entire countries. When churches plan together to spread the gospel throughout every part of their country, they can be mobilized to aim at eventually reaching every people group. Montgomery is well aware that churches can be spread geographically and still miss many people groups. The DAWN movement works with every national DAWN project to help stretch their vision to plant churches among every people.

D. "Outside-In" Thinking. Churches grow best when the circumference or horizon of the vision is an entire city, people or country. Instead of designing strategies from the inside of the church looking out toward possible new members, the vision is reversed. Start by looking at the entire city, country or people (from the outside), and then look to the church (looking in) in order to conceptualize how to reach them. It's simply a matter of intending to reach every circle and setting of humanity with a living church.

E. The Shopping Window of God. The vision of the Church saturating the earth with Christ's glory requires a different sort of church than traditional institutional churches most known for their buildings and programs. Wolfgang Simson calls for churches that multiply rapidly and powerfully because they are reduced to the elemental simplicity of a household-based "cell church" model.

Read Montgomery, "His Glory Made Visible: Saturation Church Planting," pp. 606-612 (all)

Read Simson, "The Shopping Window of God," p. 608

Conclusion of Certificate Level Readings for this lesson.

Credit Level Guide Notes continue...

VII. Bringing Forth the Blessing: Beyond Dependency

The movements that we hope to see planted in every people will express the beauty and redeemed values of their particular culture. The churches will manifest the beginning of God's blessing upon the entire society. They will display the goodness and power of God, bringing glory to Him. Part of the story of any missiological breakthrough is the record of God's provision and blessing. This does not mean that every church or people is wealthy. What it does mean is that God is honored as the one who blesses the nations. How can missionaries and interested churches help to be a blessing to the nations? Be careful. Quite often generosity is carried out unwisely, undermining the display of God's greater goodness for a people.

Glenn Schwartz warns that unwise generosity can set in motion a debilitating dependency. He recommends aggressive and balanced efforts to mobilize local resources.

A. **Destructive Dependency.** Dependency can result from poor foresight by missionaries. Some of the sources of dependency are:

1. **Failure to teach about giving.**

2. **Constructing buildings.**

3. **Paying leaders.**

4. **Subsidizing programs.**

B. **Mobilizing Local Resources.** A few simple principles will help keep wealthy Western churches and missions from hindering the life of new movements.

1. **Teach about giving.**

2. **Give involvement and responsibility to the local people** to construct the buildings that they need and to support their own leaders in an appropriate way.

3. **Do only what is reproducible.**

4. **Limit outside funding.**

Read Schwartz, "Dependency," pp. 592-594 (all)

VIII. Bringing Forth Maturity: Helping Others Follow The Holy Spirit

The Great Commission focuses on bringing about movements that obey everything that Jesus commands. How can missionaries encourage radical obedience to Christ without imposing their own cultural ideals as the paragon of Christian maturity? How can missionaries be patient when new believers appear to be in no hurry to repent of sins that seem so abhorrent from a Western viewpoint? How do missionaries collaborate with the Holy Spirit to bring about strong movements of dedicated, life-transforming obedience to Christ?

A. The Challenge: The Initial Point of Repentance. Dye describes a missionary named Pete who made the issues of polygamy, smoking and betel nut chewing to be central in the initial steps of repentance and maturity. These were behaviors that bothered Pete most. However, they were not items about which the Holy Spirit was bringing about conviction or which the people of that culture regarded as matters of primary importance.

B. The Standard: A Universal Definition of Sin. Scripture does offer universal moral principles. How these are followed may be different in various cultural settings. This does not at all mean that missionaries embrace situational ethics. There is right and there is wrong. While the essence of the commands and principles are clear, the cultural "edges" are defined differently in different societies. How can missionaries help people follow Christ according to the Scriptures and in keeping with their culture?

C. The Progressive Change: The Role of The Holy Spirit. The key truth in Dye's article is that God is continually guiding each person into greater spiritual maturity, love and obedience. There are, in fact, many occasions for repentance in the life of any believer. If this is true of an individual believer, it is just as true regarding the journey of a people in following Christ together. The growth in righteousness of a church, and therefore, of an entire society is progressive. The role of the missionary starts becoming clearer. Instead of imposing a set of standards, the missionary can help bring about an allegiance to Christ by training leaders to follow the Holy Spirit in accordance with the Scriptures.

D. An Approach: Allowing the Holy Spirit to Convict and Transform. A six-point chart on page 471 outlines a way for missionaries to encourage a Christ-focused obedience.

Read Dye, "Toward a Cross-Cultural Definition of Sin," pp. 469-473 (all)

IX. Case Studies in Church Planting Movements

As you read these two case studies, watch for the principles of this lesson being played out in different settings.

A. **Family Ties.** The gospel is extended along the relational webs of family and friends.

1. **Family connections.** Key leaders within families and friendship circles were encouraged to take the primary role in welcoming new inquirers.

2. **Home settings.** In both cases, the most dramatic growth takes place when the meetings are kept small and located in homes.

B. **Growth in Obedience.** The obedience to Christ in both cases would be suspect by some Christians.

1. **Class sin?** In the Latin case, people are being welcomed to follow Christ without having to deny their class and wealth as a first step of repentance. In fact, many of them are retaining those family and social connections to draw others to Christ. At the same time, they are extending blessing and fellowshiping as a larger family of God with churches from other social classes. There are distinctive congregations. But in their mind, there is not a divided Church. What do you think?

2. **Ancestor honor?** In the Hakka case, people are welcomed to honor their dead ancestors with traditional music while being careful to convey that they are not worshiping the ancestors. Some leaders would think that this is going too far. For many Hakkas, it became possible to follow Christ without denying their families. A radical break from idolatry would happen when the Holy Spirit Himself brought about conviction.

Read Boehr, "A Work of God Among the Hakka of Taiwan," pp. 673-675 (all)

Read Taylor, "An Upper Class People Movement," pp. 690-692 (all)

14 Pioneer Church Planting

Studying this lesson will help you:

- *Describe why church planting among unreached peoples is difficult, feasible and crucially important.*

- *Describe what "extraction evangelism" is and how to avoid it.*

- *Describe how a "conglomerate" church forms and evaluate its potential for multiplying throughout a people group.*

- *Evaluate the practicality of focusing on one people group in culturally distinctive churches which aim not to be exclusive or divisive.*

- *Explain how culturally diverse churches can lead to reconciliation and unity.*

- *Describe why new converts often experience great scorn and disfavor from their people and yet should be encouraged to remain in relationship with their people.*

- *Describe why new converts can aspire to exemplify the finest ideals of their people.*

- *Use the "C-Scale" to identify and compare contextualization of new churches in a Muslim society.*

- *Describe some guidelines to guard against syncretism in pioneer church planting.*

Now we come to the strategic heart of this course. The plight of unreached peoples is not that they have not heard the gospel. The real tragedy is that they have never seen how Christ can be followed by their people without committing what amounts to cultural suicide. There is no indigenous church, and therefore, there is no way to multiply congregations. This lesson is how to bring about the all-important beginning—the missiological breakthrough.

Recall the image of the gospel being brought as a seed to new soil and being allowed to bear fruit indigenous to the new culture. To push the analogy a step further, pioneer church planting aims to nurture entire groves of such living expressions of Christ's kingdom. The new churches bear the same fruit of Christ's character, but usually on stalks and branches of social customs which appear quite alien to the missionary's home culture.

We'll face two key issues about pioneer church planting. First, the issue of encouraging a church movement to express the cultural identity of a single people group. Some have looked on such culturally-focused churches as exclusive or even racist. Others point to the value of penetrating many different people groups with distinct, but not divided church movements.

Second is the issue of the radically different cultural complexion of the churches that grow in frontier mission situations. Is it sound practice to encourage movements of believers to follow Christ without extracting them from their cultural roots? Most say yes until some of those cultural roots appear to be vestiges of religious practice or belief that seem to be "non-Christian" to Western believers. To what extent must we "de-Westernize" our message in order to evangelize unreached peoples in the simple power of biblical truth?

We must have God's wisdom about these complex matters. We have about 10,000 more beachheads to establish. Every one of them will be different in some way. There is no standard plan or formula. To step right into the fray we'll dig into contemporary cases of pioneer church planting.

BREAKTHROUGH To breakthrough is to begin the finish. From Satan's point of view, a missiological breakthrough permanently penetrates the darkness of his domain. From God's point of view, He is at long last welcomed, known and followed. From the people's point of view, breakthroughs introduce enduring hope. Breakthroughs are turning points in history. It's hard to imagine being part of anything of more enduring significance.

I. A Church in Every People

Donald McGavran makes the surprising statement that "It is usually easy to start one single congregation in a new unchurched people group." What is truly difficult, but essential, is planting not one, but a cluster of growing churches which reflects the cultural soul of the society. This missiological breakthrough is so crucial that McGavran states that the goal for mission should be to plant "in every unchurched segment of mankind" a cluster of growing congregations.

A. Conglomerate Churches and Extraction. Follow McGavran's description of how "conglomerate" churches are gathered. He calls it the "one-by-one out of the social group" method. "Extraction" is the practice of urging an individual or family to divorce themselves from their family and culture in order to follow Christ. The impetus for extraction can come from a combination of missionaries and local churches pulling the convert toward a foreign or Christianized sub-culture. Alternatively, extraction can take place when members of the local culture ostracize or "squeeze out" the follower of Christ from their society. Either way it's extraction. It invariably slows down, and often entirely freezes, a movement to Christ. The churches that result from evangelism by extraction are "sealed off" from the culture instead of permeating the entire people group with the life and message of Christ.

B. Seven Principles for Beginning Christward Movements. Each one of the following principles could be expanded with libraries of research and illustration. You'll find that some of them review what you've covered in earlier parts of this course. Seek to grasp them well enough to identify when or how they are being implemented in the case studies that follow.

1. **Aim for a cluster of growing churches.** Always aim to plant a movement of multiple congregations. When there are several congregations there is a rich web of friendships and supportive relationships which can withstand outbursts of hostility from those who oppose the movement. A cluster of congregations can more clearly display what it means to follow Christ in many different settings and sites.

2. **Concentrate on one people group.** As missionaries aim to draw converts from one segment of society, it may be a sociopeople, such as the taxi driver illustration, but as the church forms, it will have a "built-in social cohesion" in which "Everybody feels at home." The sense of belonging is far more crucial than most Americans realize in the societies of the 10/40 Window where most unreached people groups reside.

3. **Encourage converts to remain with their people.** Encourage every member of the new church to remain in close contact with his kin.

   • **Trophies of extraction evangelism?** Missionaries should be dismayed when converts are cast out from their families. Instead, some missionaries have actually commended the new believer for "paying the price" to follow Jesus. Social exclusion may take place, but severance from one's people should never be reckoned as a standard price for following Jesus.

   • **Patiently bear disfavor.** McGavran recommends coaching new converts to aspire to exemplifying all their society's ideals. To do this they must retain ties and identity with their people. This can be more costly than accepting the status of an outcast.

- **Retain most cultural practices.** There are areas where new converts cannot remain one with their people, such as idolatry or obvious sin. But in most matters they can continue to embrace the values and practices of their people.

4. **Encourage group decisions for Christ.** Group decisions can bring about a "critical mass" of new believers who can stand together, resist mild or severe ostracism, and more likely present an effective invitation to the rest of their people to join them. McGavran suggests delaying baptism until there are large enough numbers to withstand ostracism.

5. **Aim for a constant stream of new converts.** Why would missionaries ever fail to aim for a steady stream of new believers? It's quite common. There is a window of time during which new believers have great power to tell their story persuasively. Missionaries very often fail to maximize this optimum by preoccupying these potential new messengers with teaching. Of the two "evils" of too little teaching or a sealed-off community, the missionary should always favor keeping new believers in life-giving contact with their community. The extremely brief period of instruction that Paul offered to churches shows that the Holy Spirit can be trusted to bring people out of darkness into light.

6. **Help converts exemplify the highest hopes.** Pioneer church planting is successful when the churches have "witnessed" (as defined in Lesson 5) in such a way that the value of following Christ can be observed. The church should aspire to surpass the ideals of their society. Every feature of noble character and wisdom that the people group has valued can probably be found in Christ. The new churches must realize that they exemplify the hope and destiny of their people.

7. **Emphasize brotherhood.** God unfolds the process of transforming complex societies over many years. At issue is the message at the moment of missiological breakthrough. McGavran recommends celebrating brotherhood from the first moment, but looking forward to days when God will bring about truly transformed societies.

- **Celebrate equality within imperfect social institutions.** All persons are equal in Christ. However the initial thrust of the gospel is not necessarily the challenging of evil social institutions.

- **Obedience to Christ in every segment.** The best way to achieve reconciliation of the races and peoples of earth is to see many from every segment and race introduced to an obedient relationship with Christ. Under Christ's lordship genuine brotherhood, justice, goodness and righteousness can be increased.

I have written very boldly to you on some points, so as to remind you again, because of the grace that was given me from God, to be a minister of Christ Jesus to the Gentiles (literally: nations or peoples), ministering as a priest, the gospel of God, that my offering of the Gentiles (peoples) might become acceptable, sanctified by the Holy Spirit.

Therefore in Christ Jesus I have found reason for boasting in things pertaining to God.

For I will not presume to speak of anything except what Christ has accomplished through me, resulting in the obedience of the Gentiles (peoples) by word and deed, in the power of signs and wonders, in the power of the Spirit; so that from Jerusalem and round about as far as Illyricum I have fully preached the gospel of Christ.

And thus I aspired to preach the gospel, not where Christ was already named, that I might not build upon another man's foundation; but as it is written, "They who had no news of Him shall see, And they who have not heard shall understand."

—Romans 15:15-21

In Romans 15:15-21 we find Paul's reason for writing the book of Romans: to encourage fellow believers to align their lives with him in a specific dimension of God's mission purpose. Does Paul operate with a sense of priority? What rationale does he offer for that priority? How does Paul's communication of the gospel result in both the "naming" of Christ and the building of foundations? What kind of foundation was Paul building? Consider how God-focused Paul was about his mission. Where in this passage do you see reference to him accomplishing his mission in the triple dynamic of working from God, through God, and to God again? How can you live your life simplified so much that what matters most is what Christ accomplishes through you among the nations, and that your identity ("or boasting") is what takes place unto God from the nations? Or is this kind of focus in life only for a few apostles?

Read McGavran, "A Church in Every People: Plain Talk About a Difficult Subject," pp. 617-622 (all)

Mustafa doesn't know what to do about being baptized. He had been carefully completing a correspondence course about Jesus for months. He had kept the whole thing a secret from his Muslim family. A missionary from America had been visiting his small city for a few weeks. Mustafa had met with him secretly a few times. The man had urged him to be baptized, pointing out the verse in Mark chapter 16 in which Jesus seems to require baptism to be saved. He was confused because the correspondence course had assured him that he was saved by trusting Christ only a month ago. Before the man left town, he said he would be eager to baptize Mustafa. But Mustafa is thinking about his brother Tariq, who has just won great prestige for the family by being recommended as a professor in the university. He is also wondering about his sister Fatima, who is engaged to be married into a very important family. The marriage, and the professorship will bring lasting honor to his entire clan. But if he is baptized as a Christian, he will bring so much dishonor on his family that the marriage will likely be called off. The professorship may not be confirmed. Mustafa thinks he may be ready to suffer to be a Christian, but he may force his sister to such dishonor that she might never marry. Was it right to condemn his sister to singleness and suspicion that she was actually a prostitute? The missionary had urged him not to harden his heart to Christ's call. But his heart was torn for his family. What should he do?

A tentmaker missionary in a Muslim country explains that the joy in his life comes from obeying Jesus. "How do you know what He tells you?" asks Abdul. The missionary replied, "I read the Injil (the Gospels), His book. I have promised to do whatever He tells me from His book." Abdul asked if he could also read the book. The missionary agreed upon three conditions. First, that Abdul would invite a friend to examine the Injil with him. Second, that the two friends would promise God to obey anything Jesus told them to do. And third, that they would tell their parents and important people in their families what they were doing before they started. They agreed. Within a few weeks, both Muslim men had begun to obey Jesus as they sensed Him speaking to them from the Sermon on the

Mount. Their families were curious and observant about what would happen in their lives. Months later, after Abdul had read most of the New Testament, had learned to pray, had experienced repentance and had pledged his entire life to following Jesus, he read the words about baptism. He sensed Jesus instructing him to be baptized. He had always kept his family informed about what Jesus was directing him to do. So he announced that he wanted to be baptized. What did they think? His uncle was furious, and threatened to kill him on the spot. But the aged grandmother rose to Abdul's defense, arguing that Abdul had become the finest person in their family since he began doing what Jesus told him to do. It would never do to punish the only kind and trustworthy person of the family. And God had answered his prayers. Abdul was no longer hindered from following Christ and continued in close relationship with his family.

How did this missionary practice what George Patterson calls "obedience-oriented evangelism?" Which of the seven principles from McGavran's article do you see at work in this case?

II. Unity and Uniformity

We return to Ralph Winter's important address at Lausanne in 1974. He presented what he felt to be "the most important issue of evangelism today." It is still of vital importance 25 years later. He rightly turns to Scripture for wisdom on these matters. Winter points out a common presumption of American culture-Christianity that there ought to be just one national church in a country. The rest of his presentation challenges the parallel assumption that distinctive church planting movements are necessarily divisive.

A. **Unity and Liberty.** The key point is that Christian unity cannot be healthy if it infringes upon Christian liberty.

1. **Christian unity** is not a matter of reversing denominationalism, but of celebrating a healthy diversity within the worldwide Christian Church. Winter likens the Church to an orchestra with churches of different cultural backgrounds playing their very different cultural instruments to the same score of the Word of God.

2. **Christian liberty** can be seen in the diverse congregations of Paul's day practicing different lifestyles regarding diet, Sabbath-keeping, and so on. Paul was determined to allow Christians to follow different Christian lifestyles. He was opposed to anyone who would try to preserve a single pattern as normative for all Christians. The gospel required diversity with regard to peripheral matters. In fact, this concern is what finally brought about his martyrdom. The gospel should not result in or preserve alienation between cultural traditions. Instead, by affirming the liberty of different segments of society to retain elements of their lifestyle that are not contrary to the gospel, these peoples are being welcomed into the world Christian family. They flourish under the Word of God which ultimately calls for the elimination of every kind of prejudice.

B. Unity is not Uniformity. Winter discusses why we should aim to plant different churches for different people groups.

1. **The power of attraction.** The example of a "youth church" shows the potential for unified groups attracting many other people of the same type. Such an approach is encouraged if it is recognized that the "youth" church is a means to attracting many other young people. Should we use this strategy with an "ends justifies the means" pragmatism? Winter says that the powerful strategic idea that more people will follow Christ if they can join their own kind of people is grounded on the firm biblical truth of Christian liberty.

2. **Never exclusion.** Winter responds to the critique that churches which target a particular social group are thereby excluding others. The diversity of churches does not imply forced segregation. Churches have become diverse because given freedom to choose, people consistently seek fellowship with others most like themselves. God is not threatened by diversity, He created it. Biblical unity does not require uniformity.

> **Read Winter, "New Macedonia: A Revolutionary New Era In Mission Begins," pp. 349c-353**

III. Can Jesus Be Followed in a Muslim Way?

As the remaining unreached people groups are approached with the gospel, there is an urgent need to de-Westernize the gospel message, and to stand ready to welcome new movements toward Christ that are faithful to the biblical essentials. A Muslim convert from Asia called Shah Ali (not his real name) presents his story with the help of Dr. Dudley Woodberry. Ali points out two primary problems in Muslim evangelism. First, Christianity was perceived to be foreign. Second, relief efforts sponsored by Christians were perceived as manipulative.

Numbers are not mentioned in this article, but this movement is one of the largest movements of Muslims to faith in Christ ever in history. There are thousands following Jesus in this way. The success of movements such as this heightens the controversy about them. All the more reason for you to understand the issues. In the years ahead it will be important for many mission leaders and supporters to be well-acquainted with these issues.

A. Christian Faith in Muslim Dress. In addressing the problem of Christianity being perceived as foreign, Ali describes four different aspects to a strategy of radical contextualization.

1. **Presenting the Message in contextualized ways.** Ali used Qur'anic vocabulary and other terms which were thought of as specifically Islamic to present Jesus. Muslim theological terms were used such as "Allah" for God and "Injil" for the gospel.

2. **Messengers retain contact and identity with community.** In one experiment that failed, twenty-five national (not foreign) couples were sent into Muslim villages. Only one of them was from a Muslim background. Though the workers were accepted as helpers, they were not accepted as credible messengers. Subsequently, only workers from Muslim background were sent. They were all sincere converts from Islam who had chosen to retain features of their Muslim cultural heritage, even though they were committed to following Jesus. They continued to sincerely refer to themselves as Muslims (which

means "submitters to God") and found ways to publicly pray to Jesus Christ with forms of ritual prayers which would be recognized as honorable. They filled their prayers with biblical meaning focused on Christ.

3. **Encouraging the movement in relevant forms.** New converts were encouraged to follow Christ openly, but to continue to use the mosque (the Muslim place of community prayer and teaching). Islamic leaders have been encouraged to follow Christ, but to continue their role of influence. The term "Messianic Mosque" refers to a mosque that is dedicated to following Christ even though some forms of Islamic faith and practice are retained by the believing community.

4. **Following Christ as a completion.** Perhaps the most radical idea is that Muslims might find Jesus to be the one who *fulfills* their culture rather than one who condemns it. Jewish believers have long embraced Christ as the fulfillment of their Jewishness, and regarded themselves as "completed" Jews. This idea is abundantly clear from Scripture. Can this same idea of completion be applied in any way to other religious traditions? Some think so. Others do not.

B. **Toward Responsible Self-Help.** The second major problem Ali encountered was the perception that when Christians offered humanitarian help, it was an inducement to follow a foreign religion. The standard approach to the charge that humanitarian efforts by Christians have been manipulative and coercive has been to divorce evangelism from development efforts in this largely Muslim country. Ali's co-workers chose not to follow this approach. Instead, they sought to integrate church planting, evangelism and development efforts. The main feature of the integration is that workers are not foreign, all people in the communities are served, regardless of their interest in or willingness to convert to Christianity. The development strategies are renewable and are carefully designed to mobilize local resources with no handouts.

> **Read Ali and Woodberry, Case Study: "South Asia: Vegetables, Fish and Messianic Mosques," pp. 680-682 (all)**

IV. Contextualizing Christ-Centered Communities

Is it possible to go too far in making the gospel accessible to Muslims such that we end up with a diminished, or even sub-biblical, version of the gospel message? How can we evaluate the movements that result with respect to biblical requirements and the wide array of diverse denominational traditions? Read so that you can begin to evaluate mission efforts with a respect for the complexity of the issues and the boldness that we must find to apply the lessons of Acts 15 in our day.

A. **A Spectrum of Options.** John Travis (not his real name) presents a spectrum of options developed by field workers and Muslim converts for expressing identity as a community of followers of Christ in a Muslim situation. Keep in mind that Travis is referring to the identity of communities of faith, not necessarily the identity of missionaries who might approach Muslim communities. Be sure to grasp the difference between C-4 and C-5. Most of the concerns being raised seem to be in this range of the continuum of options.

> **Read Travis, "The C1 to C6 Spectrum," pp. 658-659 (all)**

B. A Critique of Over-Contextualizing Messengers or Movements? Phil Parshall presents a critique of efforts which allow or even encourage Muslims to remain in mosque worship patterns as a standard expression of following Christ. In reading this article carefully, keep in mind that the C-1 through C-6 spectrum does not refer to foreign Christians presenting themselves as Muslims. The issue is how shall Muslims who follow Jesus identify themselves? What kind of movement shall the new Christward movement portray itself to be? Carefully sort out the three distinct ideas of contextualizing the message, the messengers, and the movement which results.

1. **A continuum of contextualization.** Parshall presents a continuum of contextualization which is very simple. On one end are efforts of "Contextualization" by which he means efforts to present following Christ within the context of cultural and social forms which are recognized by the respondent community. On the other end of the spectrum is "Syncretism," which is a blending of Christian faith and non-Christian beliefs and practices which seems sufficiently alien to the biblical message that it becomes doubtful that the adherents are following the essentials of biblical faith. He marks a great divide between them. He offers his view that C-4 efforts are bold contextualization, but that C-5 efforts are usually syncretistic. In his view, "Messianic Mosques" go too far in attempting to present the gospel in a way that is accessible to Muslims.

2. **Mosques redeemed?** Parshall presents his concerns in reference to a movement of "Messianic Mosques" in Asia which has recently been the subject of careful research. He reveals some aspects of that research. He challenges the idea that mosques can be redeemed.

3. **Missionaries deceptive?** Parshall tells the story of a worker who falsely presented himself as a Muslim.

> **Read Parshall, "Going Too Far?," pp. 655-659 (all)**

Conclusion of Key Readings for this lesson.　　　　　　　　　　　　　　　　　　

V.　How Shall They Follow Jesus?

John Travis responds to Parshall's critique. Consider the way that he poses the questions and deals with the issues. His approach is consistently from the viewpoint of the potential converts, that is, he asks "What shall a Muslim do to follow Jesus?" Parshall's questions and guidelines are usually framed from the viewpoint of what missionaries ought to do.

A. Continuing in Community. Travis describes how some C5 Muslim converts participate in mosque meetings in order to keep their relationships vital and the community leaders from being shamed. Without deception or secrecy they are able to continue to present the Bible (*Torah* = the Law, *Zabur* = the Prophets, *Injil* = the Gospels) to many throughout their community, resulting in a steady stream of new believers in Jesus.

B. Concerns with Parshall's Critique. The research regarding the movement in Asia is again considered.

1. Recognizing the long process. The new believers are part of a highly resistant group which has rebuffed the gospel for centuries. What is the place of the Holy Spirit to work over the years to come?

2. Examine the fruit. An important criterion is transformed character and lasting fruit of the Spirit.

3. Was there any other way? There would be no movement to examine without this radical approach. What can we learn? How can we exploit this experiment in contextualization for practical wisdom we need for the many thousands of other people groups?

C. Difference between C5 Believers and C5 Missionaries. Travis is concerned as well with C5 missionaries. While allowing the possibility that God may lead a few specially-called people to be C5 missionaries, he points out that every Muslim convert is forced to find a place on the "C" scale. How shall they follow Jesus? The primary issue is C5 believers.

D. Rejecting Divergent Beliefs. What about the Qur'an and Muhammad? Though Travis does not state it this way, it's worth considering that denying the prophethood of Muhammad never saved anyone in God's sight. Correction of error is not a saving act of cross-cultural communication of the gospel. Travis reports that in his experience, it is possible to remain a part of the Islamic community and not affirm standard Muslim theology. New believers soon find that they cannot affirm all that is taught about the Qur'an and Muhammad.

E. Guidelines Regarding Syncretism. Travis offers a list of seven guidelines. They differ from Parshall's list of five guidelines in this important way: Parshall's list concerns what *missionaries* should do to avoid syncretism; Travis' list concerns what *converts* should do to avoid syncretism. We need both lists. Compare the lists. As you study them, consider which of them may be specific for Muslim situations. You might perhaps discover an underlying principle for most or all of the guidelines which makes them applicable to converts from other religious traditions.

1. Jesus Christ alone is Savior.

2. Follow Christ in community with other believers.

3. Study the Bible.

4. Renounce and be delivered from occultism.

5. Religious customs are not performed to earn merit.

6. Religious beliefs are examined in light of Scripture. Beliefs are judged or reinterpreted so that they are either maintained, modified or rejected according to biblical standards.

7. Show evidence of new birth and growth in grace.

And it came about that for an entire year they met with the church, and taught considerable numbers; and the disciples were first called Christians in Antioch.

—Acts 11:26

Do you have to be a Christian to go to heaven? Trick question. The term "Christian" occurs only three times in Scripture. What the term means in Acts 11:26 is not precisely clear. Did the followers of Christ call themselves "Christians" or is this a label placed on them by unbelievers? The only other two occurrences of the label in the Bible are Acts 26:28 and 1 Peter 4:16. In both of those passages, the word "Christian" seems to be a pejorative term, a slang term of derision. Does the Bible require a person to declare themselves to be a "Christian" in order to be saved? Without question, believing and following Christ is required for salvation. But what about the label? How should we use the label today? What about sensitive situations in which the very term "Christian" is associated more with the Crusades or with Western television morality than with Jesus?

Read Travis, "Must All Muslims Leave 'Islam' to Follow Jesus?" pp. 660-663 (all)

VI. How Shall This People Find God's Way to Follow Jesus?

The thrill of pioneer church planting should not be seen as a dry matter of theological argument. Church planting among unreached peoples may be the most fantastic miracle that ever takes place. The theological issues leap off the pages of books and are played out in high-stakes reality. There are long years of tedious labor and outbreaks of deadly persecution, but there are also gorgeous displays of worship, astounding answers to prayer and heroic stands of faithfulness.

A. **Reflect on the Cost and Feasibility.** We want you to come to recognize how challenging it will be to launch church planting movements in the estimated 10,000 unimax people groups yet without a church. Starting these movements is so incredibly difficult that it might be considered almost impossible. Even so, the actual stories of how God accomplishes the impossible show us that pioneer church planting really is feasible. Nothing could be more certain than that people groups will be reached. They will be reached because of who God is, because of the power of the gospel, because of the hunger of people to find and follow God and because of the amazing determination and resourceful zeal of God's people throughout history. Apostolic passion is not diminishing in our day. Ordinary people are expecting great things from God and attempting great things for God. In fact, two of these case studies were written by former students who found themselves working directly with unreached peoples, partly because of taking this course.

B. **Recognize Principles in Action.** Read the following stories for the joy of tracing God's hand in very recent history. Look carefully for the outworking of the following principles. Some of these restate the principles of McGavran outlined earlier in this lesson. Others reflect ideas presented in earlier lessons in this course.

1. **Focus on one people group.**

2. **Seek a pathway for people to follow Christ** while remaining part of their people. Refuse extraction evangelism.

3. **Followers live out the ideals of their people.** Christ is seen as the redemption, and not the condemnation, of their culture.

4. **Contextualization** often encroaches on the margins of syncretism. Contextualization is risky, but is usually a worthwhile risk.

5. **Local believers are usually the true leaders** and church planters. Missionaries are usually facilitators, coaches and trainers.

6. **God's hand is revealed** by answered prayers and divine intervention.

7. **Persecution is standard.** No movement stands unless it is tempered by the fires of hostility and persecution.

C. **A Muslim Story.** Paul Pearlman describes another mission effort among some Muslims in Asia. Note the willingness to experiment with form adaptations, and the readiness to adjust missionary lifestyle in radical ways. Look for the seven principles mentioned above which are at work in their strategy. What kind of understanding was there regarding finances? How was God glorified by the missionaries and their converts?

Read Pearlman, Case Study: "Reaching the Baranada People of Barunda," pp. 683-686 (all)

D. **A Buddhist Story.** Brian Hogan describes how a work in Mongolia began with a sociopeople comprised of teenage girls, and how the movement developed until it was able to impact the mainstream of society. Note how the missionary team involved the merging leadership in dealing with potential syncretism and the name for God. How was leadership development a key part of what was accomplished? Look for the principles listed above at work in this story so that you will be able to detect how those principles work out in actual cases. How has God been glorified in Mongolia by these new churches?

Read Hogan, Case Study: "Distant Thunder: Mongols Follow the Khan of Khans," pp. 694-698 (all)

E. **A Hindu Story.** Dean Hubbard tells the story of an effort which ended up reaching more than one people group in India. How did God use a partnership of local leaders and expatriate servants? How did God demonstrate His power? Watch how persecution hit the new movements. Sometimes churches didn't always recover, at other times, outbreaks of persecution advanced the movements greatly. Note carefully how the people were encouraged to follow Christ without betraying their families. How did these movements bring glory to God?

Read Hubbard, Case Study: "A Movement of Christ Worshipers in India," pp. 698-701 (all)

Conclusion of Certificate Level Readings for this lesson.

Credit Level Guide Notes continue...

VII. The Unavoidable Risk of Contextualization

Charles Kraft would probably extend Parshall's two-part continuum of Contextualization and Syncretism to a three-part continuum: Contextualization as a narrow, difficult, but necessary middle ground, surrounded by syncretism on both ends of the scale.

A. Two Paths to Syncretism. Kraft describes "two paths to syncretism":

1. **Too careless?** One path is allowing the receiving people to attach their own worldview assumptions to Christian practices. External practices are imported. Internal belief structures are not changed.

2. **Too careful?** The other path is when sincere missionaries import both a worldview package as well as a recommended pattern of behavior. Their intent is to guard new converts from ever experiencing even a moment of theological error, and to bestow upon them the great blessing of living as Western Christians do. The result is usually an isolated, conglomerate church which is perceived by the larger society as a foreign religious intrusion.

Kraft recommends that we avoid both paths by operating with a "deep trust in the Holy Spirit," by quickly and steadily turning the attention of new believers to the Scriptures, giving them enough encouragement and freedom to make biblically informed decisions.

Read Kraft, "Culture, Worldview and Contextualization," pp. 390a-391a

B. Back to Basic Assumptions About Culture. Kraft lists five insights about God's work within culture. Consider the messianic mosque experiment from these five angles.

Read Kraft, "Culture, Worldview and Contextualization," pp. 391b-391d

VIII. Are We Ready for Tomorrow's Kingdom?

Ralph Winter provokes our thinking by exposing some elements of pagan culture that have been part of mainstream Christendom for centuries. Winter suggests that the only way to not sink into a blinded syncretistic culture-Christianity is to attempt to convey the gospel to other cultures. Mission endeavor might be the only way to keep the faith pure. Winter points out that the largest growing edge of biblical faith is comprised of those whom many would consider "outside and beyond" Christianity. Among the movements that might offend or disappoint most American evangelicals are: The huge waves of "African Initiated Churches," the almost unseen movement of unbaptized caste Hindus in India, and the house church movement in China. Without endorsing these movements, each of which carries apparent aberrations from the faith which are quite significant, are we prepared to work or walk with these phenomena in some way? How shall we depend on the Holy Spirit? How shall we scrutinize our own traditions? How shall we delve more deeply into the Scriptures for a more profound grasp on the essentials of faith and obedience?

Read Winter, "Are We Ready for Tomorrow's Kingdom?" pp. 369-370 (all)

IX. Turning Muslim Stumbling Blocks into Stepping Stones
Warren Chastain challenges both our assumptions about success and our impressions about the impossibility of evangelizing unreached peoples. One key idea underlying Chastain's thinking is that the people may be more resistant to our presentation rather than to the gospel itself. Who is to say how resistant they are to Christ Himself presented powerfully in keeping with their culture and worldview? Just because a people group has resisted previous efforts does not at all mean that they will remain resistant to all future efforts, or the efforts of other more appropriate messengers.

A. Our Stumbling Blocks. The American success mentality may be diverting many from the difficult work of pioneer church planting. Challenge the "bottom-line" mentality in your own thinking. Why should one be willing to labor for a lifetime with little success?

1. **God draws the real bottom line.**

2. **Fill our minds with "harvest mentality."** Chastain brings new vocabulary to the idea of a missiological breakthrough. He calls it a "primary expansion of the gospel" among all people groups. He urges us to be confident in the knowledge that Christ has mandated such an expansion and to exert faith that "the gospel really is the power of God."

B. Muslim Stumbling Blocks. Consider how barriers in the Muslim mind may actually be turned into bridges for gospel communication. These kinds of considerations might give the impression that the gospel should be communicated in an argumentative way to correct error. The real value of this discussion is to point out the challenging, but possible mission of persuading Muslims to follow Jesus. Every pioneer church planter must dig deeply into the worldview of the receiving people in order to communicate effectively, as well as to recognize the points at which the Scriptures may be addressing their concerns (points in which Westerners are not even slightly interested).

> **Read Chastain, "On Turning Muslim Stumbling Blocks into Stepping Stones," pp. 650-654 (all)**

X. Evangelizing Animistic Societies
Pioneer church planting is also necessary among animistic societies. Alan Tippett presents some of the worldview assumptions of animism. Animism is a worldview that regards the physical world as being filled or "animated" by spiritual beings. Tippett believes that animism underlies many other religious systems and should not be regarded as strictly primitive or tribal. Don't get bogged down in the definitions of animism. Focus on the view of conversion as a group experience and how Tippett expands on the idea that evangelization will in some way require the planting of a church. Give your attention to the six problems that Tippett identifies which outlines church planting among face-to-face societies. Several of the issues he raises have wide application to urbanized peoples from face-to-face societies who find themselves in the midst of modernity.

1. **Encounter.** Tippett points out that conversion is a process. Nevertheless he extols the value of making a definitive act of commitment to the Lord. People should not drift into the Christian faith. What are the issues regarding timing and in hostile situations where a developed religious system carries centuries of animosity toward the Christian faith? Consider how Tippett's challenge may be inappropriate for many situations in which a premature open encounter would almost certainly result in the gospel being soundly and officially rejected, making evangelism virtually impossible for years.

2. **Motivation.** Mixed motives may be the reason for many cases of mixed theology.

3. **Meaning.** Consider this insightful reading of Acts 14!

4. **Social structure.** The organizational structure of churches should reflect or be compatible with the familiar structures of their society.

5. **Incorporation.** One of the greatest challenges in any kind of society is to form a new structure of brotherhood and service when such a structure or trust relationships may be nonexistent.

6. **Cultural void.** Part of the challenge of urging the people to continue in their culture is the gaps of practice when certain practices are rejected as incompatible with faith in Christ. Should substitutes be introduced? Which elements can be preserved and made "truly Christian?"

Read Tippett, "The Evangelization of Animists," pp. 623-631 (all)

XI. Forming Fellowships

Two case studies will help round out the vision of forming viable fellowships in diverse cultures. Contrast these cases with respect to the environment of hostility to the gospel. "Sarabia" is a situation where Muslim opposition to the faith warrants a quiet, almost clandestine approach. The radio churches literally broadcast their presence in the streets. The stories also contrast with respect to the number of church planters and years of effort required. Both stories point out the importance of training leaders. Note that most of the Sarabian believers initially encountered the gospel through the radio. But this does not mean that they experienced the rapid breakthroughs in Andhra Pradesh, India.

Read Livingstone, Case Study: "Sarabia: An Indigenous Arab Church," pp. 688-690 (all)

Read Mial, Case Study: "The Impact of Missionary Radio on Church Planting," pp. 675-676 (all)

15 World Christian Partnership

The "perspectives" you've gained in this course give you a vantage point from which you can behold your God accomplishing His purposes. You can now see how swiftly God's hand is moving because you have observed the Ancient of Days pressing His purpose through all the days of history.

Hope helps you see what is not yet visible. You can pray on, even when you don't see immediate answers because you can see His glory coming like the dawn on every benighted people and city. You may never be able to read your Bible again with a self-centric viewpoint. You are going to see Christ, and Him glorified everywhere you look. He may not be honored yet, or even named, but you can see His day as surely as Abraham saw Isaac coming. Now you know what the increase of His kingdom might look like in terms of new churches, transformed communities and reconciliation between the peoples. You have traced the facts of the numerical increase of His kingdom. More people are being drawn under the blessing of His lordship than ever before. You can feel the spiritual war raging, but you can see His glory coming. Yes, you see things differently now.

This lesson is about how that vision can integrate your life for His global purpose. We'll learn about the crucial role of senders and the special work of mobilization. We'll mark out the pathway of becoming an effective missionary. We'll discover the value of strategic partnerships.

Now that you have perspective on the world Christian movement you can no longer be an onlooker. Step into the movement. God gives you a place and a role. When God calls anyone, He does not call people to go away from Him to distant places. God always calls His servants closer to Himself. He may call you to be closer to Him as He works among the poor of Cairo, or the Hindus of Delhi, or the Muslims of Jakarta. He may call you to be with Him as He renews His churches in America to risky faith and blazing hope. You may not know where you will go, or what He wants you to do years from now, but you do know the One who has promised to fill the earth with glory. You have embraced the purpose upon which He has set His own passion. You are free to follow Him with the same single-hearted hope.

TEAMWORK The only heroes who operate alone are figures of fiction. The true stories of accomplishment and significance always unfold as stories of teamwork. In Christ, one's life is multiplied by others. The only way to exchange the illusions of fame and self-importance for God-granted greatness and blessing is by walking in partnership with others.

I. World Christian Discipleship

Living decisively for God's purpose is not a rare or extravagant calling. Every Christian follows the God of all nations. It shouldn't be surprising to discover that God intends for every Christian to enjoy having a part in His world-sized purpose. Understand how Bryant uses the image of "the Gap" to describe God's unfinished purpose.

A. What it Means to Be a World Christian. David Bryant revived the term "World Christian," defining it in terms of the priority of completing the task of world evangelization.

1. **World Christians described.** World Christians are not any better than any other Christians. They are simply taking God's global cause seriously and personally. Three of Bryant's descriptions are particularly significant:

   • **They take a stand with personal responsibility.** World Christians in effect, say, "Among every people group where there is no vital, evangelizing Christian community, there should be one, there must be one, there shall be one. Together we want to help make this happen."

   • **Integrating priority.** World Christians are "day-to-day disciples for whom Christ's global cause has become the integrating, overriding priority for all that He is doing for them."

   • **Location is secondary.** "They are heaven's expatriates, camping where the Kingdom is best served."

2. **Becoming and growing as a World Christian.** Bryant identifies three steps. By working through this course you are probably well along in this process. How can you help others to grow through these same steps?

   • **Step one: Catch a world vision.** How has this course changed the way you see God working in His world? What other ways are there to grow in this vision?

   • **Step two: Keep a world vision.** Probe your heart to check your willingness to grow as a World Christian. There are three questions under the section "Step Two: Have I kept a world vision?" Read them out loud to yourself.

   • **Step three: Obey a world vision.** If someone were to pose these questions to you three months or a year after finishing this course, how do you think you would answer? Would it help you if someone did in fact check with you three months or a year from now?

> **Read Bryant, "What it Means to Be a World Christian," pp. 702-704 (all)**

B. World Christian Lifestyle is a "Wartime" Lifestyle. Unless you deliberately press your *values* to be in alignment with your *vision*, you will end up losing your vision. Lesser values and cultural habits of heart will prevail so that your vision will eventually fade. Ralph Winter proposes a bold, decisive reconsecration to live for God's purpose. Winter challenges the assumptions underlying traditional American lifestyles. Winter does not subscribe to the idea that if we do with less, then poor people somewhere else in the world will have more. Be sure to understand that Winter's appeal is not based on the commonplace idea that it might be noble to redistribute wealth so that everyone has enough.

Instead, Winter says that strategic simplicity releases wealth to be allocated where it is most effective in Christ's war to redeem the nations. Ultimately, worthy lifestyles are not built around deprivation in order to bring equality. Worthy lifestyles are instead focused on better allocation of resources for God's kingdom victory. The bonus is living free from the self-inflicted damage of traditional American lifestyles. Winter is enough of a realist to urge Americans to find creative ways to break into such liberating lifestyles with others of like mind.

Read Winter, "Reconsecration to a Wartime, Not a Peacetime, Lifestyle," pp. 705-707 (all)

"He who loves his life loses it; and he who hates his life in this world shall keep it to life eternal.

If anyone serves Me, let him follow Me; and where I am, there shall My servant also be; if anyone serves Me, the Father will honor him.

Now My soul has become troubled; and what shall I say,

'Father, save Me from this hour?'

But for this purpose I came to this hour. Father, glorify Your name."

There came therefore a voice out of heaven:

"I have both glorified it, and will glorify it again."

—John 12:25-28

In John 12:25-28 Jesus reveals the inner workings of His soul at the time that He was making the most important decision of His life. He reveals His choice in the same breath as He invites His friends to follow Him. The strong implication was that they would in some way face the same life-shaping decision. He was making the public appearance that would result in His death on the cross days later. Why would this particular time be the moment that Jesus would describe His soul as being troubled? What do you see in the verses that indicate that He was weighing an important decision? He mentions two different options which loomed before Him. The two options were embodied in two different prayers. What were the prayers? What would the Father have answered to either prayer? What parallels do these prayers have for Jesus' followers today? Jesus describes the single criterion which helped him choose a life path for God's greater glory: "But for this purpose I came to this hour." Do you know the purpose for which you have come to this hour? What might unfold in your life if you were to ask God to glorify His name with your life regardless of the short term outcome? In what way would you be following Jesus by praying and living for this purpose?

II. Serving as Senders

God wants every believer to live in the joy of fulfilling His global purposes.

A. The Role of Senders. Missions is not just for missionaries. For every effective missionary we find a dozen or more people who support missionaries and boost the cause of missions. The life of sending can be particularly challenging because sending is voluntary and most senders remain immersed in their home culture. While a missionary's work is cross-cultural, a senders work is counter-cultural. Senders must regularly remind themselves of their purpose and seek out accountability to stay on track. There are two general categories of sending:

1. Specific sending supports missionaries.

2. General sending advances the larger global cause. This kind of sending includes many general efforts of intercession and mobilization.

B. The Work of Mobilization. Mobilization is a specialized kind of sending which lifts the vision and involvement of many other people in the work of completing world evangelization. Mobilization includes mission education, organizing persistent prayer for unreached peoples and mentoring would-be missionaries and mobilizers to reach their best effectiveness.

C. Core Activities of Sending. When Christians are challenged to "pray, give or go" in a perfunctory way, there is not a sufficient sense of ownership and participation for people to seriously integrate their lifestyles and life choices around God's global purpose. When senders seek to fulfill God's purpose by living in the clear role definition of a sender, they invariably find themselves contributing in three ways:

1. **Serving.** Senders find relational ways to support frontline missionaries and those who are part of the mission infrastructure which enables frontline missionaries.

2. **Giving.** Senders give with a sense of partnership toward accomplishing specific strategic goals. Their generosity flows from the simplicity of their lifestyles.

3. **Praying.** Senders pray *with* missionaries instead of merely praying *for* them. In this way they come to enjoy a sense of partnership in the task instead of responding passively as an occasional donor.

Read Hawthorne, "Senders," pp. 708-713 (all)

III. Join the World Christian Movement

Throughout this course we have been tracing the development of the most significant movement in history—the World Christian Movement. It is certainly the longest-running movement, if we trace its beginnings to Abraham. There is no question that it is the most influential stream of human activity the world has known or will ever know. There is no real way to be a Christian without being a part of this incredible movement.

A. Become a Student of the Mission Industry. To move beyond a spectator status, it's crucial to become acquainted with the heart of the movement: the professionals and organizations that sustain work so significant that it takes several generations to fulfill. We speak of the highly developed mission enterprise which can properly be called the "mission industry."

1. **Mission agencies.** Place great value on these incredible institutions. You've already traced the heritage of these organizations throughout history. They are not add-on or stop-gap structures making up for a temporary lapse in local church obedience. Mission agencies express the life of the Church in powerful ways, and enable the obedience of many churches. Get acquainted with the different types and accomplishments of the amazingly diverse world of mission agencies.

2. **Training institutions.** Do more than learn about schools and training opportunities or regard them as something for young people to work through. Enroll yourself in a course of learning beyond Perspectives. Perhaps of even greater importance than continuing as a learner is to mature in your role as a mentor to others. Collaborate with training institutions and your local church to maximize the effectiveness of others.

3. **Associations and societies.** The mission industry is filled with serious professionals. Why not gain the professional skills that you will need as a mobilizer or a missionary by linking with the larger World Christian Movement through publications and conferences?

4. Local churches. Understanding the role of your local church is important. Don't expect too much or too little. Local churches gain wisdom and vision from a dynamic partnership with organized mission structures. Mission agencies need the support and prayer that local churches can offer. Part of understanding the place of local churches in the mission industry is to recognize that churches often need to be called again to their primary mission and place in world evangelization. Mobilizers are needed for this task.

B. The Essential Role of Mobilizers. If the total task is held in view, then it becomes obvious that mobilizers are as essential as missionaries to the World Christian Movement. Mobilizing is so strategically necessary that full-time mobilizers should be considered equally worthy of mission budgets. How does Winter encourage you to mobilize yourself?

C. Knowing God's Will. Winter challenges many of the frustrating myths believers have about knowing God's will. Be sure to comprehend the value of placing His cause above your career. Be able to explain the ways of God with regard to how much God lets us know about His will before we do it.

Read Winter, "Join the World Christian Movement," pp. 718-723 (all)

Conclusion of Key Readings for this lesson.

IV. Charting A Path To the Nations

Stephen Hoke and Bill Taylor point out the importance of stepping boldly into what you have been learning. The distinction between those who go and those who send takes on a wonderful life-giving flavor with the terms "goer" and "grower." Master the approach that Hoke and Taylor present as if God were calling you to be a "grower" who will counsel and coach dozens of aspiring missionaries to reach their highest effectiveness. Perhaps you know the Lord wants you to be a "goer." The value of each step will be obvious. Keep in mind that not everyone will need to work through these steps in the precise sequence in which they are ordered. Grasp the total picture of the wisdom that is distilled in these paragraphs:

A. Phase One: Getting Ready—Stretching. More "steps" are part of the initial phases. Each of the four steps mentioned in this section are beginnings of life-long growth and learning.

B. Phase Two: Getting There—Linking. Relationships with mission agencies and hands-on learning with missionaries are the primary features. It's not so much a search for what you would like to do. It becomes a process of discovery of what it would be best for you to do.

C. Phase Three: Getting Established—Bonding. Learning goes on, either as an apprentice to a seasoned missionary, or as an able mentor to others.

Read Hoke and Taylor, "Charting Your Journey to the Nations: Ten Steps to Help Get You There," pp. 714-717 (all)

V.   The Awesome Potential of Local Churches

George Miley expresses the high hopes of many, that their church will become a sending base for ministry to unreached peoples. Miley points out that churches are incredibly varied. Each church is laden with God-given potential and resources that can powerfully advance world evangelization. Some churches will express that life through traditional channels. Some churches are coming to grasp the total task of world evangelization. As a result of owning their part in the total task, some churches are aspiring to focus their energy on one of the remaining unreached peoples as a way of making a strategic contribution. They take on a particular people with a "whatever-it-takes" zeal. Miley calls this approach "people-group focused mission." Miley has observed hundreds of churches for years attempting this kind of mission. He points out that it can be done poorly or it can be done well.

A. People Group Focus Pursued Poorly. Miley lists five things to avoid. Study them carefully. You may be in a position to advise a church in years to come at some of these critical points.

B. People Group Focus Done Well. Many churches are doing a fantastic job. Their effectiveness has much to do with attitudes of humility and patience. One key feature of churches which are effective in evangelizing unreached people groups: They either form a partnership with an established mission agency, or they end up forming a new mission agency. Miley describes again the familiar distinction between modality and sodality using the term "apostolic structures" and "pastoral structures."

> Read Miley, "The Awesome Potential for Mission Found in Local Churches," pp. 729-732 (all)

VI. World Christian Partnership

We are part of a global mission force. Completing world evangelization is a task to be shared by churches from all over the world. Western Christians continue to have a valuable role in the task, but increasingly, the most viable role for Americans will be found in dynamic partnerships with churches and agencies from all over the globe. We are enjoying a day of maturity in partnerships as never before. Why are these partnerships important to you? In a matter of months or years you may have opportunity to be part of forming a strategic partnership. Within days you might be approached by a mission agency with an appeal for funds. What are the most important principles to observe? Zeal for strategic action has moved some to be overly eager to enter partnership arrangements that were ill-advised. Like the people-group focused mission mentioned above, partnership can be pursued poorly, or it can be done well.

A. The Power of Partnership. Phill Butler introduces the terms "strategic alliances" and "strategic evangelism/church-planting partnership." Butler discusses four aspects of partnerships:

1. **The value of partnerships** can been seen in the biblical values expressed by partnerships and by the effectiveness and efficiency of partnership.

2. **The dynamic of partnership** can be seen in the word-by-word definition of "strategic evangelism/church-planting partnership."

3. **The shape of partnership** can be seen from the different viewpoints of the one being evangelized, the field workers, the emerging church, the non-Western church, sending churches and donors and finally, from the viewpoint of God.

4. **Examples of partnership** amidst unreached peoples display the potential of agencies and churches working together.

Read Butler, "The Power of Partnerships," pp. 753-758 (all)

B. **Lessons of Partnership.** Bill Taylor outlines five of the major challenges that he has faced as he encourages partnerships in mission training throughout the globe:

1. **Keep listening and learning.** Partnerships ultimately bear fruit as people grow through mistakes and maintain listening relationships even when efforts fail.

2. **Share ownership.**

3. **Evaluate comparisons of cost-effectiveness.** A common appeal coming to American Christians is the challenge to fund national missionaries. The appeal is usually made with charges that mission agencies are sub-biblical while national workers are far superior at a fraction of the cost. This assessment of the value of mission agencies is without basis in either history or the Bible. National missionaries may at times *not* be the most strategic personnel for the task of church planting among unreached peoples. They may be the least likely to penetrate barriers of prejudice that are the greatest hindrance for unreached peoples to follow Christ. Just because an evangelist is from the country of India does not at all mean that he will have any access or persuasive power among other castes, languages and urban networks in India. It is false to assert that funds allocated for American missionaries deprive non-Western missionaries. We often see that the more people give toward their own missionaries, the more funds are released in the long run for all kinds of opportunities. Why not increase all categories of giving, and do it wisely?

4. **Enter with humility and wisdom.**

5. **Wise churches recognize what they cannot do** and what they can do. Taylor proposes two levels of partnerships between local churches and mission agencies: training and member care.

C. **Principles of Fully Functioning Partnerships.** Taylor finishes with five simple principles. They aren't hard to understand but they aren't always observed. To comprehend these tested principles, try to recognize how each of them may be at work in Taylor's example of the "Deep Sea Canoe Missionary Movement," at the opening of his article. Can you imagine yourself or your church involved in such a partnership?

Read Taylor, "Lessons of Partnership," pp. 748-752 (all)

Conclusion of Certificate Level Readings for this lesson.

Credit Level Guide Notes continue...

VII. Tentmakers

More than ever, we are seeing God send His people out as tentmakers. Ruth Siemens defines what tentmakers are and offers some of the strategic values of this approach in the biblical record. Tentmakers are missions-committed Christians who support themselves abroad in secular work, as they engage in cross-cultural evangelism on the job and in their free time.

A. What are Tentmakers? Siemens presents seven important characteristics of tentmakers.

1. Tentmakers use trades or professions to support themselves. There is actually a continuum of valid options between tentmaking and the standard model of the missionary who receives support from donors or churches.

2. Tentmakers do cross-cultural work.

3. Tentmakers do full-time ministry.

4. Tentmakers do workplace evangelism.

5. Tentmakers accomplish specific ministries.

6. Tentmakers are not second-rate witnesses.

7. Tentmakers are not "lone rangers."

B. Practical Values for Tentmaking. Siemens further presents seven further points portraying the strategic value of tentmaking. Tentmaking is not a strategic concession to get into so-called "closed countries." The professional roles of tentmakers position them in strategic settings. Their self-support can accelerate the launching of new missionaries. Like no other time in history, an international job market provides opportunities to live fruitfully and freely in almost any region or country in the world.

C. Biblical Reasons for Tentmaking. Two valid biblical models should be recognized: Peter demonstrated a *donor support* model. Paul demonstrated a self-*support* model. The study of Paul's practice and stated intentions regarding his work highlights the great strategic value of self-supporting missionaries in planting self-supporting churches. Paul's credibility was enhanced. He was also able to move rapidly in strategic identification with the people that he was reaching.

Read Siemens, "Tentmakers Needed for World Evangelization," p. 733-741 (all)

VIII. Reaching the World that God Brings to Us

Another way of working to fulfill the Great Commission is to reach people with the gospel who have been brought near to our homes and churches. A missionary should not be defined by the geographic distance he travels. The primary feature of a missionary is crossing cultural distances to communicate the gospel. One important category of missionary which God has used since biblical days are those who introduce international visitors to the living God. Tom Phillips and Bob Norsworthy describe the strategic opportunity in our day of reaching international students while they are visiting home communities of Christians. Every year in the USA, there are over 550,000 international students and scholars living in American cities. It's a highly strategic ministry to befriend these students, serving them in the name of Christ, and seeking sensitive ways to invite them to follow Christ. It is an accessible ministry. Most sincere Christians find it not only possible, but greatly enjoyable to enter such strategic friendships along with others of their church family. Like any authentic ministry, it can be demanding and stretching. But like few other ministries which touch the unreached peoples of the world, it is a feasible ministry. Much can be accomplished by teams of everyday Christians extending neighborly kindness.

Read Phillips and Norsworthy, "The World at Your Door," pp. 742-743 (all)

Both tentmaking and international student ministries might appear to be evidence that the day of standard mission agencies is passing. Look again. Both models of ministry (tentmaking and ministry to international students) are enhanced enormously when there is connection to mission agencies. Increasingly, standard mission agencies are enlisting missionaries who will carry out their ministry as self-supporting tentmakers, but also enjoy the huge benefits of partnership with an established mission agency. In the same way, the most effective ministry to international visitors is done in league with others. Several mission agencies specialize in this approach.

IX. Integrate Your Vision

As you seek to live out the vision you have gained in this course, be wise in finding a dynamic balance. Healthy world Christians become so convinced that God is indeed blessing the world through His people that they conduct their lives in a glad confidence. Healthy world Christians do not become eccentric, obnoxious single-cause advocates. Instead, they steadily evaluate and integrate every aspect of their lives by the purpose of God as reflected in the Great Commission. Since God Himself is accomplishing His purposes, but graciously beckons His people to join Him, world Christians can enjoy the same gracious urgency, integrating their lives instead of fragmenting their churches.

Bill and Amy Stearns present a way to fulfill God's purpose as if it were a "Family Business." With care and patience, healthy world Christians find ways to encourage healthy churches to exert themselves powerfully to bless the nations.

A church begins to be diverted from its fullest purpose unless it aims at the fulfillment of all of God's purpose. There is something powerful about owning the entire purpose of finishing the total task of world evangelization. It is obvious that while a church can own its stewardship in the total task, God will only give to a local church a specific part to play. With the total task as a guiding and defining purpose, any local church can grow in all four of the following dynamics.

A. God blesses His people to strengthen the church.

B. The church is to be a blessing to its own people group.

C. The church is to be a blessing to every people—including reached peoples.

D. The church is to be a blessing to every people—including unreached peoples.

Read Stearns, "The Power of Integrated Vision," pp. 724-728 (all)

Vision to Action

The Vision to Action exercises are practical ways to integrate the Perspectives vision with the realities of daily living. They can be done in any order, but you'll find that they roughly correspond to the content of the fifteen lessons. Together they are a powerful package of helps toward World Christian discipleship. Some Perspectives classes may assign and use them in different ways. They may be done with others in your class or with a mentor.

1. Breaking into Significance

Living a life of significance means aspiring to a life purpose beyond the confines of your own interests, or even beyond your lifetime. How do you lay hold of a personal destiny that makes sense in the larger scope of history? The answer lies in the fact that you are Abraham's child-in-faith. Your best destiny lies in taking hold of the purpose God gave him. Using a timeline, break out of the confines of personal gratification to God's glorification as a life ambition.

2. Praying with Purpose

Prayers should emerge from problems but can be framed and articulated powerfully according to the promise/purpose of God. Using "the Lord's Prayer" as a template, write out a prayer and a prayer plan to follow for a week. Learn to pray your way toward something God is doing, instead of merely praying for things that God may grant.

3. Reading the Bible as a Book of Hope

How do we read Scripture with eyes to see what God is doing, and with ears to hear what He is promising? Look for more than mere helps to survive life. Learn four practical ways to step each day into the grandeur of a global story in order to lay hold of the significant life to which Christ is calling you, in keeping with His purpose.

4. "Sending Grace" Inventory

What gracing/gifting has God given you that enables you to participate in His global purposes? Using a checklist of possibilities, identify what God has poured into you that is valuable to Him and to His purpose. You are probably far more wealthy than you realize with what matters most.

5. Value-Added Missions

Compare your church's mission activity with the church of Antioch in the book of Acts. If missions is draining your church, then there may be discoveries in store for you that the Antioch church found. Missions added to their church even while they gave away their best people. Find the features at Antioch that may help your church receive all that God may be wanting to bring about.

6. Praying With, More than Praying For

Learn an exhilarating way to pray for missionaries. Pray with them. Pray according to a biblical passage of promise. Write the prayer down, and mail it. Learn the joy of communicating with mission workers as colleagues in God's purpose. Leave behind the task of hero maintenance. Get on level ground with missionaries before the throne of God. Connecting with missionaries in what matters can multiply your prayer life instead of just adding minutes of prayer rituals.

7. Praying with the World

Finally, millions of people are agreeing with you—when you pray with global resources that align and fortify your praying. Choose one of three resources to use as a tool: Operation World, the Global Prayer Digest, or the Pray Through The Window calendar. Learn how to pray for what matters.

8. Lead the Way in Prayer

Organize and lead a prayer meeting for mission concerns. Invite friends of your church to join you in one powerful 15 minute prayer session.

9. Giving with Purpose

Begin to give boldly and openly, countering the standard American custom of amassing private wealth. Grow toward greater simplicity a step at a time. Learn how to give with others by making a donation together as part of the exercise.

10. Wake Up to the World

Design a plan for bringing about a greater awareness of the progress toward completing God's purpose in the world. Mobilize one relationship at a time. Share what you are learning with another acquaintance in a way that will help encourage them in what they already see as God's call on their life.

11. Interview an International

Enjoy a conversation with an international visitor. Thaw some of the ice of isolation in our society by simple friendship. Learn what topics make for easy engaging conversation that can lead to wider friendships with their friends and family. An invitation to a meal or an offer to help with errands is a good first step in friendship.

12. Lifestyle Choices and Life-course Decisions

Scrutinize some of the daily lifestyle choices (patterns of accumulation, time use, pain avoidance, privacy, etc.) in light of the values of the kingdom of God. Then examine one or two of the defining life-course decisions you have made. Learn how your course of life can be affected by the commanding vision that you choose.

13. Three Roles with One Vision

Try out different futures for size. Spin out a scenario of your life in the three roles of Sending, Welcoming, and Going. Explore how each of these roles might fit you and the vision God is giving you.

14. Vision Lift and Value Shift

Design a path of ongoing learning, increasing prayer and mission activity with a classmate, or better yet, a respected leader in your life. Discuss the vision-building activities you want to continue as a part of your way of life. Describe the ways that you will be a mobilizing influence in a local church. Consider how you might provide leadership with a few others, offering and/or receiving accountability as agreed.

15. Next Step Check

What next steps will you take in the next six months to live out what God has given you during this course? Write a letter to yourself. Give it to a friend who agrees to mail it back to you in about three months. Parts of this course are still under construction. Contact your Perspectives class coordinator or your mentor for the update that you will need to fulfill this part of the course. Or you can check the Perspectives website (www.perspectives.org) to learn about these materials.

Name:_____   Date: _____   ____/20pts

1. Match the stage on the left with the phrase that describes it. (2 pts)

    ____Pioneer Stage   a. missionary works by invitation

    ____Parent Stage   b. participating as equals

    ____Partner Stage   c. initial contact

    ____Participant Stage   d. expatriates train national leadership

2. What caused confusion and tension during the two transitions between the three Protestant mission eras? (2 pts)

3. Briefly explain the difference between E-1, E-2 and E-3 evangelism. (3 pts)

4. Which type is considered the highest priority from a strategic viewpoint? Why? (1 pt)

5. Non-Western missionaries _____ North American and European missionaries. (circle one) (1 pt)
    a. are in desperate need of training before they can be released by
    b. are finally shifting to unreached peoples, leaving the inlands areas to
    c. are avoiding countries where there is work already being done by
    d. are growing numerically faster than
    e. are cheaper to send and therefore better than

6. For each of the following situations, decide whether it should be evaluated on the "P-Scale" or the "E-Scale". Use "P" or "E" to answer. (3 pts)

_____ An Anglo-American shares the gospel with a Mexican migrant farm worker.

_____ While in the airport in Johannesburg, a South Korean missionary shares the gospel with a Japanese businessman.

_____ A church in India invites a high-caste Hindu woman to social gathering. She leaves when they serve beef.

_____ An Iranian Muslim cleric remains a secret believer for fear of being seen as a traitor.

_____ A Norwegian missionary goes to Siberia and witnesses to atheistic Russians in Siberia.

_____ An unchurched couple has marriage struggles so they check the Yellow Pages for a church with free counseling.

7. Define the term people movement with reference to kinship and to the decision-making process. (2 pts)

8. Identify the strategic focus, leaders, student movement and primary geographical sending base associated with of the Three Eras of Protestant mission history. (6 pts)

	1st Era (1792-1910)	2nd Era (1865-1980)	3rd Era (1934-????)
Focus			
Key Leaders			
Student movement			
Primary Sending Base			

Name:_____ Date: _____

On this page, describe some of the things you have sensed to be most important to you after the first five lessons of Perspectives. You can organize your response in any number of ways. You may describe content items that have been particularly surprising or challenging. You may want to describe how you sense God has been speaking to you. Or you may choose to present something like a personal journal entry describing changes you are experiencing because of this course. There are no right or wrong answers.

Name:_____ Date: _____

Respond to what you have learned in the History section of this course (Lessons 6 through 8). There is no correct answer. You will be graded on the thoughtfulness and depth of your interaction with material learned in this class. Below are three possible ways of organizing your response. You may choose one of the ways or come up with your own way to express your response. Limit your response to the front of this page.

   1. Impact from the past. Select one idea, movement, personality or statement that has made an impact on your views, hopes or life decisions. For example, describe how an idea or movement has encouraged, dismayed or informed you.

   2. Meet history. You might choose to do some time travel in your response. What era or place in mission history would you want to visit with the idea of bringing back valuable insights for missions today? Where would you go? Who would you seek out?

   3. Back to the Future? Identify one point of history that you would like to have turned out differently. How would you like to have altered history? What would be the outcome of these alterations?

Name: _____ Date: _____

Respond to what you have learned in Lesson 9. There are many possible ways to frame your response. How did the lesson build hope or bring discouragement? Which ideas do you most want to retain and why? What did you find most surprising? Which part do you think you are most likely to recount to someone else? Your comments will be evaluated on the basis of the personal application and thoughtful dialogue with the material.

Name: _____ Date: _____

Respond to what you have learned in Lessons 10 and 11. Choose one idea or concept that was startling, pertinent, significant or outrageous to you. Describe the idea and your response. Limit your response to the front of this page.

Name: _____   Date: _____

Respond to what you have learned in the Strategic section. Select an idea that was significant to you and describe its impact on your thinking, lifestyle, obedience or mission involvement. Here's another option: Frame your answer in the form of a journal, chronicling how the class material impacted you as you processed Lessons 12 through 14. Your response won't be evaluated on the basis of your opinions or values but on how well you demonstrate thoughtfulness and personal sensitivity to the material. Limit your response to the front of this page.

About the Author

Steven C. Hawthorne

Steve had to sneak his way into Urbana '76, InterVarsity's triennial Missions Conference. At the time, he was not at all interested in missions. He simply wanted to hear the biblical exposition of John Stott, one of the plenary speakers. Steve discovered after arriving at Urbana that the conference was sold out. He decided to sleep on a dormitory floor, eat out of vending machines and pay his registration fee by way of the offering in order to take in the conference. The opening address of John Stott forever changed his life. It was called "The Living God is a Missionary God." That address is now Chapter One of this book. The next day Hawthorne met Dr. Ralph Winter, who introduced him to the biblical certainty and the strategic possibility of completing world evangelization. Steve signed up then for a correspondence course called *Understanding World Evangelization* which eventually became the *Perspectives* course.

While completing a Master's degree in Cross-Cultural Studies at the School of World Mission at Fuller Theological Seminary, Steve helped as a class assistant for the Institute of International Studies at the U.S. Center for World Mission. In 1981, along with the community of mission mobilizers at the USCWM, he co-edited the *Perspectives* material with Dr. Ralph Winter.

Steve now directs WayMakers, a mission mobilization ministry focused on activating hope for Christ's greater glory in a prayed-for world. Steve helps churches and mission agencies cultivate maturity in intercession, research, and church planting among unreached peoples and in cities throughout the USA. Before founding WayMakers in 1994, Hawthorne served with the Antioch Network as an advisor to local churches endeavoring to send church planting teams among unreached peoples. Earlier, he served as vice president of Caleb Project, a ministry aiming to mobilize students with vision to complete world evangelism. Before that he worked as executive editor of World Christian Magazine. While working to portray unreached people groups in World Christian Magazine, he conceived and launched the research and mobilization effort called "Joshua Project," a series of field-based research efforts among unreached people groups. For years, Steve recruited, trained and labored with teams who carried out relationally-based field research identifying unreached peoples in world-class cities in Asia and the Middle East.

He has become a spokesperson for a growing global movement of on-site intercession known as prayerwalking. He co-authored with Graham Kendrick the book *Prayerwalking: Praying On-Site with Insight*. He also edited the widely used handbook to short-term mission service called *Stepping Out: A Guide to Short Term Missions*. He says of his writing and speaking, "I like to commit arson of the heart."

Now living in Austin, Texas, Steve and his wife, Barbara, experience the joys of parenting three daughters, Sarah, Emily and Sophia.